WHY POSITIVE THINKERS HAVE THE POWER

Why POSITIVE THINKERS have the POWER

KEN BOSSONE

JAICO PUBLISHING HOUSE

Ahmedabad Bangalore Bhopal Chennai
Delhi Hyderabad Kolkata Lucknow Mumbai

Published by Jaico Publishing House
A-2 Jash Chambers, 7-A Sir Phirozshah Mehta Road
Fort, Mumbai - 400 001
jaicopub@jaicobooks.com
www.jaicobooks.com

Published in arrangement with
Frederick Fell Publishers, Inc
c/o Rights & Distribution, Inc.
2131 Hollywood Boulevard, Suite 305
Hollywood, Florida 33020, USA

WHY POSITIVE THINKERS HAVE THE POWER
ISBN 978-93-86867-23-0

First Jaico Impression: 2017

Printed by
Trinity Academy For Corporate Training Limited, Mumbai

Endorsements

"It's so refreshing to read and hear about positive people and positive thinking. Ken Bossone is the first to document it correctly.

—Roxanne Batson

Managing Partner-Women Corp.com

"Ken is so amazing, he puts others before himself with his book and demeanor."

—Susan Barnes

Author, Businesswoman and two-time Guest on the Rachael Ray Show

"Ken's book is excellent-a lot of research went into it." It proves with humor and seriousness alike that you can really enjoy finding the true way to success and happiness. You will not be able to put this fantastic book down."

—Len Johnson

CEO Pac West Chem-author and Business and Marketing Guru

"Ken Bossone has delivered an inspiring compilation of research and true stories of why positive thinking works.
I got hooked and just had to share parts of the book."

—Debbie Wolf

Associate Producer, Inside Success Radio

"What a motivating read! Be proactive and learn the real positive thinking, the most essential ingredient to happiness, health and abundance."

—Dr. Proactive (Randy Gilbert)

"Ken Bossone's book uses real life examples and the wisdom of some of history's greatest thinkers: Lance Armstrong, Vince Lombardi, Oprah, Einstein, Winston Churchill, Bruce Jenner, along with a host of everyday people who have done extraordinary things because they believe in positive thinking. An inspiring must read book."

—Stacey Kannenberg

Author, Publisher of Children's Books and Successful Businesswoman

"Ken's examination of this innate capacity we all share to excel moves the gender forward from self-help to self-realization. Great motivational material."

—Christine Patti

Certified Natural Health Professional

Endorsements

Ken was a fun and motivating guest. He delivered well-researched stories and insights from his book to our listeners. He is an expert on sharing positive thinking."

—Jodie Lynn

International Award Winner, Syndicated Parent/Health Columnist, Author and Radio Host

"This book is really different. It is specially written for people who want to be different and MAKE a difference. Ken reveals in plain English what turns the timid into Tigers."

—Sharon Iezzi

Inspirational Speaker and Writer

"Ken is an advocate of his sincere message. Think Positive! It is evident that Ken has burnt a lot of midnight oils' to do the research. His book is a must for every household."

—Fatima Gulamhusein

Business Analyst

"I whole heartedly endorse Ken's book to all those who are ill or well, as it can do nothing but motivate and help to enhance one's power over difficulties or affliction. Ken's book has the power to pull you onto the path to greater well-being if you put into practice its teachings."

—Dr. Amaya Caso

LDS Hospital Salt Lake city, Utah

"Very, very insightful-challenging and very well thought out."

—R.T. Jones Bishop

African American Bishop-Pastor

"There are many reasons why Ken's book should be in everyone's library. You will need this book many times in your life. Be prepared."

—Thelma Gray

Advertising Federation of America Woman of the Year Award,
Public Relations Hall of Fame Member

"Finally a book that shows why men and women do not meet goals and proves conclusively how to change that around to a positive conclusion."

—Glenn W. Turner

Sharecroppers Son, Hair lip, 8th-grade Dropout,
Turned multi-millionaire and American of the Year

To my three children:
Christopher, Eileen, Andrew
More than anything, I want them to be with me
as a family again.

And to God

About the Author

Ken Bossone is president of the World Positive Thinkers Club, which includes more than 500 celebrities of the sports and business world. Members include Donovan McNabb, Brian Westbrook, Andy Reid, Tom Brady, Bill Belichick, Lance Armstrong, Payton Manning, Mrs. Ruth Peale, and the late Dr. Norman Vincent Peale, and the late Margaret Gorman (the first Miss America). Cal Ripkin Jr. is also a card carrying member. The club was started by Ken in 1995 and there are no dues at present. Plans are to eventually use funds to help hungry children, and the club has adopted a child in Appalachia with a monthly donation.

Ken is a published author, has written a series of Positive input children's stories, articles for Personal and Executive Excellence and Leadership Excellence magazines. His first book and tape series "Win at Buying and Selling came out in 1995. He is a financial and business advisor with a flair for creating and evaluating business plans. He won the prestigious "Parent to Parent Adding Wisdom Award" for this book and "Business Book of the Year," is director of sales for IDCure.com and is on the Faculty of the Internet Masters Program.

He was named one of the three top athletes in school and in his senior year was scouted by the Pittsburgh Pirates. Ken volunteered to serve his country in the Army, serving time in Korea where he earned the black belt in Karate. During his tenure in the Army he was named Outstanding Soldier of the Guard every time he pulled guard duty, as well as earning letters of commendation and was named Soldier of the Month.

After the Army he started his career in sales and has won awards such as top producer of the month; most sales produced for a new agent and salesman of the year. He was a director of sales; one of the youngest regional sales supervisors in the insurance business, and was a training director, traveling around the United States conducting sales seminars. Part time Ken owned his own Karate dojo and taught self-defense to police departments, college students, YWCA, YMCA students, as well as conducting adult night school classes.

For the past 10 years he has put his career on hold to research and write why people don't reach goals and to discover and share the real secret of those who do. During his research and ten year journey he discovered the **three-word motto** of all winners, which he happily promulgates in this astounding, totally enjoyable book. It was not all fun and games, as Ken paid the ultimate price, by facing his own unbelievable personal tragedies and hardships, which you will read about, but never once lost his positive attitude.

This book is like none other before, and a true self help book has reached the book stands. Don't read this book if you don't like to get involved by doing a little work to achieve the rewards mentioned in the poignant pages.

"If you want to leave footprints in the sands of time, you must wear work boots."

Table of Contents

INTRODUCTION 15
BEGINNING NOTE 19

CH 1. The Positive Thinker Sees the Invisible, Feels the Intangible, and Achieves the Impossible 21
CH 2. Dare to Risk 35
CH 3. You Do Not Have to Be a Victim of Your Circumstances 55
CH 4. Be Persistent as a Squirrel 77
CH 5. Positive Thinkers are Happy and Have a Great Sense of Humor 87
CH 6. Don't Be Satisfied With Average 105
CH 7. The Great Comebacks 115
CH 8. Ordinary People Can Become Extraordinary 127
CH 9. Don't Itch For Something You are Not Willing to Scratch For 145
CH 10. Faith in Yourself is Your Real Attitude 155
CH 11. Who is the Best? 167
CH 12. Are Women Better Positive Thinkers Than Men? 179
CH 13. Positive Thinking, Nutrition, and Faith Improve Your Health 197
CH 14. Mind Over Matter 219
CH 15. The Positive Thinker Puts it All Together 233

EPILOGUE 239
INDEX 249

Introduction

This book was written with one main purpose in mind. That purpose is to change you to a daily Positive Thinker. It is a labor of caring and hope, and the firm belief that you can accomplish anything you set your mind to. Hundreds of others written about in this book, including myself, are living proof that you can keep a positive attitude through pain and suffering. And it is about my close to 10 year search for the main ingredient all winners possess, which coupled with goals assures success and happiness.

I searched for close to 10 years to find out what drove people on and on in the face of defeat and adversity. What was it they did, or said, or thought? I wanted to know what drove them. Was it goals? Having a goal is nothing new. Man has had goals since the beginning of time, and goals are part of the equation. Hard work wasn't the ingredient I was looking for. Hard work has always been necessary to accomplish anything. After all, the only thing that sits its way to success is a chicken. And the only place where success comes before work is in the dictionary. Was it intelligence, I asked myself during my research? No! Many brilliant men and women wind up in skid row. Was it wealth? No! Many wealthy people are not happy, and many commit suicide. What I discovered shocked me. It is a **three-word motto** coupled with goals! It surprised me because it was so simple.

I discovered this life-changing motto long into my research while watching a middleweight championship-boxing match with Sugar Ray Leonard and his opponent. It opened my eyes to head along that path to find the secret, which you will discover later in the book. Two words Sugar Ray Leonard's' opponent spoke give you a strong hint. The words were negative in content. But they were strong words. They were so strong in fact, that he became instantly known the world over as a, "quitter."

I am convinced without a shadow of a doubt that the positive **three-word motto** (which is opposite words from the words Leonard's opponent spouted) coupled with goals is the main ingredient needed for winning and happiness. You will discover it for yourself as you turn the pages of this exciting and profound book. This motto is imbedded in every winners mind and very soul. It is the fuel that drives men and women onward through hell, if necessary, to work hard and achieve their goals. And the main goal in life is happiness. Anyone who denies they ultimately want happiness is just kidding himself or herself and not being totally straight forward.

This book is laced with humor, coupled with many pragmatic quotes from the living and deceased pundits of the world such as Shakespeare, Cicero, Marcus Aurelius and Confucius. There are poignant stories from the great thinkers, leaders, and winners who graced this exciting planet, like Napoleon, Lincoln, Teddy Roosevelt, Eleanor Roosevelt, Benjamin Franklin, Eisenhower, Jeanne Holm, (the first woman two star general), Dr. Joyce Brothers, Sandra Day O'Connor, Dian Fossey, Oprah Winfrey and many other winners who still inhabit this exciting planet. There are provocative stories about athletes, like Mickey Mantle, Lance Armstrong, Mohammed Ali, Jackie Robinson, Jesse Owens, Tom Dempsey, Rocky Marciano, Gene Tunney, Babe Zaharis, and Billie Jean King, as well as many other champions. These Positive Thinkers overcame extreme difficulty and went on to greatness. They have faced obstacles and heartache as you and I have. That is part of daily life. Every one of these people started as an average or below average citizen. The difference was they were dreamers. They felt compelled to control their lives and not allow adversity to control them. Once they dreamed, they then took a certain step towards that goal and burned three words into their whole being. They went forward towards that goal, never looking side-to-side, or backward. They were focused and they became winners. But once they took that three-word oath, they were already winners and they were convinced that that they would not fail attaining the coveted goal.

There are too many people who are defeated by the everyday problems in life. They go through life struggling, and sometimes complaining to those around them that they have not been given a fair shake in life. It is a fact that some people get a better break than others, but that is because the person who was afforded the break really wanted the opportunity to be rewarded for his or her extra efforts.

It actually took me close to 10 years to write this book, because when I started writing it, I realized that the only way to write a book about overcoming turmoil, setbacks, heartache, loss of family and friends, death threats, poverty, hunger, losing all one's possessions and still be able to think positively through it all, I would have to experience a few or all of them. I did not plan my misfortunes, believe me, but fate has a funny way of making things happen. And I have experienced every one of those setbacks. I have sent out hundreds of letters and e-mails seeking funding for a self-published/25 city book tour, so that I can get this extremely important, life-changing book in your hands.

During the early part of the 20th century, America's most prolific writer, F. Scott Fitzgerald, wrote, "Show me a hero and I will write you a tragedy." Unfortunately Fitzgerald had his own personal tragedy in the form of a bottle, bearing the alcoholic elixir that has destroyed many lives and families.

The alleys of the world are filled with people who have lost everything through natural disasters, or through war. For them it is a physical tragedy. But the alleys, streets, and mental hospitals are also filled with those poor souls who have given up hope of overcoming the burdens of life. That is a mental tragedy. Both tragedies can be rectified, however the easier tragedy to avoid is the mental. With proper thinking we can control our mental lives so that the negative thoughts cannot be allowed to dominate and control our minds. With the proper positive attitude we can stay focused, and negativity will not be allowed to control our thinking. With the **three-word motto** I discovered, and am now passing on to you, your life will become much easier to endure. Life is tough out there, but you ought to be glad you don't live in Rodney Dangerfield's neighborhood. He once said, "It was so tough in my neighborhood that after the opposing team sacked the quarterback they went after his family."

It is not my desire to minimize the problems of this wonderful, but sometimes disappointing world. My desire is to help you learn how to overcome them. There are no people in this world that have not faced a life-threatening situation or physical or mental hardship. But the Positive Thinker refuses to allow these dire circumstances to overpower his or her will to stay focused on the positive outcome. A classic example is the story of Mrs. Maxwell Rogers, who weighed all of 123 pounds. Her child was pinned beneath the wheels of a car in Tampa Florida in 1960. Her desire to remove that child from a life-threatening situation gave her the strength to lift that 3,600-pound car to save her loved one.

I attended college briefly and will not pretend to be a scholar. I am a student of the world of hard knocks and am self-taught in most of what I have learned. So I am a man who came from a simple beginning and I love the average folk. I have met with people such as great athletes, presidents of companies, and workers on the assembly line, and I am confident that I can relate to all of them. They all ultimately want the same thing. Happiness is the goal of everyone but it will never be attained without the proper positive attitude. Until you firmly believe that you can overcome any obstacle, you

will never attain that happiness, and in this poignant book you will learn the **three-word motto** of happy winners.

Why is it a supervisor on an assembly line can be given a rush order and will think it can't be accomplished, while another supervisor in the same plant, with the same rush order, will jump right in with the belief that it can be accomplished? And guess what? That supervisor completes the rush order, while the other supervisor loses time complaining and focusing on reasons why the order can't be accomplished.

There is challenge to your beliefs, and controversy, particularly in the 12th chapter, which is titled "Are Women Better Positive Thinkers than Men?" The 13th and 14th Chapters also challenge your beliefs. I suggest you continue to keep an open mind, as you did when you had the good sense to choose this exciting book. As you read through these pages you will find out why, and you will read many stories of people who turned failure into success. Most importantly, you will also discover the **three-word motto** to winning in life and achieving the goals and happiness you seek. Now face it, is there anyone that doesn't want to know how to attain happiness? And what is true happiness? Here is how President Franklin Delano Roosevelt described it in his first inaugural address, in 1933, "Happiness lies not in the mere possession of money; it lies in the joy of achievement, in the thrill of creative effort. The joy and moral stimulation of work must no longer be forgotten in the mad chase of evanescent profits."

Open the book now and have a ball reading about the palpable, wonderful world of Positive Thinkers. Oh, and don't forget a highlighter, because I might give you a quiz of two hundred questions after you finish reading the book.

Beginning Note

One of my firm convictions is that most people are basically ambitious. They are not lazy and want to improve themselves. You have just proven that, because you picked this book to help you become a better, happier person, and learn a life- changing **three-word motto** to assure you of meeting your goals, leading to greater peace of mind. At the end of this book is an alphabetical listing of names of people or things quoted or written about. Since this is a self-help book I purposely did not number the pages they are on, because it will stick in your memory if you do some of the work. So when something written about a particular individual or item moves you, go to the back of the book and put the page number next to the name. "Anything worth having is worth working for," is an old tried and true adage, which continues to hold true. This book is intended to be a true self-help book that is different from any before it, by getting you involved. After all, winners never appreciate something they did not have to do a little work for, and the only place success comes before work is in the dictionary. The best do the little bit more, that is why they are the best, and I am presuming you want to walk on that hallowed ground reserved for winners. You certainly didn't purchase this book to just to kill some time.

"If you wish to leave footprints in the sands of time you must wear work boots."
— Author unknown

One very important action you must take while reading this book is to highlight important sentences. The reason for that is at the end of each chapter is a progress task (main thoughts and challenges) for you to perform. So while my intention is to feed you with positive thinking and many poignant stories of winners, those stories have a purpose. Use a highlighter for the lines that jump out at you and write your notes on the page at the end of each chapter. If I did not advise you to do the above task I would be doing you a grave injustice. So if you will now retrieve the highlighter you can continue to the next paragraph.

Before you start on this exciting journey I want you to help me help you one more time. Right now I want you to lean back and relax and take a deep breath and then close your eyes for 30 seconds. During those precious 30 seconds I want you to breathe slowly and deeply, and concentrate and continually repeat these following six words. "I will keep an open mind."

THE POSITIVE THINKER SEES THE INVISIBLE, FEELS THE INTANGIBLE, AND ACHIEVES THE IMPOSSIBLE

"Impossible is the word to be found in the dictionary of fools."

—Napoleon

Do not start reading without a highlighter at the ready position.
Let's start off with a B a n g

Why did you pick up this book? Was it because you know the way to succeed in the wonderful game of life and be happy is to be a Positive Thinker? That puts you in a rare class of people! When you picked up this book and started reading, you dared to let positive thinking enter your mind. There is a very special reason why people win, which you will learn, and you will read how the winners overcame and still overcome the impossible. The winners do not believe in that word! It is not in their vocabulary. It certainly wasn't in the vocabulary of Fanny Blankers Koen, of the Netherlands, who was 30 years old with two children when she won four gold medals in the 100-and 200-meter dash, the 80- meter hurdles and the 4 X 100 meter relay in the 1948 Olympics.

If you get one thing from this book, it will be that the true Positive Thinker believes he can overcome any obstacle. Henry Ford, (about whom one teacher said, "He is a student who shows no promise"), the great automobile magnate who changed the way products are manufactured said, "Man can do what ever he can imagine." And by the way, Henry Ford meant to include women in his statement. I am convinced of that because I have watched many women overcome adversity, and Ford's wife was his driving force.

During the 1984 Olympics I watched a woman overcome the impossible. Seventeen days before the Olympics were to start this Positive Thinker was forced to undergo knee surgery. This would have devastated the average person but this beautiful lady was no average person in her thinking, because two hours after the operation she began rehabilitation. She was responsible for the women's marathon being run for the first time in the Olympics, as only a few male runners surpassed her times in the Boston Marathon. The skeptics said she would not have a chance and even tried to keep her out of the Olympic Marathon. Joan Benoit entered that marathon in 1984, and won the gold medal, and you can be sure Joan knows the **three-word motto** of all winners.

Dr. Norman Vincent Peale, author of, *The Power of Positive Thinking*, once said, "Don't tell me that miracles don't happen, or that you are doomed to failure. I have read the greatest book ever written many times from cover to cover. Nowhere in the Bible does it say man is born to lose."

Before you go any further in this book, I suggest you mark your spot here and get a highlighter if you haven't already. After all, you have paid good money for this book, so why wouldn't you do as the Positive Thinkers do? They go the extra yard and they do the basics better than the rest of the crowd. Just put the book down. I will wait until you get back with the highlighter. Do it now. I am very serious. If you do not put the book down and get a pen or highlighter to highlight you will be reported to the SPCAW. (Society for the Prevention of Cruelty against Writers).

There are many exciting stories, quotes, and words of wisdom from the Positive Thinkers of the world in this book. You will want to read them over from time to time as one or more will appeal to you. Any pundit will advise you to read a book more than once to absorb the contents better. By the third day after reading a book only ten percent is retained. Heck, I wrote this book and don't remember all that I wrote. You should go over the highlights at least once a week. "Do it now," is a wise saying when we think of an important action to be taken, as we tend to forget. And, "don't put off till tomorrow what you can do today." As motivator Anthony Robbins said, "Many people fail in life because they major in minor things." Jim Rohn also said, "I find it fascinating that most people plan their vacations with better care than they plan their lives. Perhaps that is because escape is better than change."

Why do Positive Thinkers get positive results? Why do they win more often than negative thinkers and why are they happier than negative thinkers? Why are there no statues erected to negative thinkers? What is positive thinking? What is a Positive Thinker made up of? To find the answers to those poignant questions, I will take you through an exciting journey that cost me close to 10 years of research, writing, suffering, loss of income, and property. My mission in life during those long years has been as it was for best selling author, Napoleon Hill. Napoleon was hired by the world's richest man, Andrew Carnegie, and consequently spent 20 years struggling on a paltry income to find the secrets to wealth. He interviewed 500 of America's richest men to learn their secrets. His book, *Think and Grow Rich*, is a masterpiece, and to my knowledge, still in print. I do not consider myself to be in Napoleons class, but I am on a similar mission.

Andrew Carnegie started life as a poor little Scotsman, but when he died left over $300 million to charity. Carnegie built the steel industry in America to become the most powerful industry in the world. His president, Charlie Schwab, talked Andrew into selling Carnegie Steel to the feared banker, J. P. Morgan, (one of the most powerful men in the world), for over $300 million. Naturally, Charlie was a master salesman and he achieved the sale on the golf course. Very interestingly though, historians claim that the canny Scotsman, Carnegie, wanted to sell anyway and get on with his love of philanthropy, but we will never know for sure. One thing we know for sure is that Carnegie made the world a better place than when he entered it. Because of this Positive Thinkers generosity, we have many libraries and buildings where higher learning takes place. Carnegie knew the **three-word motto**.

Carnegie and Morgan did not know they were on the same cruise ship, and ran into each other at the railing. Carnegie looked Morgan square in the eye and said, "Mr. Morgan, I should have asked for more money." Morgan chuckled and retorted, "Well, Mr. Carnegie, if you had asked for more, you would have received it." They both laughed, and two enemies became friends. Two powerful Positive Thinkers. What a team they would have made if Carnegie had not decided to retire!

By the way, Charlie Schwab and Walter Chrysler were the only two men at the time that earned a million dollars in salary per year. Both were considered master Positive Thinkers. Unfortunately, Charlie did not know how to retain money, and died abroad on borrowed money. It is easy to earn money; it is the keeping of it that is hard. In the old days a person who saved money was considered a miser, now he is considered a magician.

My mission was to find the main winning thought all winners have embedded in their minds and souls, making it guaranteed to succeed and be happier. No one paid me to do this. I just felt it was my duty to find this powerful thought, so I could pass it along and make more people happy. My goal, like Napoleon Hill's is not to become wealthy off this book. If that happens it would be nice, but I would be more comfortable now if I did not have this book to work on for the past close to 10 years.

I have run into many of the negative thinkers of the world. These people say with great conviction, "it can't be done!" or, "You are crazy to try that!" or, "You are wasting your time." or, "No one ever did it before, so you can't either." The biggest negative statement is "it is impossible." Many cynics will not take this type of book seriously, and that is a positive statement! I can assure you though, if you keep an open mind, and are in your mind a negative thinker, this book will change your attitude and your income, and above all your happiness. And if you are a Positive Thinker in your mind this book will make you a better person and you will achieve more of your goals.

After close to 10 years of research and personal experience I have become solidly convinced -Positive thinking is seeing the invisible, feeling the intangible, and achieving the impossible. I have that saying on a little plaque my oldest son Christopher gave me. He has gone through some very tough times in his life, but he continues to think positively. When the going gets tough, the tough-get-going. The Positive Thinker loves a challenge and never backs down from one.

As you go through this book you will read stories about the great Positive Thinkers and what they are really made of. As written earlier, F. Scott Fitzgerald, one of America's greatest writers, wrote in the early 1900's, "Show me a hero and I will write you a tragedy." B. C. Forbes said, "History has demonstrated that the most notable winners usually encountered heart-breaking obstacles before they triumphed."

You will read about overcoming tragedy, like Joni Earickson Tada, who is paralyzed from the neck down from a diving accident. These stories are mainly to encourage you, and to make you think for a moment and say to yourself, "wait a second, if he or she can do that, so can I!" Mostly, this compelling book is about discovery of a **three-word motto** all the Positive Thinkers have burned into their whole soul and mind, which leads to winning and happiness. Some have done that consciously and some subconsciously. But be your own person and do not try to imitate them.

Just follow their lead. Keep an open mind, relax, and enjoy life. It is full of delightful surprises.

During the joy of writing this book, I never found it difficult to comprehend what people have had to go through to attain their goals and aspirations. We all have faced a crisis at one time or another during the course of chasing the dream. However, you have to realize that a crisis is nothing more than opportunity riding on dangerous wings. Winners have faced many negative thinkers along the way who tried to discourage them. Like the tall man who walked into a shop in Dayton, Ohio, where his sons were working. "Boys," he said, "why don't you quit your foolish tinkering with that silly machine? You are not going to make it work. You are not going to fly-no, one is ever going to fly, so long as the world stands." He then added. "Even if anybody ever does invent a machine that will fly, it certainly won't be anyone from Dayton, Ohio." Ironically, noted astronomer, Simon Newcomb, in 1903 stated, "It is just common sense to keep both feet firmly planted on the ground." Newcomb then went on to say, "Aerial flight is one of that classes of problems with which man can never cope." But in 1903, Orville sent his father a telegram stating, "Success assured, keep quiet." On a cold windy day on December 17, 1903, at Kill Devil Hill, five miles south of Kitty Hawk, North Carolina, the Wright Brothers made history by flying 120 feet for 12 seconds. The longest flight of the day was 852 feet. Even two years later the skeptics in Europe did not believe man could fly after hearing of the Wright Brothers success. The Wright Brothers knew the **three-word motto**.

What would the world be like if the Wright Brothers, who started as simple bicycle mechanics, had listened to their father, or the military men who said the airplane had no practical purpose? What if they had taken to heart the statement of Lord Kelvin, President of the Royal Society in 1895? Kelvin said, "Heavier than air, flying machines are impossible." Thank God the Wright Brothers did not listen to Kelvin, because Kelven also said that radio had no future and that x-rays would prove to be a hoax.

What if they did not believe Napoleon's statement to one of his generals, who was afraid during a certain battle, telling Napoleon that a certain objective was impossible to overcome? Napoleon countered, "Impossible is the word to be found in the dictionary of fools." That general went on to win that battle. By the way, Napoleon lost a third of his battles, but he always kept a positive attitude. He knew the **three-word motto**. The reason Napoleon had his hand in his shirt so much was because he had a skin disease that caused him to continually scratch his chest. How about that for a little trivia!

Someone else would have made a heavier than air machine fly in time, but the Wright Brothers had a steely determination. It is also known as persistence.

"The power to shape the future is earned through persistence. No other quality is as essential to success. It is the sandpaper that breaks down all resistance and sweeps away all obstacles. It is the ability to move mountains, one grain of sand at a time."
— President Calvin Coolidge

They knew that they had to use the research of those before them. You do not try to reinvent the wheel. Knowledge is power, however they knew that imagination is the switch that turns the power on. And so they imagined and dreamed. Henry Wadsworth Longfellow made a statement that aptly applies to the Wright brothers when he said, "The heights by great men reached and kept were not attained by sudden flight, but they, while their companions slept, were toiling in the night."

The Wright Brothers made it happen years sooner than any other person because of their belief in themselves and positive thinking and oh yes, they knew the **three-word motto**. They researched and tested, and researched and tested some more. They were scorned as not being scientists and the negative critics stated that they just happened to be lucky. [I personally believe that luck is preparation meeting opportunity]. However, they used mathematics and results from other scientists and did their own testing. The great French philosopher Valery, stated, "Science is a collection of successful recipes." They created a wind tunnel, tested over 200 types of wing surfaces and took angles into account. They researched the findings of Otto Lilienthal, and their second glider had similar curvatures as those used by Lilienthal in 1896. They also followed the research of Samuel Peirpont Langley, who started his research in aerodynamics in 1886 with the help of Charles M. Manley, a Cornell graduate with a degree in engineering. They did their homework, and if that is not what a scientist does then the world really is flat. The great poet, Robert Frost said, "Do not follow where the path may lead. Go instead where there is no path and leave a trail."

Because unbelievers would not put credence in their machine, the Wright

Brothers had a hard time selling the United States government on the idea of the importance of airplanes. Finally, in 1908, the Wright Brothers were commissioned to build 'Jenny's' for the Army, but we had no real effective Air Force to start WW I. The Wrights even faced the ultimate insult of their own government, which stated they did not invent the first heavier than air machine to fly. That is why until 1948, the worlds first plane did not land in the famous Smithsonian Institution in Washington, D.C. Initially, they gave Flyer I to the Kensington Museum, in London in 1928, for display.

The point is they never gave up through adversity and the negativism they had to face. They were Positive Thinkers, and they knew the **three-word motto** of all Positive Thinkers, which you will learn soon. They were two people who saw the invisible, felt the intangible and achieved the impossible.

The Wright Brothers are a shining example of how a Positive Thinker thinks and reacts; especially how he or she reacts to the negative thinker. The hardest obstacle a Positive Thinker has to overcome is the negative thinker. The negative thinkers are everywhere, trying to discourage others from succeeding. Don't let them sway you on the exciting trip to your goal. Remember, as Hannah More stated, "Obstacles are those frightful things we see when we take our eyes off the goal." The Wright Brothers dreamed and dared to risk, as do all Positive Thinkers. They never took their eyes off the goal.

And they were patient. If the Wright Brothers had listened to some of the negative aeronautical engineers of the day, they might not have flown.

Let's go a little farther into the history of the lighter than air craft, by listening to what a professor of aeronautical engineering at Cambridge told Frank Whittle when he examined the strange engine Frank was working on. "Your plans for a jet engine are interesting, but it will never work." Another negative thinker proved wrong.

You have heard the old story of the bumblebee. Aeronautical engineers today can prove to you that by using the laws of physics and aerodynamics, it is impossible for the bumblebee to fly. His wings have too short a span for his size and weight, and so, in their scientific thinking he should not attempt to try to fly. Let me add a twist here. If the bumblebee could understand the scientific reasoning, and he was a negative thinker, he would think that scientific logic must be right and so he would not attempt to fly. But on the other hand, if he were a Positive Thinker, he would thank them for their advice and continue to fly leaving that melodic buzzing in his wake.

Perhaps you have heard the old story about the hot dog stand during the depression. The owner through receipts from the stand sent his son to college, and when the son came home for semester break he advised his father that things were terrible. He advised his uneducated father not to spend so much money on supplies, to cut back on buns and hotdogs and to not stay open so long. His father thinking his son knew better than he did exactly as the son advised, and sure enough the business turned out as his son had said the rest of the businesses were faring. That successful little hot dog stand went out of business. Isn't it interesting how many successful businesses were started during the depression!

Don't listen to the negative thinkers. Follow your dream, and as I wrote before, use your imagination, because knowledge is power, but imagination is the switch.

Webster's newly revised copyright pocket dictionary gives several definitions of the word impossible. Webster leaves the door open with the definition, "unlikely to take place or be done." So you see, while some think the word impossible means that a thing never can be done; others think there is a good chance it can be accomplished. Webster does say "unlikely." He does not say, "Cannot be accomplished."

The Positive Thinker realizes that to be successful in his venture he must, take the course opposite to custom. Earl Nightengale, a very successful businessman, author, and motivational speaker said, "The opposite of success is not failure, it is conformity. It is acting like everyone else." So dare to be different. Don't be a sheep, which are notorious followers. Mark Twain (Samuel Clemens) said, "The secret to success is finding out where every one is going and then get there first."

A few years ago the television show 'M*A*S*H' was a big hit. One of the stars, Loretta Switt, a tall green-eyed blond, played the part of 'Hot Lips Hoolihan,' a nurse who has occasional mixed emotions pertaining to her duties. Loretta did what every successful person does. She dared to dream. She said when interviewed, "Ever since I can remember, I not only wanted to be an actress, but I also knew that I would be one. When I was a little girl, each time I went to bed at night, I created roles for myself and acted them out in my mind before going to sleep. I rehearsed and rehearsed all my fantasies until they were as real as my real life." Loretta firmly believes that you can will almost anything to happen if you work at it hard enough. All Positive Thinkers think like that!

America's sport, baseball, had cloudy beginnings. One supposed credible story is that General Abner Doubleday was credited with creating the grand old sport which Americans, and eventually much of the world, have come to love. Because baseball was once a big part of my life, I decided to do some research on the game. What I discovered surprised me and caused me to change some of my attitudes towards the great game. I have more of a positive feeling now considering what the founders of the game went through.

First off, Abner Doubleday did not start the game in 1838 as reported by Albert G. Spalding, of Spalding Sporting Goods fame. Doubleday was still on campus at West Point, and not in Cooperstown organizing the game. The game has its roots as far back as 1700, as an offshoot of the English game, rounders. And even the ancient Egyptians had a bat-and-ball game. Albigence Waldo, the surgeon with General George Washington wrote about watching troops batting balls and running bases during lulls in the fighting during the revolutionary war. And as a matter of fact novelist Samuel Hopkins Adams grandfather claimed he played 'baseball' in Mr. Mumford's pasture in 1820.

Throughout history baseball had obstacles such as injuries, and some religious zealots who declared it should not be played on Sunday. There have been strikes by the players and umpires. Gambling flourished early on and there was the famous Black Sox Scandal in 1919, which nearly closed down the game until a Positive Thinker with skinny legs came along. He changed the game of baseball with his hard hitting and great fielding. The era of the home run came about because of this great Positive Thinker. The writer, W.O. McGeehan, wrote, "Babe Ruth with his bat pounded baseball back into popularity. He swings with the utmost sincerity. When he hits the ball it goes into wide-open spaces. When he misses, he misses with vehement sincerity." Babe Ruth had his critics and share of negative thinkers. Some writers vilified him for his drinking, womanizing and eating habits, but the Babe never missed a game on purpose. He loved the fans, and especially children. This Positive Thinker is credited with helping to save baseball, and Yankee stadium was constructed and referred to as, "The House That Ruth Built." Even Tris Speaker, one of the great baseball players of that time criticized him and said, "Ruth made a big mistake giving up pitching." Isn't it interesting that some people have to find fault in something or someone great? The Positive Thinker does not take the criticism too seriously, because he has complete confidence in his abilities, and he knows the **three-word motto**.

Babe Ruth was a tremendously gifted athlete and Positive Thinker, and one night at a Society dinner for charity in Wilmington, Delaware, he became "tipsy" by two in the morning. He jumped into a roadster with a boxing promoter friend; drove to Camden, New Jersey, 25 miles away and partied until nine in the morning. He arrived at Shibe Park in Philadelphia that afternoon without any sleep. One of his teammates suggested he looked ready for the funeral home. Babe, the consummate Positive Thinker, calmly stated, "Don't worry about it kid, I'll probably hit one out today." His first time up Ruth crunched an outside pitch into the left field stands. He then proceeded to hit two triples and one more home run to right field, as well as making two great running catches in the outfield, (those were the days before players used huge gloves to catch the ball). I remember reading that if Babe Ruth were playing today, he would be earning the biggest salary in the major leagues and half owner of the Yankees.

Babe was the most photographed man in the world and was better known to most foreigners than President Calvin Coolidge. He was once told that he made more money than the President, and he jokingly remarked that he had a better year. Babe Ruth knew the **three-word motto**, and Positive Thinkers have a good sense of humor, too, as you will find out by reading chapter six of this book.

All Positive Thinkers have great confidence in their ability, and thanks for the Positive Thinkers, or baseball might not have survived the negative thinkers who were out to close down the game. On August 30, 1881, a New York Times editorial stated that "Baseball had become a dangerous sport." A statistician reported that in the last ten years up to 1881, the annual number of accidents caused by baseball was 37,518, of which 3 percent were fatal. There were 25,611 fingers broken, 11,016 legs broken, 1,900 eyes permanently put out and 1,648 ribs fractured. That should have been ample reason to shut the game down. The positive side to those statistics is that those negative aspects along with the drinking, gambling and rowdiness of the players and fans caused those who were concerned about the integrity of the game to decide to invite the fairer sex to the games, thereby leading to a "purifying element." The Ball Players Chronicle stated that the presence of ladies "purifies the moral atmosphere of a base ball gathering." And so Ladies Day was born, designating the last Thursday of the month for wives, daughters and girlfriends to watch the games free of charge. The result was that the ladies had a positive calming effect on the players and fans as well as boosting attendance. And Mabel Hite, the famous actress and wife of Giants player Mike Donlan, enthusiastically claimed, "There is nothing I delight more than sitting in the grandstand. I'd rather be a baseball player than a worker in any other profession under the sun." Stella Hammerstein, the actress daughter of Oscar Hammerstein would sometimes be late for a performance because she would not leave a game in progress. Several pages later on you will find out about how the lovely fairer sex had another positive affect on the great game of baseball. I would like to add a personal comment by stating that I have been to many baseball games, both professional and amateur, and the female fans can be just as boisterous and enthusiastic as their male fan counterparts.

Baseball employs thousands of men and women and brings joy to millions who watch this great game. It gives hope to many boys like me when I was young. It proves you can grow up and do anything you want if you want it bad enough, while thinking positive.

I will not reveal my real age yet, but up until the summer of 2001, I played baseball (hardball) on Sundays, and one of my former Sunday teammates was a positive thinking 76 year old piano tuner.

In essence, the Positive Thinkers overcame the ranting and attempt at sabotage of the negative thinkers to wipe out the great game. If the owners of the teams had listened to Clark Griffith, the owner of the Washington Senators, when he said, "There is no chance whatsoever of night baseball ever becoming popular in the bigger cities," (he said this after President Roosevelt pushed a button in 1935 that ignited 632 lamps lighting up Crosley Field in Cincinnati), then baseball might not have survived. The workingman could not get to day games as often without taking sick or vacation days. So, Larry MacPhail, the positive thinking, daring manager of the Cincinnati Reds, risked every penny, and 20,422 fans showed up that night to witness history. See if you can find many baseball games played during the day now, other than weekends, Pennant series and the World Series. Positive thinking changed the game for the better, and has brought happiness to millions around the world.

What if the Positive Thinker, Judge Roy Hofheing, had listened to the skeptics? If he had, the eighth wonder of the world would never have been built. It was built in 1965, and was first named after Harris County in Texas. Judge Hofheing charged one dollar per person for a tour, and took in a million dollars letting people tour the Houston Astrodome, the first indoor ball field.

One of the saddest stories I ever heard was about an important game where a pinch hitter struck out without swinging his bat. He never took the bat off his shoulders as three pitches whipped by him for strikes. His manager walked up to him and asked him why he had never even swung the bat. In truly negative fashion he exclaimed, "I was afraid I would miss." Needless to say, he did not last long in the majors.

Babe Ruth, Reggie Jackson, Willie Stargell, Mike Schmidt, Bobby Bonds, and Mickey Mantle are among the leading homerun hitters of all time, and they are among the leaders of home run hitters who struck out the most. The Positive Thinker is never afraid to swing. Most home run hitters (with a few exceptions, like the great Ted Williams, who blasted 521 home runs) strike out often, because they are Positive Thinkers and are not afraid to swing. The Positive Thinker standing at the plate waiting for a fast ball knows he only has four tenths of a second to swing at a 90 mile per hour fast ball after it leaves the pitchers hand, and that a curve ball can veer by more than 17 inches. This does not deter him as he is convinced that he will make contact three out of ten times and be successful. He is willing to risk embarrassment by not getting on base seven other times. That is just like life. We do not get on base all the time, but we have to swing, and we have to laugh and not dwell on the misses, of which there are many. As the great African American pitcher and Baseball Hall of Famer, Sachel Paige said, "Never look back, something might be gaining on you."

During my research I discovered that women played baseball as early as 1875. Women wore as much as thirty pounds of clothing, including floor length skirt, underskirts, long sleeved high neck blouse, and high button shoes. Later in the early 1900's they were known as "Bloomer Girls." I discovered that Jackie Mitchell was signed to a men's minor league contract, and you will discover in Chapter 14 what an impact she made. In 1952, Eleanor Engle signed a men's minor league contract with the AA Harrisburg Senators, and in 1998, lla Bordes pitched and won a men's minor league game 3-1. That year, two Major league teams contacted her. Soooooooo,

I guess women can play hardball, as the movie, A League of Their Own, staring Tom Hanks, Gina Davis, and Rosie O'Donnell, based on a real life women's baseball league in the 1940's proved. Were they Positive Thinkers? You bet! Did they know the **three-word motto**? You bet!

A very interesting court order from the Supreme Court in 1974 ruled that the Little League was discriminating by banning girls from participating. The irony here is that the press claimed it as a legal victory: however if they had done their homework they would have discovered many instances where women participated in baseball as players. As a matter of fact, in 1928 a Positive Thinker named Margaret Gisolo played American Legion Junior Baseball in Indiana, helping her team win the state championship.

One of the important qualities about a Positive Thinker is enthusiasm, and his or her love of the game, be it sport, business, or hobby. When you are around the Positive Thinkers you will notice that enthusiasm, and it emits itself to those around them. They have a certain air of confidence and love the game of life.

The following prose has always been a great help to me in my thinking, and I want to share it with you.

ENTHUSIASM

"Enthusiasm is the greatest business asset in the world. It beats money and power and influence. Single handed the enthusiast convinces and dominates where a small army of workers would hardly raise a tremor of interest. Enthusiasm is faith in action; and faith and initiative rightly combined remove mountainous barriers and achieve the unheard of and miraculous. Set the germ of enthusiasm in your business; carry it in your attitude and manner; it spreads like contagion and influences every fiber of your industry; it begets and inspires effects you did not dream of; it means increase in production and decrease in costs; it means joy and pleasure and satisfaction to your workers; it means real life and virile; it means spontaneous bedrock results—the vital things that pay dividends."

— Author Unknown

"Flaming enthusiasm, backed up by horse sense and persistence is the quality that most frequently makes for success."

— Dale Carnegie

"I rate enthusiasm even above professional skill."
— Sir Edward Appleton

The winner has goals; knows the **three-word motto** and has self-confidence. He follows the advice of the great African American tennis player, Arthur Ashe, winner of the 1975 Wimbledon and 1978 U. S. Open tennis championships, who said, "One important key to success is self confidence. An important key to self confidence is preparation."

If you want to lead the orchestra, you have to put your back to the crowd. To be successful and happy, swing often, prepare, think positive, set goals and learn the **three-word motto**.

MAIN THOUGHTS AND CHALLENGES

1. Go back to the beginning of this chapter and review the highlighted sentences.

2. Place the highlighted page numbers on this sheet.

3. Write down the most important highlight and why it is so important to you.

4. Write down what you have overcome in your life that you thought impossible.

5. Now write what it is that you consider impossible or hard to overcome in your life or the life of your family.

6. Finally, put on your sheet your main goal in life. Think carefully if you do not already have a goal, and then write it down. Remember that goals must be specific, motivational, relevant and reachable. You must use a calendar specifically for goals. When you finally discover the **three-word motto** you will realize how very reachable goals become. As you go through the chapter review at the end of each chapter you will understand why the calendar is necessary.

Chapter 2

DARE TO RISK

*"Take calculated risks.
That is quite different from being rash."
—General George S. Patton*

Did you ever start out to set a record knowing you could lose your life in the process? How about a world record while only having the sight of one good eye; flying in a plywood airplane, 27' 7½" wide with one 500 horsepower motor, while flying at a top speed of 150 mph? Wiley Post and his navigator, Harold Gatty, decided in 1931, to fly around the world, a trek of over 15,000 miles, intent on beating the record set by the "Graf Zeppelin" in 1930. The Zeppelin left Lakehurst, New Jersey for an around the world trip and arrived back at Lakehurst 21 days later.

Wiley and Harold not only took on the record, but also did it during a time when the airplane was in doubt as a safe flying machine (due to the safety record of the blimp). So they were out to prove the safety of the airplane as well, while setting a new standard.

Not only did they have the distance to consider, but also knew they would be flying "blind" over much of the ocean. There were no modern flying aids as there are today. There were many other considerations, like unfamiliar landing strips and foul weather. They also knew that by not carrying spare parts they were risking the record, because a blown tire or broken shock in Siberia could mean a month delay in getting spare parts.

A winner knows that both preparation and research are needed to set any record. So they made sure every single detail was covered, including how much personal clothing they could bring along. Every item the plane carried had to be carefully thought out to reduce the flying weight. A major consideration was computing the fuel consumption based on the weight of the plane.

When they finally roared down the Roosevelt Field runway at 4:55PM on Tuesday, June 23, 1931, the skeptics shook their heads and wrote them off.

These intrepid men almost didn't make it as their motor sputtered over the ocean. Wiley had to use all his flying skills to re-start the motor and one more obstacle was out of the way. After landing in Blagoveschensk, Russia, the Winnie Mae's wheels sank in the mud during heavy rain, and as the wheels sank deeper, it looked as if their quest for the record had come to an end. But these two winners knew the **three-word motto**! They recruited non-English speaking natives and a few horses to pull the plane out of the mud. The same thing happened to them in Alberta, Canada. But 8 days, 15 hours, 51 minutes later they settled on the runway at Roosevelt Field, New York. Once again the hoards of skeptics were silenced. It is so much fun to accomplish something the critics say can't be done! Winners dare to risk it all.

A few years later, Wiley Post and the great humorist Will Rogers left for another record-breaking trip, but never returned. That is the price we must pay sometimes to achieve greatness and prove the skeptics wrong. Sometimes the skeptics are right in their prognostications, so let's face it, even a broken clock is right twice a day.

During the depression, new businesses were started, while many business leaders were committing suicide after losing it all. These daring entrepreneurs who started the new enterprises during the great depression were not afraid to risk. They knew like the turtle, you only make progress when you stick your neck out.

"Some men have thousands of reasons why they can't do what they want to; all they need is one reason why they can."
— Willis Whitney

In my business, I find capital for start up entrepreneurs. I have the greatest respect for these people, because they are what make this country so great. They are willing to take a risk and earn a piece of the great American dream. They cause the economy to continue to grow and create jobs for people. However, some of these start-up entrepreneurs give up when the going gets rough and the negative thinkers get the best of them. But the real Positive Thinkers stay the course and get funded. And the cream-of-the-crop stays positive and does not land on the trash heap of failures. Daniel Webster said, "Failure is more from want of energy than want of capital." Positive Thinkers see problems every day, and they take to heart part of a speech the great minister and Positive Thinker, Dr. Norman Vincent Peale, who wrote the best selling book, *The Power of Positive Thinking*. Dr. Peale, who was my mentor, said in a speech, "Problems constitute a sign of life; the more problems you have the more alive you are. The fellow with 10, tough, man-sized problems is twice as alive as the poor, miserable, apathetic soul who only has five. And those of you here today who have no problems whatever, I warn you, you are in great jeopardy. You are on the way out and don't know it. The minute this meeting is over, you better head for home and go to your room, shut the door, get down on your knees by the bed, pray to the Lord, and ask, "What is the matter Lord, don't you trust me any more? Send me some problems." Napoleon Hill was commissioned by Andrew Carnegie to interview 500 of America's richest men, and write a book on how they got to be in that enviable position. Napoleon Hill spent 20 years gathering the information, writing volumes, and wrote, The Science of Personal Achievement, which ultimately led to the best selling book, *Think and Grow Rich*. He could have turned down that assignment and led a comfortable life, but he was willing to risk failure and hard financial times. Carnegie assured him that if he researched for twenty years, he would then be able to write and show the "average" person how to become wealthy.

Napoleon had to hide for a year, because thugs were out to kill him. They believed he was involved with a newspaper publisher who was writing stories exposing those same thugs. After the year of hiding he found he now had no publisher, as the thugs had killed him. Also, his influential business manager had died. So he had to start looking all over again for both a publisher, and a business manager. Talk about persistence! He knew the **three-word motto**. Napoleon knew he had to risk it all to get his great findings in the hands of the average man. He knew that with this knowledge he could make more people wealthy, and in turn, strengthen the economy. Napoleon finally found a new publisher and backer, and wrote the book *Think and Grow Rich,* which became an overnight best seller. Napoleon Hill knew the **three-word motto**.

I once wrote an article for Personal Excellence magazine. In that article I quoted W.C. Fields, who said, "If at first you don't succeed, try, try again, then quit. There is no sense in making a fool of yourself." I countered that with, "I know many fools who have risen from the ashes of defeat to build new businesses and succeed. Someone once said, "Out of the ashes of defeat grow the flowers of success." You can't achieve the impossible without attempting the absurd.

One of my favorite Presidents, Teddy Roosevelt, lost his wife and mother on the same day. What a crushing blow to any person, let alone a future President. Teddy moved to South Dakota. He lived as a cowboy for three years before he came back and took on the Tammany Hall politicians in New York and eventually became President of the United States. Teddy said, "The credit belongs to the man who is actually in the arena. Whose face is marred by sweat and dust and blood; that strives valiantly; who errs and comes short again and again. Who knows the great enthusiasms; the great devotions; and spends himself in a worthy cause; who at best, knows the triumph of high achievement; and at worst, if he fails, at least fails while daring greatly, so that his place shall never be with those cold and timid souls who know neither victory nor defeat." T.R. knew the **three-word motto**, and I will repeat his powerful quote later in the book. Hope you highlighted T.R.'s quote.

This is what life is all about to the Positive Thinker. While it may be agonizing at times when we face terrible obstacles in our lives, it is life. But, we all face trials and tribulations. Why not face them knowing positively that you will overcome all that are thrown at you? Now I know you will say, "But Ken, how about the people who find out they have a terrible disease?" Let me answer that real life crisis in two parts. First off, it has been proven conclusively that many diseases are mentally induced, such as ulcers. Ulcers are not the result of what we eat, but what is eating us. And it has been medically proven that arthritis and bursitis are often linked to people who are rigid and mentally restrictive. So, by thinking positive, you can avoid those types of problems. Watching the foods we eat and not smoking can avoid cancer. Cirrhosis of the liver can be avoided by limiting our alcohol intake. In other words, we can avoid risking most of the physical ailments with proper diet and exercise, and a good frame of mind. We can risk giving up the things we like to enjoy a healthier life. If we do contract a disease, it, and even the big C, (cancer) can be overcome. Many people I know, including doctors, know of people who have conquered cancer and many other diseases by positive thinking, prayer, and nutritional products like colostrum. One in particular was a beauty queen who won a major beauty contest. She soon developed the deadly disease, lupus. This former beauty queen developed skin lesions on her face, which formed ugly scabs. She went from doctor to doctor with no cure in sight. She became almost bald and grew a beard. Her teeth became loose, her vision and hearing deteriorated, and she developed terrible headaches from the drugs she took. Finally, after being given only a few months to live, she tried to take her life, as she was in excruciating pain. But suddenly a miracle started taking place. To make a long story short, she became a Positive Thinker and a firm believer in miracles. She put her trust completely in God's hands. Two months later the warts and lesions disappeared, as well as all the other effects of lupus.

Now the Positive Thinkers leapt for joy, but the negative thinkers took their normal route, by declaring it was simply the drugs that saved her. If that were true, then all the doctors and specialists she met with had lied to her, because they told her the drugs would not arrest the disease. The doctors claimed all they could do would be to alleviate the pain. Chapter 15 is spent going into more detail as to how positive thinking cures illness and can prevent it. Positive thinking does improve your health, as you will see as we go more in depth with confirmed stories in later chapters.

It is inescapable to avoid crisis in our lives, and while a hermit avoids the problems people bring, he still has to live with his own thoughts. Those thoughts can be terrifying when he remembers why he dropped out of society. That same hermit still has to face the dangers all humans have to face in regards to their health, be it physical or mental. After all, we can't get away from ourselves. There is an old saying that applies here, "A ship in a harbor is a safe place, but that is not what ships are built for."
— William Shedd

One of my favorite customers lives in Virginia in a little out of the way town named, of all places, Dixie, which was next to the Fort Union Military Academy. Dick lives in a beautiful home, which was Dicks and his wife's dream home built according to their specifications. Dick was one of the nicest people I have ever met, but in a few short years he lost his wife and daughter in tragic circumstances. I remember asking myself, why does this have to happen?

Why do people have to suffer? In one of Saint Paul's letter to the Romans he exclaims, "I reckon that the sufferings of this present time are not worthy to be compared with the glory, which shall be revealed in us." I called Dick several years ago and he acted as happy as I had known him before the tragedies. It didn't surprise me, because Dick was always happy and a positive thinker.

In 1949, an automobile accident almost killed one of the world's greatest athletes. The doctors doubted he would ever walk again, let alone play sports. But the doctors didn't realize this great athlete knew the **three-word motto**. Seventeen months after his accident, Ben Hogan won his second U.S. Open golf title at Merion, Pennsylvania. [I have played Merion, and have never played a tougher course]. In 1951, he went on to win the Open again, and the Masters. Winners know differently than skeptical doctors. They are willing to risk embarrassment and pain to win, and they know the **three-word motto**.

Does the name, Frank "Spig" Wead, mean anything to you? Frank fell down the stairs of his home, paralyzing him from the neck down. The doctors said he was to be bedridden the rest of his life. Three years after starting rehabilitation at San Diego Naval Hospital, he regained the use of his fingers, and finally was able to walk on crutches. [John Wayne starred in the Movie, 'Wings of Eagles' with Maureen O'Hara, Dan Daily and Ward Bond about Spig]. Several years later in 1930, you would have known him as one of the most successful screenwriters of all time. He was also responsible for helping to develop the mini-aircraft carriers, (Jeep Carrier) which helped win the war against Germany and Japan.

Speaking of movies, let's get into the risks many actors, directors and producers take making movies. Many times they take a risk on a questionable movie and they have to pay the consequences if it flops at the box office. Many careers have gone down the tubes or at the very least have taken a nosedive and many films have bankrupted producers and backers. Yet they take those chances, because they are risk takers, like Jack Lemmon was in the highly popular film, Some Like It Hot. Jack was having dinner in Dominique's, in Hollywood when the great director. Billy Wilder approached Jack about a role in Some Like It Hot, with Marilyn Monroe and Tony Curtis. It is about two men who witness the St. Valentines massacre, and they have to hide, forcing them to dress up as two women. Jack said, "I knew I would be taking a chance on it. It was a delicate situation, but worth the risk."

To prove how great a risk movie making is, take the case of the movie It's a Wonderful Life, starring Jimmy Stewart, Donna Reed, and Lionel Barrymore. The interesting thing is that the movie has been played more than any other has in the history of movies. The reason unfortunately is that the copyright was not renewed which placed it in the public domain. The great director, Frank Capra, William Wyler, George Stevens and Sam Briskin had formed Liberty Pictures, and they wanted Frank Capra to direct It's a Wonderful Life as their first venture. They were positive it would be a hit, so they risked everything but it failed miserably and bankrupted the company. Yes there are risks in life, but we just go on to the next challenge when we fail.

Remember that when you dare to risk, you will have the negative thinkers telling you it can't be done. And even after you accomplish your dream, another group of negative thinkers will pop up and say that it will never last, or it is not very practical. A classic example was when the telephone was invented in America by Alexander Graham Bell, on March 10, 1876 in Boston. Bell spoke the famous words to his assistant, "Mr. Watson, come here; I want you." The head of the British Post Office laughed and said, "We have no need of such a thing; we have plenty of messenger boys."

When you dare to risk, you are actually making a bet on yourself. You are using courage to take a calculated risk and bet your ideas will be fruitful. Life is not just courage on the playing field or battlefield. Life itself takes courage to face. You must never stand still when faced with an obstacle, because that causes you to become nervous. You will feel trapped, and, as a result of constant indecision, you will eventually encourage physical problems. When faced with an obstacle, the Positive Thinker does not rush right in like a bull in a china shop. He or she sits down and analyzes the problem, and if it does not require a decision immediately, he will think it over for a day. If it does require a decision immediately, he will still take his time to think it over, but he or she will make a decision. He or she will stand behind that decision regardless of the consequences.

Lee Iacocca, the great businessman, and risk taker, felt that introverts, (the non-risk takers), were probably that way because they must have made the wrong move in a marbles tournament or game of checkers when they were young and made up their minds they were never going to take a risk again. As successful as he was, Iacocca admits he made his share of mistakes but he knew that was part of the growing process.

One of the great exponents of the risk philosophy was the first commissioner of baseball, Judge Kenesaw Mountain Landis, and Judge Landis ruled baseball with an iron fist. Baseball was in disarray and needed a savior. Babe Ruth was not enough to save baseball as gambling was flourishing in those days. Judge Landis took over and drew up rules for the owners and players to stick by. If anyone broke the rules Judge Landis would investigate and if the infractions proved correct the guilty party was drummed out of baseball with no provision for re-instatement. Once Landis made the decision it was final regardless of what the fans, owners, players and press thought of his decision. He risked being unpopular, but he was a man of conviction and integrity.

The Positive Thinker knows that when he risks he takes the chance of failure, but is willing to risk it. And as 1948, Nobel Prize winning author, T. S. Eliot, put it so succinctly, "Only those who risk going too far can possibly find out how far one can go."

"The most important thing in life is not to capitalize on your gains. Any fool can do that. The really important thing is to capitalize on your losses. That requires intelligence and makes the difference between a man of sense and a fool."

— William Bolitho

author of Twelve Against the Gods.

General R. E. Chambers, former chief of the Army's Psychiatry and Neurology Division, stated, "Most people don't know how brave they really are. In fact, potential heroes, both men and women, live out their lives in self-doubt. If they only knew they had these deep resources (courage, and faith), it would help give them the self-reliance to meet most problems (take risks), even a big crisis."

The Positive Thinker knows that some decisions will be wrong, like the 40,000 mistakes Thomas Edison made until he invented the light bulb. Edison knew the **three-word motto**. And speaking of inventors-many people think only of men when it comes to inventing. Did you know that a woman invented Kevlar, which is made up of aromatic polyamide fiber, is five times stronger than steel on a weight by weight basis and is used in bulletproof vests? The famous actress, Hedi Lamar, invented frequency hopping during World War II, to keep the Germans from jamming American torpedoes. This is the technology, that is used in cell phone technology today. Next time you smoke a cigar think of the actress, Edie Adams, who invented the cigar ring.

Of course, the negative side to taking a risk is those poor souls with "gambling fever" who crowd the gambling tables night after night. They are betting on themselves but the house is betting that it will win. And so the house to stay in business has to make the odds in its favor. Many an aspiring gambler has left a gambling establishment with no money for the groceries that week. Have you ever heard of many gaming houses going out of business except for poor management? The one time owner of the Philadelphia Eagles gambled away his fortune and lost the team. Know the limitations. A man who made his living by owning a string of one armed bandits said he had nothing but contempt for the foolish people who are so naïve as to imagine that they can beat a machine that is already rigged against them. And one of the best known bookmakers told Dale Carnegie of Carnegie Adult Night Schools that with all his knowledge of horse racing he couldn't make money betting on the horses. And yet in 1910 people bet six million dollars a year on the races. That was six times as much as the national debt back then. Just imagine what is bet today. Ahem: Imagine what the national debt is today. Again I repeat, know the limitations.

Patrick Henry, Samuel Adams, Thomas Jefferson, Benjamin Franklin and all the signers of the Declaration of Independence, along with George Washington had a huge decision to make that involved a tremendous risk. Our Positive Thinking forefathers were willing to risk everything for their countrymen, including their own freedom. They were not just going to challenge the King of England's taxes and authority. They were putting their lives on the line. Once the 56 men signed the Declaration of Independence on July 4, 1776, in Independence Hall, (then known as the state house), in Philadelphia, Pennsylvania, they became outlaws and were considered traitors to King George III. That meant they could lose their properties, families and their lives. And dear reader that is exactly what happened to some of them. Those intrepid men became criminals and were hunted by the British troops. When Patrick Henry made his famous speech ending with, "give me liberty or give me death," a tidal wave started which could not be stopped and thousands of lives and families were destroyed so that future generations would not have to live under a despot but in a free society under a republic type government. These sagacious men were willing to make the ultimate sacrifice, knowing some of their neighbors were loyal to the King. George Washington and many others gave up the comfort of their estates so that men could pursue the rights of free people. They also had to face the most powerful army on earth, but through their faith in themselves, and God, and with courage and positive thinking they overcame the impossible. They knew the **three-word motto**, and were willing to risk it all.

Bob Bush made a split decision in World War II to risk it all. His Medal of Honor citation states: "In this perilously exposed position, he (Bush) resolutely maintained the flow of life-giving plasma, (a wounded officer was lying in the open on a ridge top, and Bush ran to his aid). With the bottle held high in one hand, Petty officer Bush drew his pistol with the other and fired into the enemy ranks until his ammunition was expended. Quickly seizing a discarded carbine, he trained his fire on the Japanese firing point-blank over the hill, accounting for [the deaths of] six of the enemy despite his own serious wounds and the loss of one eye suffered during the desperate defense of the helpless man."

This brave man drove off the rest of the Japanese soldiers and then evacuated the wounded officer. Bob was willing to pay the ultimate price to save a fellow human being. The Congressional Medal of Honor calls for bravery above and beyond the call of duty. Today, this positive thinking man, who made a decision to act above and beyond the call of duty, has a very successful lumber and building supply business.

And so, is that the ultimate risk one must take? Is a father or mother laying down his or her life for loved ones the ultimate price? Is it a relative, or a stranger giving a healthy body part, so that another may live? Is it a person giving up a loved vocation so that a son or daughter can have constant love and care while in their baby and toddler years? Is the ultimate price a person leaving their job to start up an enterprise, so that they can be their own boss and build a garage operation into a multi-million dollar empire, like Positive Thinker Bill Gates? Is it giving up home and loved ones to keep ones sanity after constant abuse from a spouse? Is it putting a career on hold to take care of an ill, aging parent? Is it leaving your beloved country to become citizens of another country, where they can practice religious freedom and enjoy free speech? No matter what my opinion is, this is the real point: there is a price to pay for greatness or love, or success or peace of mind. And if you are not willing to pay the price, I do not condemn that decision, because we all do not think alike. One person's goals are not the same as another's. But if you are not willing to take a risk for your goals then do not expect people to follow you or help you. Oh, and don't be naïve enough to think you will achieve those goals if you are not willing to pay the price, for that is also an insult to those who have been willing to pay the price to achieve theirs.

Is the risk $50 ? That was the price Dr. Horatio Nelson Jackson was willing to lose in 1903, when someone made the statement that no one could drive across America in one of those new horseless carriage machines. Dr. Jackson bet the doubter $50 that he could drive from San Francisco to New York in three months. This was a daunting task, because there were no reliable roads or maps and certainly no signs showing the way. Dr. Jackson bought a 1903 Winton, which had no windshield and had a motor with only twenty horsepower. This price payer was about to make history, but it was not going to be easy, due to the many obstacles, that do not face drivers today. Consequently he became lost many times along the way because of numerous reasons, including bad directions by well wishers. Did he win the bet? If you want to see how it turned out a movie was made with Tom Hanks titled, Horatio's Drive, with an actual 1903 Winton.

Life is full of surprises no matter how we plan it. In his play Macbeth, Shakespeare wrote "Out, out brief candle! Life's but a walking shadow." Theodore Roosevelt said, "I wish to preach not the doctrine of ignoble ease, but the doctrine of the strenuous life." LaBruyere said "Life is a tragedy for those who feel and a comedy for those who think."

"

Every life is many days, day after day. We walk through meeting robbers, ghosts, giants, old men, young men, wives, widows, brother's-in-law, and ourselves. But always meeting ourselves."

—James Joyce

You can read all kinds of books on the bookshelves telling the secret to success, and years ago I stumbled onto the secret of success through reading about people who achieved it. Earl Nightengale, Dr. Norman Vincent Peale,

Napoleon Hill, Dr. Maxwell Maltz, Andrew Carnegie, and W. Clement Stone, to name a few, as well as many other people with sagacity throughout history, such as Plato, Socrates, Confucius, Marcus Aurelius, and many others have all disagreed on many different subjects. But every one of these erudite people has agreed "you become what you think about." If you think success, you become successful; if you think failure, you become a failure. But, and this is the great alternative-but-what do you have to do to become successful? It is not enough that you have to think success to become successful. Shortly, I will tell you the most important three-word part to the equation, that when coupled with goals will lead you to being happy and successful. Every good book you read will tell you that to be successful you have to have goals. Webster's dictionary defines success as "the satisfactory accomplishment of a goal sought for." Then there is the definition of success by one of the zaniest professional baseball players to ever wear a uniform, Bob Uecker. Bob once said, "My career is a confirmation of one of the basic laws of success: Anything is attainable if you don't need it." Of course Bob speaks with tongue in cheek, because while Bob was a mediocre ball player in his own opinion, he went on to be a success in broadcasting and on television with his popular comedy series, Mr. Belvedere and as an announcer. Just recently this mediocre ball player was inducted into the Baseball Hall of Fame for his baseball broadcasting ability. My own personal opinion is, while some ball players are mediocre in the major leagues, and others become stars, just getting to the majors is considered being successful.

As a matter of fact, you will have to go through what I have been through, or close to it. And I am not kidding. You must be willing to suffer. You must be willing to sacrifice. You must be willing to eat peanut butter and jelly sandwiches without the peanut butter and jelly. And let me tell you right here and now, brother or sister, if you are not willing to sacrifice, if you are not willing to face anxiety, if you are not willing to put off the bill collectors, then don't plan on becoming a winner. But, "Happy the man, and happy he alone, he who can call today his own: he, who can secure within, can say: "Tomorrow, do thy worst, for I have lived today."— Author unknown

And remember, tomorrow is a mystery; yesterday is history; today is a gift, that is why it is called the present.

Every single person who made it to the top had to sacrifice and take risks unless they inherited wealth. And even those people had to face obstacles in their personal lives. Many of them took their own lives, because they were not allowed the luxury of facing obstacles in their early lives. They were pampered and coddled by others when they faced obstacles in childhood. Others eliminated their problems for them. When they faced crises in their grown up lives, they crumbled. It reminds me of a roommate I lived with. Six of us rented an old mansion in the area near Valley Forge, Pennsylvania. One of our roommates was a recent graduate of a prestigious college. He came from a very wealthy family and his father did everything for him. This young man never worked a day in his life. After a three-month stay with us, he informed us he was going to New York to take on Wall Street and, "show it how things were done." I remember several of us shaking our heads and wishing him well and in my heart I did not give him much of a chance. But myself being a Positive Thinker, I felt he might be different. So off he went to take on powerful Wall Street as a stockbroker.

A year later almost to the exact day, he called us and asked if he could get a room back. The roommate who replaced him had just left, so, fortunately for him, we did have a room available. When he arrived at the house he had a dejected look on his face and his shoulders were slumped. He barely spoke above a whisper. He stayed in his room, rarely leaving except to eat. He had never had to fend for himself, and Wall Street had gobbled him up and spit him out as flotsam. In my opinion, this is a message to all parents to allow their children to take risks and fend for themselves at times.

The problem is, he was conditioned like the cricket in a jar. When you put a cricket in a glass jar with a lid, the cricket will jump and jump and jump. He will bang his head on the jar, and he will be conditioned to jump no higher than the lid. That is proven when you remove the lid after a while. He has become so conditioned that he can't jump higher than the lid, so he stays in the jar. That is what happens to people who have everything done for them. When they go out into the cruel world they bang their heads against the lid, because their thinking controls them.

In 1910, Manuel L. Quezon decided he was going to become president and free his fellow Philippine citizens from bondage. Twenty-four years and six months later, he did become the first president of the new nation. He knew the **three-word motto**, or he would have never stayed the course to accomplish that great achievement. He dared to risk a comfortable life to lead his country out of the dark ages.

If you are not prepared to pay the price by taking risks, don't set the goal, for no port is the right port for a ship without a rudder. And speaking of taking risks, try diving for sixteen years off the coast of Florida looking for the treasure from the Spanish ship, Neustra Senora de Atocha that sank in a hurricane in 1622. Mel Fisher paid a terrible price during those hardship years, including the drowning of his son and his daughter in-law. He almost lost his own life, but he kept daring to risk. Mel was determined and refused to give up. His stick-to-it-iveness paid off when he finally discovered over $400 million of sunken treasure in 1985 after years of painstaking searching. A movie was made about his search, in which Cliff Robertson played the part of Mel, and Loretta Switt played his wife.

You must be willing to pay the price. But, as Horace said, "Riches either serve or govern the possessor." Cyrus stated, "No good man ever became suddenly rich." So take adversity and give it a purpose. You must also find a mentor to learn from. We need mentors to help us climb the mountains we face in life. Everyone needs someone to draw strength from. I draw my strength from God, and I would not have had the strength to go through the years of my life (particularly the last ten) without leaning on Him. And, of course, I also followed the lessons of Dr. Norman Vincent Peale.

You need hope to carry on the struggle. You must remember that it is when things seem worst, that you mustn't give up. You will want to give up. Oh, how you will want to give up. But, you must have faith in yourself and God. Oh, I know the atheists and new age thinkers say there is no God, or that you yourself are a god, but the old saying holds true, "there are no atheists in foxholes." And, in mans arrogance, we have been shown time and time again that we are not gods. We think we can go it alone, and don't have to depend on anyone but ourselves. But if that is true, why do so many of these people see therapists on a regular basis? One of the designers of the Titanic boasted, "Even God can't sink this ship." There have been many other unsinkable ships built throughout history, like the battleships Bismarck, and Yamato, which are rusting on the ocean floor.

Through all the hardships you must never build a case against yourself, and remember that ultimately nothing matters anyway. So, why worry? The word worry comes from an old Anglo Saxon word, Weirgon, which literally means to strangle or choke. In other words, when you worry, you are actually strangling off your air supply, damaging your body, and shortening your life. "Though life is made up of mere bubbles, tis better than many aver. For while we've a whole lot of troubles, the most of them never occur." —Nixon Waterman. Why Worry?

One of the keys to control worry is to relax physically. That will cause a mental relaxation as well. Too many people are rushed, and too busy to take time to relax, they say. That has to change. You need to force yourself to go to a quiet place for 21 minutes a day to relax, and close your eyes and get away from it all. Visualize yourself on a beautiful island relaxing. This will cause a "dehypnotizing" effect from the negative influences. Simply let go and relax your muscles, one by one. Now focus on your island. After that mental picture has formed, relax again and form a picture of your goal. Another method is to go back to a happy time in your life. Visualize the images. Pay attention to details like sounds and physical feelings. We should do this daily, and in the same place and time. We need a quiet room, a decompression chamber of sorts. We need to depressurize from the daily tensions in life so that we can return the next day ready to take on the "real world."

Dr. John A. Schindler, stated, "Regardless of the omissions and commissions of the past a person has to start in the present to acquire some maturity so that the future may be better than the past. The present and the future depend on learning new habits and new ways of looking at old problems. There simply isn't any future in digging continually into the past."

You must remember to take the clear road on the mistakes of the past. Everyone, including Einstein and Bill Gates, has made mistakes. But they were willing to take risks. These mistakes are necessary in the learning experience, and this is a proven theory. Just remember that mistakes are all right as long as the eraser does not wear out before the lead in the pencil.

Dorothea Brand explains how she became a more productive and successful writer. Dorothea had witnessed hypnosis and read a sentence by psychologist, F.M. H. Myers, that she claimed changed her life completely. Dr. Myers explained that the talents and abilities displayed by hypnotic subjects were due to a "purgation of memory" of past failures, while in the hypnotic state. Dorothea reasoned, "if that were possible under hypnosis—if ordinary people carried around within themselves talents, abilities, powers, which were held in and not used merely because of memories of past failures—why couldn't a person in the wakeful state use these same powers by ignoring past failures and "acting" as if it were impossible to fail?" Dorothea decided to try it and acted, "as if," with amazing results. Her production and sales had increased many times over and she became an accomplished public speaker, much in demand. Before this change, she was terrified of public speaking.

Professor William James advised us as far back as 1899, "When once a decision is reached and execution is the order of the day, dismiss absolutely all responsibility and care about the outcome." In other words, you should not worry, but if you have to worry, do it before the action is to take place. Because once the action takes place worrying will not affect the outcome. Just relax, "Taking no anxious thought for tomorrow."

Dr. Matthew Chappell, stated, "The only cure for worry is to make a habit out of immediately substituting pleasant, wholesome, mental images, for unpleasant "worry images." Each time the subject finds himself worrying he is to use this as a "signal" to immediately fill the mind with pleasant pictures out of the past, or in anticipating pleasant future experiences. In time worry will defeat itself because it becomes a stimulus to defeat itself." You must not have the attitude, "I hope nothing happens." That is defeatist.

One successful method of overcoming worry is when it happens to you, simply snap your fingers twice, or pinch yourself twice or say "stop" twice. This will always be your signal, like the ringing of the bell for Pavlov's dog. (Pavlov was a psychiatrist, who proved the theory of conditioned reflex). It will become automatic after a while. Did you highlight this paragraph?

Dr. William Osler talks about "day tight compartments." "Look neither forward nor backward beyond a 24-hour cycle. Live today the best you can. By living today well you do the most within your power to make tomorrow better." And dare to risk making tomorrow better. Winners that are willing to risk know the **three-word motto**.

Professor William James commented about the attitude of Saint Catherine of Genoa, when he wrote, "She took cognizance of things, only as they were presented to her in succession, moment by moment. To her holy soul, the divine moment was the present moment … and when the present moment had established itself and in its relations, and when the duty that was involved in it was accomplished, it was permitted to pass away as if it had never been, and to give way to the faces and duties of the moment which came after."

In 1944, Dr. James Gordon Gilkey, gave a sermon titled *Gaining Emotional Poise,* and it became a best seller. Dr. Gilkey found after many years of counseling, you develop a bad habit of feeling that you should be doing many things now and that leads to breakdown, and worry, as well as other problems. His solution was to take things in single file by visualizing an hourglass where the grains of sand drop one by one.

Remember, as Dr. Peale said, "The more problems you have, the more alive you are." So, when funds are low and debts are high and you want to smile, but you have to sigh, when care is pressing you down a bit, rest if you must.... Very shortly I am going to give you the **three-word motto** of how to stay positive and meet your goals in life.

Put your plan together first.
"Effort only fully releases its reward after a person refuses defeat."
—Napoleon Hill

One of the most important processes you should go through during your quest for your goal is to stay motivated. The best way to do that is to read your goal to yourself every day when you wake up in the morning, and right before you retire at night. It is extremely important that you read motivational books, such as *Think and Grow Rich,* and/or *Grow Rich With Peace of Mind,* by Napoleon Hill. One of the most important books that should be daily reading is "*The Power of Positive Thinking*", by Dr. Norman Vincent Peale. Zig Ziglar wrote a profound, must-read book titled, *See You At The Top*. I am firmly convinced that these and How to Win Friends and Influence People, by Dale Carnegie, should be required reading in high school. Hopefully this book will stay on your reading list. You must also limit reading negative information, such as the newspaper, and magazines. If you have to stay on top of the news, just be aware of the headlines. They pretty much say it all. In another chapter I will tell you what the experts tell you to do to get to the heart of the story while not reading the whole negative article. Watching the late night shows is enjoyable, because they have humor laced with some important news. Staying positive is more fun than staying negative anyway, so give your mental attitude an edge. You will find that you will be a happier person eliminating the negative influences in life. You will also find most people are attracted to Positive Thinkers.

"A positive attitude is contagious, but don't wait to catch it from others. Be a carrier."
— Anonymous

What is the key once you set a goal? Stay with me for a while. There is the only one way to become a winner. You must have the **three-word motto** embedded in your brain, your heart and soul. You must grit your teeth every day and repeat the **three-word motto** often. It all starts though by daring to risk.

God has a plan for each of us. And as I sit here working my fingers across the keyboard I realize my life has happened so fast, and that eventually nothing matters when they shovel the dirt on your coffin.

One of my early heroines was a great lady by the name of Sally Starr. She was a big TV star in the 50s and early 60s, but the studio eventually canceled the children's show she was the host for. When you thought of Philadelphia, Pennsylvania, you thought of former police Commissioner and Mayor Frank Rizzo, Sally Starr, and newscaster, John Facenda. The stories about the struggles that she faced after being terminated by the television station fill a book she has written. Sally has fought her way back after terrible tragedies and heartache. Sally lost everything, and she is indicative of the Positive Thinker you can't keep down forever. Sally is a fighter. She became my friend later in my life and I can assure you that she knows the **three-word motto**.

John Facenda had a heavy cross to bear as well, because his wife whom he adored had become ill and wheelchair bound. But John was a positive person and it was a comfort to hear his melodic deep voice. Frank Rizzo was a very positive person too. He had a radio program in which listeners called in to air their disagreement with the present economy, city administration, or any subject. Frank would always have a positive reply by comforting the person, telling them they were lucky to live in the greatest country in the world. Frank was not afraid to take on controversy while he was Commissioner of Police, and then Mayor and was known as a no nonsense administrator. He continually risked the ire of the press, but he was a man of his convictions and stayed the course to rebuild the great city of Philadelphia. I talked with Frank Rizzo before he passed away and I am convinced he knew the **three-word motto**.

Regardless of a person's occupation, we are all endowed with a very important factor called human dignity. We are all made by God and He gave us all good qualities, but even if you do not believe in that philosophy, we must realize it is our obligation, and not only that, it is our inalienable right to live with dignity. And quite frankly, in my opinion, we should treat all others with dignity. Our great statesman Ben Franklin said, "When you are good to others you are best to yourself."

If you want to think of dignity, think of the youth in Athens. He had a speech impediment, and people laughed at him when he gave his first address. Now that is a definite loss of dignity. What would you do if that happened to you? Would you vow to never talk in public again, like many aspiring public speakers do, or would you stick out your chin and vow to work harder to be the best, and say to yourself "I'll show them!"

This youth, who lost his dignity, was orphaned at seven and his guardians misused his estate leaving him barely anything. When he became of age he sought justice, and won some damages after pleading his own case. He had a long way to go as a public speaker though. To learn to speak distinctly, he spoke after putting pebbles in his mouth and reciting while running. He even shouted over the loud roar of the waves to give his voice strength.

Demosthenes greatest speech was given in 330 BC, and it propelled him to fame as one of the greatest orators in history. This poor boy with a speech impediment grew to be a man who stood tall and spoke with dignity. A fellow senator said, "When I speak, the people say, 'How well he speaks,' but when Demosthenes speaks the people say, 'Let us march!"

And to round out taking a risk: John Wong, and his partner, Casey Lau, launched ActionAce.com in 1997 with their pooled savings of $100,000 and a clear goal: "Do something fun, where we won't have to work." They began by selling a product they knew well--old comic books. But soon they decided the serious money was in other playthings. Today their Web site is Hong Kong's leading Internet toy seller; they are said to have grossed more than $1 million last year, and the city's venture capitalists are wagering big bucks that the company has only begun to grow.

"Progress always involves risk. You can't steal second base with your foot on first base."
— Author unknown

DARE TO RISK

To laugh is to risk appearing the fool. To weep is to risk appearing sentimental. To reach for another is to risk involvement. To expose your ideas, your dreams, before a crowd is to risk their loss. To love is to risk not being loved in return. To live is to risk dying. To believe is to risk failure. Because risks must be taken, because the greatest hazard in life is to risk nothing. The people, who risk nothing, do nothing, have nothing, and are nothing. They may avoid suffering and sorrow, but they cannot learn, feel, change, grow, love, live. Chained by their attitudes, they are slaves; they have forfeited their freedom. Only a person who risks is free. —Author unknown

"Let me dare to risk it all to make others happy and in turn I am fulfilled."
— Anonymous

"You must do the thing you think you cannot do." Eleanor Roosevelt
"If you risk nothing you risk even more."
— Anonymous

MAIN THOUGHTS AND CHALLENGES

1. Go back to the beginning of this chapter and review the highlighted sentences.

2. Place the highlighted page numbers on this page.

3. Write the most important highlight and why it is so important to you.

4. Write on your sheet a risk someone in your family or a friend has taken.

5. Write on this page what you are willing to risk to achieve your main goal.

Chapter 3

YOU DO NOT HAVE TO BE A VICTIM OF YOUR CIRCUMSTANCES

As you grow older you will discover you have two hands.One for helping yourself and one for helping others."

—Audrey Hepburn

Academy Award winning actress

Don't ever try to convince a true Positive Thinker that you are the victim of your circumstances, and therefore can't do anything about it. If you were formed by those circumstances, then you can be re-formed by other circumstances.

One of my favorite movies is "*My Fair Lady*" with Rex Harrison and Audrey Hepburn. In the movie, two English gentlemen make a bet. Rex bets he can take a guttersnipe and turn her into a real lady of sophistication. Audrey is his challenge and what a challenge. Her face is dirty, her clothes are ragged and filthy, and she speaks with a Cockney accent. In time, with patience, coaxing and threatening, she is transformed into a real Cinderella. The hardest part was the mental preparation to convince her she could actually become a real lady. She keeps insisting, "I can't do it." I remember once when I really got into positive thinking and I saw the movie again, a quote came quickly to mind. "Success comes in cans, failure comes in cants."

No one is born with many different personality traits. They come slowly over time and so slowly can be replaced. That is why brainwashing works.

The opposite of "My Fair Lady" is what happens sometimes to very successful people. I am talking about the ravages of drugs and drinking. For example: some years ago after being discharged from the Army, with motion picture photography school and photography experience behind me, I went into skid row in Philadelphia, Pa., with my brother. He was assigned to film a story on skid row, as a cameraman with Channel 3 in Philadelphia. To this day I will never forget the men we met there. I am talking about very successful, prominent men. One skid row resident was a former lawyer. Another was a former director from Hollywood, and still another was a well-known doctor. The personality metamorphosis that took place was pathetic to say the least. Here were men who were at the top of their profession once and now were living in poverty wearing rags and dependent on alcohol. We interviewed them at length, and most gave the same reason why they turned to alcohol. I prefer not to get into that reason, because it will ruffle many feathers. But the point is they went from success to failure.

"Most of the shadows of this life are caused by standing in one's own sunshine."
—Ralph Waldo Emerson

Washington Irving wrote, "Little minds are tamed and subdued by misfortune; but great minds rise above it." You can alter the negative traits after you finally come to the realization that you really, truly want the good things available to come into your life. You must also come to grips with the nature of your fears, and doubts. In the majority of cases people never examine the origin of their fears, nor do they have any idea of the number of fears bothering them.

The two most destructive fears a person must face are first: self-created, and second: adopted. Self-created fears come from inferiority feelings. They come from a physical limitation, or an emotional shortcoming. These fears are justified but with positive input will be overcome. What is that positive input? First, if you are really sincere about becoming a positive person you must wash the negativity out. Giving up negative habits does that. One of the easiest ways to accomplish this is to write them down on paper. Then you must stare at them and ask yourself if they are doing you any good in your life. Then you must resolve to get rid of them, but understand that you need two things to do this. First off, you must get help and second, you must have patience, all the while knowing positively that once you know the **three-word motto** you will succeed.

One of the most damaging negative habits is the negative news you read or see almost daily, which I wrote about earlier in this book. Now granted we need to know the happenings to keep current and not be ignorant of what goes on around us. But all stories happened before. There is just a different twist and different people in them. According to Ron Stables of Effective Reading Systems, you can get at least 80% of the information you want from the newspaper article simply by reading the first and last paragraph; looking at any captions and quickly skimming the rest. Positive Thinkers just look briefly at the headlines, and if it is of earth-shattering importance will glance briefly through the article. Positive Thinkers limit their input of television news and negative leaning movies and television shows. In my personal opinion, Oprah Winfrey gives the best positive input of all the shows and I watch her every chance I get.

Positive Thinkers refuse to listen to gossip and dirty stories. They are usually looking at the good side of life. They are usually involved in community activities to help their fellow man. The Positive Thinker reads positive input books and success stories. He or she reads history of successful people. The Positive Thinker has positive input sayings around his house or office.

A classic example of reading the negative news concerns a former heavyweight-boxing champion of the world. He had been reading the newspapers, and all they said was how he was going to lose the championship fight. He had awakened from a nightmare, which showed him being mauled and bleeding, sinking to the canvas and being counted out. As he sat and remembered the nightmare he couldn't stop trembling. He said, "Right there I had already lost that ring match which meant everything to me—the championship. Through the newspapers I was losing the battle in my own mind. I realized part of the solution was obvious. Stop reading the papers. Stop thinking of the Dempsey menace, and Jack's killing punch and ferocity of attack. I simply had to close the doors of my mind to destructive thoughts—and divert my thinking to other things."

Gene Tunney went on to defeat the "Manassa Mauler" in that championship fight on September 23, 1926, and in a rematch, beat him again. You will read about Tunney in another chapter.

Dempsey admitted that worry was his biggest opponent, so he would give himself pep talks during his fights. He kept saying repeatedly to himself, "Nothing is going to stop me. Nothing is going to hurt me. I won't feel his blows. I can't get hurt." He prayed before every meal, and speaking of meals Jack owned Dempsey's restaurant at 36 W. 33rd Street, New York, which still stands today. Yogi Berra once said, "Nobody goes there anymore it's too crowded."

Remember one very important thing - you must never try to develop another person's personality. These stories you read are for inspiration and knowledge only. You must decide to put you in the middle, and completely focus every bit of your interest on numero-uno. But never forget to be of service to the less fortunate.

President Teddy Roosevelt was voted "Man of the Decade" for the years 1900 to 1910. Teddy also won the Nobel Peace Prize for settling the Soviet-Japanese wars. He said later in his life, "Having been a sickly boy with no natural bodily prowess, and having lived much at home, I was at first quite unable to hold my own with boys of rougher antecedents. I was nervous and timid. Yet from reading of the people I admired I felt a great admiration for men who were fearless and who could hold their own in the world, and I had a great desire to be like them." He did not say he wanted to be just like them. He said he had a desire to be like them. He knew that he could never be just like them. He didn't have their body strength, intelligence, looks, height or weight. He was small and scrawny. But he realized that he had to pay a price to gain strength and stamina. After all, he had a terrible case of asthma, and there were times he was close to death. However, he built up his strength slowly by exercise. He became a voracious reader, and he imbedded the **three-word motto** into his very soul.

Al never went past grade school and had doubts about his abilities. But one day he woke up and decided that he would not allow his mother to work as hard as she did to support the family. And so he started reading all he could get his hands on to get an education, because he knew that knowledge is power. Almost by accident a neighbor asked him to run for politics locally. Al did not know a thing about local politics so he read and studied the issues. Al eventually became a member of the New York assembly from 1903 to 1915, and then was elected sheriff of New York County until 1917. He then was asked to run for state representative and the rest is history. He continued his reading into the early morning hours, getting, at most, around four hours of sleep a night. Al Smith was elected governor of New York four times and became the greatest living authority on the government of New York State. In 1928 he was elected to represent the Democratic Party in the presidential election that year, and six top universities, including Harvard and Columbia, conferred honorary degrees on him. Throughout his great career, Al Smith never lost his humility. While he served in dignified positions, and had honor after honor bestowed on him, he remembered the teaching of Aristotle, who said, "Dignity consists not in possessing honors, but in the consciousness that we deserve them."

Ben Forston was Secretary of State for the state of Georgia, and served his duties from a wheelchair he was confined to after an accident in 1929. Ben was another Positive Thinker who did not blame circumstances and proved that positive thinking over comes all obstacles. "Better to die on your feet than live on your knees." —Anonymous

Stay away from the negative thinking that traps you in the vicious circle of fear. You become convinced that you will fail, so you do not try. The Positive Thinker never fears failure, but the negative thinker has a passive attitude, which automatically produces failure and this proves to him that his fear was justified. He creates that awful circle that will never allow him to realize his hopes of being successful.

The negative thinker can and does change his thinking and circumstances to positive thinking if he really wants to become a Positive Thinker. To prove the point, a few years ago one of the great players of baseball had to retire because of glaucoma. This short, stocky resident of one of the worst projects in Chicago was told he was too small to play professional baseball. Yet, he led the Minnesota Twins to two world championships in 1987 and 1991. Kirby Puckett told of his dream as a five-year old to play professional baseball during his recent speech at his induction into the Baseball Hall of Fame in Cooperstown, New York. Kirby said, "It might be cloudy in my right eye, but the sun is shining in my left eye."

Just remember as Cardinal Newman, a great theologian stated, "Great acts take time." We can't outgrow the limits we place on ourselves: rather we should set new limits to live by.

Napoleon said, "Imagination rules the world." Einstein said, "Imagination is the world." George Scialabba said, "Perhaps imagination is only intelligence having fun."

The great Olympic decathlon champion, Bruce Jenner, looked at a photograph of his face on the body of a former Russian champion every night before going to sleep. He pictured himself night after night taking the victory lap after winning the grueling decathlon. He built up his body and practiced vigorously day after day to prepare and did win the decathlon in the Olympics. His face is now on a Wheaties box, along with many other Positive Thinkers, like the first person, two-time Olympic Pole Vault champion, Reverend Bob Richards, Mary Lou Retton, and Michael Jordan.

Neil Armstrong, the first person to take a step on the moon, dreamed as a child that he would do something big in aviation, and Billy Graham practiced giving sermons to tree stumps before he became the great preacher, known the world over. The famous comedian, Sir Harry Lauder, told the press that he could practice as much as 10,000 times before giving a performance.

Dr. Denis Waitley stated, "When winners are without, they work and practice to toughen themselves to the task. They know that imagination is the greatest tool in the universe" To prove that point and to stay on the theme of this chapter – read on about a former POW.

Every day in his lonely dank cell he imagined himself playing golf on all the different courses he had played while he was a free man. He would pick up his imaginary golf clubs and start with the driver. He would look over the fairway and address the ball. This Positive Thinker would drive the ball straight down the fairway and pick up his next club out of the bag to make his approach shot. Again the shot made its way straight towards the green. His next shot might be a pitching wedge and he would put it close to the flag. Finally, he would pull out his putter and would never need over 2 putts to get the ball in the hole. Day after day he practiced. Finally, he was released from this hell he had been in for over 5 years. He then went on a pro/amateur outing with one of the great golfers of the game. To everyone's astonishment after over 5 years of not playing golf he shot a76, and I will expound on this moving story later in the book.

As president of the World Positive Thinkers Club I have had the pleasure of writing and mailing the newsletter to hundreds of members over the last five years. In those newsletters I write about people famous and not so famous who have overcome all manner of obstacles. One such story is about, Legson Kiryia, who had a dream to go to college in America. He asked permission from his mother and she packed some cornmeal in some leaves for the journey. She had no idea her little village in Africa was over six thousand miles from America.

Legson walked for over six months, sometimes sleeping in the open fighting disease and wild animals, and then spent another six months working to be able to get to the coast. He then walked another year to get to the coast of Africa. Missionaries helped out with his visa and passport, and the students in America where he was to attend college pitched in with charity events to raise money for his passage. After over two years, he finally arrived on the college campus with one pair of shoes and a suit. Now that is a Positive Thinker.

Harry could not attend college because of financial problems, so he took odd jobs: railroad timekeeper, booker, mailroom clerk, and bank clerk. He entered World War I and participated in heavy fighting. In 1934 Harry was elected to the U.S. senate and in 1944 was selected to be Franklin Delano Roosevelt's Vice President. Harry went on to become President after Roosevelt died, and became President again in the next Presidential election, narrowly defeating Thomas Dewey. Some of our senior citizens reading this book can remember a Chicago newspaper headline stating that Dewey had beaten Truman before the election was over. Harry Truman is the last President to enter office without a college education, and he made a huge decision to drop the atom bomb on Japan to end WWII, thereby saving millions of lives. By the way, the Japanese had an atom bomb they were preparing to drop on San Francisco only eleven days later. As a Positive Thinker Truman knew, "The buck stops here."

Have you been laid off from your job recently? If you look at it in a positive light you will see that it is an opportunity waiting to happen, like the young clerk who was laid off from his job in the Salem (Massachusetts) Customs House. Well actually it wasn't he who saw the opportunity; it was his sagacious wife. Nathaniel told her the grave news and insisted on getting another job immediately, but she revealed that she had been saving money from her household allowance and it was time for him to write the book he always wanted to write. And so, with the help of a loving wife Nathaniel Hawthorn devoted the time to turn a lemon into lemonade, and two years later the best seller: The Scarlet Letter was published.

It could happen overnight and often does, but prepare for the eventuality that you will have to work long and hard at it. It is worth the price! You have to have hope and believe in yourself, and dream, and if you are a Positive Thinker and know the **three-word motto** of all winners, it will happen. Do not allow yourself to believe the negative thinkers and social engineers who say you are a victim of your circumstances. They mean well, but they do not understand that many winners started out living in the slums.

Nietzsche's formula for the superior man was, "Not only to bear up under necessity, but to love it."

One of the most important decisions you have to make is realizing from a positive standpoint, that your problems are not as complicated or as bad as you think. Emotions tend to take over and magnify problems and make them appear frightening. Furthermore, most of our problems are not deeply rooted. Some are old problems, probably, but only because looking at it from a positive angle, you never did anything about them. Perhaps you tried, but the method taken to try to solve the problem was incorrect.

The key is finding the right solution and then simply eliminate the problem. This might seem to some to be over simplifying the problem, but the major problem is some people tend to make mountains out of molehills.

Much of it has to do with our attitudes. For example: One day a man faced with moving to a new town walked into city hall, and told the clerk he was thinking of moving to the town. He wanted to know what the people were like in the town. The clerk looked at him for a moment, and then asked him what the people were like in the town he was moving from. He then proceeded to vilify the citizens of his former town in a vitriolic manner. When he finished his tirade, the clerk calmly commented, "I hate to tell you this, but unfortunately I think you will find the citizens of this town exactly like the ones you are preparing to leave." A scowl filled his face and he sullenly walked out of the hall. Several weeks later another man walked into the same city hall and asked the same clerk if she could tell him what the people were like in this town, as he had to move and was thinking of moving to her town. Again this sagacious clerk asked what the people were like in the town he was leaving. A big smile crossed his face, as he became lavish in his approbation of his former neighbors. He finished by saying that he hated to leave such fine people, but he had no choice. The clerk smiled and said, "Well I think you will find the people in this town are just like the people you are leaving."

Next time you are feeling sorry for yourself take a deep breath and think back in time about a situation you have heard about or have personally seen relating to human suffering. One such calamity happened in the Philippines on April 9, 1942, when Major General Edward King climbed into his jeep and made the heartbreaking trek to surrender to General Masaharu Homa. This surrender set in motion the infamous Bataan death march, whereby

78,000 American and Filipino soldiers, and 20,000 Filipino civilians were forced to walk over 75 miles in the searing heat to a death prison. Many of these poor starving unfortunates were murdered on the long hot dusty road, simply because they could not keep up with the blistering pace. When they arrived at the railroad station they were forced into metal boxcars with no ventilation or no room to sit or lay down, and many of these unfortunate men died where they stood. Their dignity was stripped from them as well as their clothes and shoes and personal possessions, and they were not allowed to drink water from waterfalls along the route after disembarking from the death rail cars. Fortunately, on the positive side, some of the prison guards were kind to the prisoners and became friends, and in chapter 15 you will read about a miracle that occurred in that final death camp.

Oh yes, you have it tough, as we all do from time to time, but you have to face reality and be a man or woman and keep your dignity and fight back, as those poor unfortunate American and Filipinos were not allowed to do.

With so many people in psychoanalysis today, we are trained to believe that it is a long drawn out process to pinpoint the problem and find the solution. Perhaps the following question will ruffle some feathers! Why is it that some psychiatrists and psychologists (in my opinion, in the minority, I might add) can cure the patients they deal with much faster than other of their peers? In my opinion, we are brainwashed into believing that all psychoanalysis is a long drawn out process. The true Positive Thinker like I write about in this book does not believe in that line of thinking. A classic example is about a time when a young actor asked James Cagney how often he was in therapy with a psychiatrist. Jimmy told him that he never spent time on a psychiatrist's couch, whereby the young actor expressed amazement and responded, "You must be kidding, everyone in Hollywood spends time there."

Understand one thing as you leaf through the pages in this book. This book is not intended to be a cure all. The results of your search to become a Positive Thinker and find happiness depend entirely on YOU. You must be willing to take control of your life. You must write down what is keeping you from being a Positive Thinker and vow to do something about it. I would like to suggest and even urge you to do it right now. I am very serious. Put this book down and write now what you feel is keeping you from being a full time Positive Thinker. Then come back to the next sentence. Do it now.

I will wait for you! Put your notes in the space provided below and take as long as you need.

If there is more than one problem you must take them one by one, rip them apart and resolve to rectify them. Put on the paper solutions you feel comfortable with and get good advice from those you respect and know will be positive in their outlook. It is absolutely your choice and nobody else's. You have control over the situation if you really want it. You have to take charge, just like the quarterback in a close football game. Don't be afraid or think people will deter you because they see a difference in your attitude. Do not become paranoid, because they are talking about you. It is simply jealousy. Do not be like the football fan that every time his team goes into a huddle thinks they are talking about him. "You're the man," or woman, whichever the case. Stop letting others run your life.

The student, who believes he is an "F" student in all his subjects, or even one, will find that his report card is exactly as he expected it to be. The sad thing is, he now has proof, and it takes faith in himself or another person willing to help him to get out of this negative path. A girl sitting on the sidelines at the school dance, who believes nobody likes her, will find that she will not be asked to dance. Her self-conscious expression and her unconscious hostile facial expressions will emit to those around her. A salesperson with a good self-image will undoubtedly have an easier time selling than a salesperson with a lack of confidence in his or her abilities.

Dr. Maxwell Maltz, plastic surgeon and author said, "The most important psychological discovery of this century is the discovery of the self-image." Dr. Maltz reported case histories of complete changes in personalities and character after he had performed corrective surgery on people with facial defects. He felt that the scalpel he used to correct the defects was like a "magic wand" that transformed the whole life of the patient. Shy people became bold and courageous. In one particular case, a retarded boy turned into a butterfly. He literally overnight became an alert, bright teen who became an important executive later in life. A salesman who had lost faith in himself became one of the firm's top salespeople. Everyone, regardless of whether or not he will admit it is seeking an identity, an urge to be somebody. You could take a survey and I would venture to say that 99% of the people you surveyed would admit to that not new revelation. Professor William James, one of the leaders in his chosen profession stated, "The deepest principal in human nature is the craving to be appreciated." Dr. John Dewy, another well-known pundit said, "The deepest urge in human nature is the desire to be important."

Dr. Georgi Lozanov, a top psychiatrist, has developed a method of cue-reinforced learning. His method re-teaches the mind to relax by playing soft music, psychodrama, psychology of suggestion, and listening repeatedly. Dr. Lozanov's methods have brought about a chorus of praise from educators throughout the world. First-grade students after using his methods learned over a thousand words of a foreign language in only one day. To top it off, he taught first-graders algebra and calculus so difficult most college students would have a hard time solving the problems. We are talking about six year old average children. This has opened up a whole new methodology of learning and an auspicious learning industry.

During their imprisonment in Vietnam, many of our American POW's taught each other how to play the guitar with sticks and stolen strings. And these were people who never had even held a guitar before. Some POW's even sketched piano keys on a flat board and practiced their favorite tunes. As I mentioned in an earlier chapter, a colonel played an imaginary round of golf every day for five and one-half years while in solitary confinement. The most important technique he had to use was one of self-discipline and self-image.

He had two choices. He could sit and rot in the cell or he could do something constructive. He chose the latter and for five and one-half years he teed the ball up and played a round of golf every day. His drives were hit straight down the fairway on every course he had ever played. He replaced every divot and fixed every ball mark on the green, raking the sand traps as well. He did everything a golfer does on the real course, including pulling out the flag while putting.

He proved that self-image works, because less than one month after his release from the Hanoi Hilton, he paired with the professional golfer, Orville Moody, and shot a 76 in the New Orleans Open. The news media in their unbelief congratulated him and shot questions at him like, "That was beginners' re-entry luck right?" With a broad smile on this hero's face, he retorted that he had never three-putted a green in his five and one-half years in captivity. He practiced the method of self-fulfilling winning prophecy in that dank cell for five and one-half years. He never once complained for his lack, and he knew the **three-word motto**.

If you want to talk about winning golf, follow the career of the great Lee Trevino, one of the top money winners on the PGA tour. One of the keys to his success, (even though he does not have the classic swing or a powerful body of Tiger Woods, Tom Watson or Bobby Jones), is his obsession to win. He simply expects to win. One year, while battling pneumonia he came in second in the U.S. Open. Lee visualized himself winning every match. Granted he did not win every match, but without his strong self-image and attitude he would not have won half the matches he did win. There is no one who wins all the time at everything they try. The key is they do not complain about what they lack.

The key is setting a goal, and knowing the **three-word motto**. One is not much good without the other! Nothing great was ever accomplished without goals and the **three-word motto**. "No wind is the right wind if your sails are not up." Just remember that we have a hard time doing things alone and need support, so once you make up your mind to lose weight or whatever other goal you have you must get support from another positive person. And do not under any circumstances listen to the negative feedback.

While in Korea I made up my mind that I would not sit around doing nothing but drinking beer or shooting the bull like many soldiers do. I realized that school is never out for the pro, and we must continually be learning new things, versus becoming a couch potato growing a huge gut and taking weekly trips to the drug store or doctor. And so my second day in Korea I signed up for Karate lessons at the base gym.

Now, in the space following this sentence I want you to in large letters write the words, "I will act in a positive manner to meet my goals and will memorize and practice the **three-word motto**." Go ahead, write them in the space below, and highlight them.

Think of the men who were born in log cabins like Lincoln, Millard Fillmore, Warren G. Harding, James Buchanan, James Garfield, and Andrew Jackson who went on to become President of the United States. President Andrew Johnson had the most poverty stricken, unhappy childhood of any boy who became President. Andrew Jackson's father died before Andrew was born. Lincoln, whose mother died when he was a tot read borrowed books by candlelight on a dirt floor and was considered the most skillful President in his use of the written English. Teddy Roosevelt had severe asthma attacks at night and had a speech impediment. F.D.R. ran the country from a wheelchair, and JFK had terrible back pain from a war injury and had to be helped to walk on occasion.

You must put on three 3 X 5 cards how much weight you plan to lose and by what date. These cards are then placed in strategic places like the bathroom mirror, the refrigerator, and your car dash or desk at work. You must then repeat the goal first thing in the morning, then at noon and last thing at night. You must also realize the consequences if you do not overcome the problem, such as being overweight. The next thing to do in the process of overcoming the problem is to close your eyes in a quiet environment and concentrate until you see the end result of overcoming the problem. I am very serious here. You must visualize the end result. I will prove it works with a story in a later chapter about a little boy who was the worst player on my son's baseball team.

If you are overweight, you must see yourself thinner, wearing nice fitting clothing. And most importantly, you must put the **three-word motto** on the cards and swear to abide by it.

One thing you must also realize is that it sometimes takes help to accomplish a goal. Inform your relative or friend of your goal if it is not too private, and ask them to help you. Get into a support group. They will then keep on you to make sure you are heading towards your goal. If anyone is negative and says you can't accomplish your goal go to another to help you, until you find that one positive person. Pardon my redundancy, but above all, write the **three-word motto**, which you will learn shortly on the cards too. Don't even try to accomplish your goal without the **three-word motto**. If you don't, I will report you again to the SPCAW. [Society for the prevention of cruelty against writers].

You must also read positive input books and articles every day, like Zig Ziglar's, *See You at the Top*, and listen to tapes. That sentence is so important that I will repeat it. Read positive input books and articles every day and listen to tapes. We all need to be inspired and reminded, including yours truly.

When a plumber comes to your house to make a repair would you have confidence in him if he left his tools home? He must carry tools to achieve the required result. That is what we all use when we make repairs. We all use tools. Positive input materials are your tools. Use them daily like the plumber uses a pipe wrench, and stop thinking of what you lack. Think in positive terms.

Reading positive input daily is in essence, practicing. The great actors, comedians, musicians, athletes, artists, public speakers, bow hunters, dancers, orators, salespeople, and all other great professionals will tell you that if you want to excel, and be the best, you must practice, practice, practice. You must practice and learn daily, because school is never out for the pro. And you must stop thinking about what you lack.

For example, how would you feel if your leg was broken and had to be amputated from the knee down? Suppose you were a college football player. Would you think your career was over? I suggest you ask Neil Parry how he felt when it happened to him on October 14, 2000. Neil lost a leg and is now wearing prosthesis. He is lifting weights, and working out every day, and his coach at San Jose State assures everyone that Neil will play on special teams, not just be a holder for the place kicker. Speaking of place kickers Brian Hall kicked field goals for Texas Tech. from 1974-76 with a prosthetic foot.

One of my all time favorite actors is Kirk Douglas. I have seen almost every movie he has appeared in. From Sparticus, with Jean Simmons, to Final Countdown, where he played the captain of the nuclear aircraft carrier U.S.S. Nimitz, which goes through a time warp and finds itself back in time on December 6, 1941.

Kirk wrote several books and one in particular is, My Stroke of Luck. In the book, Kirk talks about his stroke and how he almost took his own life. He talks about his coming to the realization that his stroke was a blessing, and that we are put on this earth to help others less fortunate than us. And he and his lovely wife, Anne, now do charity work. Kirk has won the Presidential Medal of Freedom, which is the highest civilian award given by the President, along with numerous other awards and honors. He now serves as Goodwill Ambassador for the State Department, and the Legion de Honneur in France. One of Kirk's favorite people is Jim MacLaren. Jim is a six-foot-five athlete, who was riding his motorcycle to school at Yale, when his motorcycle crashed into a bus, causing him to lose his right leg. Kirk writes about Jim, "He still worked as an actor and participated in triathlons, swimming 2.4 miles, bicycling 112 miles and running 26.2 miles. With his prosthesis, he became the world champion of physically challenged individuals. He never wore a cosmetic prosthesis, just a steel rod inserted in his shoe. He saw no need to cover it up." He focused on his positive not what he now lacked.

Kirk wrote, "One summer, Jim was participating in a triathlon in Orange County, and he asked me to watch him race. It was Sunday, the last day of the event. I couldn't go, so we arranged to meet at my house the next day."

"But the next day, I visited him in the hospital. He looked up at me. 'Kirk, what are the odds of me having two accidents like this in five years?' "He was completely paralyzed. He had broken his neck, as a pick up truck got in his way in the final event of the race."

Jim was smiling in that hospital room, because he is a Positive Thinker and knows he will walk again. Of that he has no doubt. "The accident has been a gift to me," he said to Kirk. He told Kirk that he didn't like the guy he used to be.

Jim now gives inspirational talks to people who are physically challenged. Kirk writes, "Why is it some people get stronger with adversity, while others shrink?"

There are so many stories of famous and non-famous people who have overcome adversity. I think of athletes who have been injured on the playing field, some of them becoming paralyzed. Some of them wallow in self-pity and stay incapacitated and some refuse to let injury lock them in a wheelchair. I think of Jim Abbott, who was born with one arm shorter than the other, and retired recently from pitching in the big leagues. Beethoven, Milton, Fanny Crosby, Ray Charles, Helen Keller, and Stevie Wonder were blind, yet they went on to greatness.

There is a wonderful young lady who lives in New York by the name of Shirley Cheng. It just so happens that if you look on the front cover of this book you will see she her endorsement, and I am one of her biggest if not her biggest fan. Shirley is a blind/disabled award-winning author, motivational speaker, self-empowerment expert, poet, author of seven books, a contributing author of eleven books, and an advocate of parental rights in children's medical care, aide/caregiver monitoring and screening for students with special needs and people with disabilities, and world peace. Many times I have talked with Shirley on the phone. She is the happiest lady if not person I have ever spoken with, and you can view her website at shirleycheng.com. Thomas Edison was mostly deaf and his laboratory burned down to the ground, yet he became the most prolific inventor of all time. Edison said, "Opportunity is missed by most people because it is dressed in overalls and looks like work."

The bankers denied a dreamer loan after loan because they felt his ideas were foolish. He never gave up his dream and finally after faith in himself and his wife's faith in him, Henry Ford changed manufacturing methods and built one of the great automobile empires. Henry Ford and his wife knew the **three-word motto**.

Ray Berry played end for the old Baltimore Colts with one leg shorter than the other. Fred Arbonis was blind in one eye and played tight end for the Kansas City Chiefs. Billy Jean King was a short, pudgy little girl, and the other children laughed at her when she claimed she would be a great champion some day. She won a record 20 Wimbledon matches and is one of the greatest tennis champions of all time. One of the only two-time Olympic decathlon champions, Bob Matthias had anemia as a child. Jim Ruyan was so sickly as a child he spent half his time in the doctor's office. He went on to break every middle distance running record. A block in football injured Bill Neider and the doctors said the knee would never bend again. He walked down to the track at Kansas University one day, and picked up a little iron ball and tossed it in anger. Little by little the leg began to bend, and he became a world champion shot putter.

A thirteen-year-old boy had injured his leg so badly in an accident that the doctor claimed the only way to save the boys life was to amputate the leg. This determined boy refused to let the doctor amputate and begged his big brother to stand guard outside the door to the bedroom where he and his other five brothers slept. If the doctor had amputated the leg this boy would never had been able to enter West Point. He would never have planned the invasion of Germany in World War II and, Dwight D. Eisenhower, would have never become President of the Unites States of America. His faith pulled him through.

Alice Marble woke up the day of the 1936 Wimbledon tennis championship match with a torn stomach muscle. The doctor advised her not to play. She was in excruciating pain, but was determined to put mind over matter and went out to win the most prestigious tennis event there is. The greatest upset in boxing history shocked the world in 1920. The newspapers were not giving the Manassa Maulers opponent a ghost of a chance. He was one of the biggest underdogs in the history of the fight game. He almost believed the stories, but stopped reading the newspapers and focused his mind on a vision of him beating the champion. Gene Tunney went on to beat Jack Dempsey not once, but twice. He had scored the greatest upset in the history of boxing until another huge under-dog named Cassius Clay, now known as Mohammed Ali came along and beat Sonny (The Bear) Liston. Ali never forgot his poor roots, and one day he was told that a home for elderly people was being torn down, leaving no place for these poor unfortunates to live, so Ali took the money out of his own account and had a home built for them.

The great poet Robert Burns grew up living in poverty and became a drunkard in the bargain. But through it all he stayed his course and the world became a better place through his beautiful thoughts. Michael Jordan was cut from his high school team, but refused to give up. He wasn't even the first player drafted after college and became one of the greatest basketball players of all time. Many say the greatest! Margaret Thacher was told England would never tolerate the idea of a female Prime Minister, (some say she made the statement herself). Jimmy Durante the great actor/comedian was warned that his big nose would keep him from entering show business. He eventually earned his own popular television show. Goldia Meir was advised that she would never see success and was criticized for her lack of education and thick accent. This New York resident of Russian Jewish ancestry eventually became Prime Minister of Israel. One of the great television broadcasters, Ted Koppel was advised strongly by his broadcasting professors not to enter broadcasting. The former owner of the Cleveland Cavilers professional basketball team, Gordon Gund, is also an expert skier and is blind.

Tom Sullivan is a great sports fan and sees the game better than anyone would hope to see. He has season tickets to the Los Angeles Lakers games, sitting right behind Jack Nicholson. Tom enthusiastically talks about the sounds of the game saying, "You can tell if a team is getting back on defense by the squeak of their shoes." He can tell by what the coach is saying whether or not the players are paying attention. He could even tell you that it was Magic Johnson by the sound of his dribble. He can tell you which referee blew a whistle to stop action by the type blast from the whistle. Tom Sullivan has written five books, including a best seller, plays the piano and three of his recorded albums have reached the top twenty. He also is a movie producer, television interviewer, actor, and motivational speaker, accomplishing all this while blind from birth.

In 1977, Bob "Butterbean" Love had to retire from professional basketball because of a bad back. This 6'8" 215 pound gifted athlete lost everything including his wife in 1983 because of a stuttering problem. In 1984 he took a job as a busboy in a restaurant out of desperation, because no one in the basketball industry would hire him for any type job. As a child he dreamed of giving speeches to thousands of people, but in those days in Bastrop, Louisiana no one knew about speech therapy to help his stuttering problem. For 45 years he dreamed that dream. He finally worked his way up to working the cash register and started speech therapy in 1986.

The therapy helped him overcome his fears, turning his life around leading to his promotion to Nordstrom Corporate Director of Health, giving speeches about self-worth and self-image. In 1989 he was awarded the Lifetime Achievement Award and gave a stirring speech about what it is to believe in yourself and deal with life.

In 1988 Gail Devers started experiencing migraine headaches and terrible pains in her feet. One doctor told her she had a severe case of athlete's foot, while others told her she was simply experiencing stress or fatigue. Gail even went through the horror of watching her face shed its skin, as well as seeing her eyes bulge. The worst was yet to come as she started shaking involuntarily, losing weight, developing insomnia, and hair and memory loss. Blood blisters developed on her feet causing swelling and yellow fluid to ooze, producing an awful odor.

Luckily, the problem was diagnosed as Graves disease, but the doctors recommended foot amputation. Gail refused to give up and after a thyroid operation she started back on the road to recovery, and even claims to be thankful for having gone through the terrible ordeal she faced daily. She was confident that her personal hell made her stronger and more determined. Gail says, "And I would tell anybody, the last three years of my life is like a miracle. If you don't believe dreams come true, look at me. You have to have faith and believe in yourself." In the 1992 Olympics, in Barcelona, Spain, Gail Devers won the gold medal in the 100-meter race and barely missed the gold in the 100-meter hurdles. Gail proved that just because life throws you a curve you don't give up once you know the **three-word motto**.

Bonnie St. John Dean wrote for Personal Excellence Magazine, which I was privileged to write for. Bonnie said, "Growing up in hospitals, in leg braces and on the wrong side of the tracks didn't stop me from believing that an African-American girl with only one leg could learn to ski. And as soon as I learned to ski a little, I set my sights on qualifying to compete in the 1984 Disabled Olympics in Innsbruck, Austria. Such a big dream, such an outrageous dream, made me stand taller just thinking about it."

"My big break came when an elite ski academy in Vermont accepted me as a student. For three months I searched for grants, scholarships, and sponsors to no avail. I will never forget when I told the headmaster I couldn't afford the tuition and had failed to find sponsors. He said, "Come anyway." I knew this opportunity would change my life."

"But the first day of school at Burke Mountain Academy, I broke my leg—my real leg—while playing on a skateboard. As the only kid there with one leg, I badly wanted to show them I could run obstacle courses, jump rope and play soccer. Instead, walking on crutches with my artificial leg, I could barely leave my room without tripping on stones in the path. Being so inept in a crowd of super athletes hurt more than my injuries. At night I cried in my pillow to keep my roommate from hearing.

"Although the doctor removed my cast after six weeks, my luck did not improve. Within a week my artificial leg broke in half. For three weeks my prosthesis roamed the country, lost in the U.S. Postal Service."

"Years later, standing on the winner's platform in Innsbruck, Austria, as the silver medal was hung around my neck, I could hear the National Anthem playing, and see the Stars and Stripes fluttering behind me in the frosty night air. Dreams of that moment pulled me through the tough times."

Bonnie is a Rhodes Scholar with degrees at Harvard and Oxford, and teaches self-motivational skills. Bonnie never thought about her lack.

I am going to be a little harsh here, but tough love never hurts anyone, so quit feeling sorry for your circumstances and stick out your chest and be a man or woman. Take responsibility for taking charge of your life and help others by giving them encouragement. You will be surprised at the calming effect it has on you. Don't blame others for your present state of affairs, be it emotional or physical, because when you point your finger at others there are three times as many pointing back in your direction. Stop being a couch potato if that is where that is where you spend most of your time. Get out and enjoy the fresh air. Walk or get a bicycle and move around the neighborhood, smiling to the neighbors, or call people on the phone if you are incapacitated physically. Get to the library and enjoy the wonderful world of adventure and history. Take up a hobby and learn the feel of accomplishment. In other words, follow the example of others before you and who had the courage to overcome pain. What has happened has happened. Face your problems, stop wallowing in victimization and play with the cards you have been dealt.

I am not talking about clinical depression here, as that takes treatment, but most other problems can be handled by your standing up and being counted.

In the beginning of this chapter, I said that your problems are not as complicated as you think. Below is a list of things you should be thankful for. Hopefully, you will realize that life is not as complicated as some people make it out to be.

I AM THANKFUL

- For the person who complains when his dinner is not on time, because that person is home with me, not someone else.

- For the teenager who is complaining about doing dishes, because that means she is home and not on the streets.

- For the taxes that I pay, because it means I am employed.

- For the mess to clean after the party, because it means that I have been surrounded by friends.

- For the clothes that fit a little snug, because it means I have enough to eat.

- For my shadow that watches me, because it means I am out in the sunshine.

- For a lawn that needs mowing, windows that need cleaning, and gutters that need fixing, because it means I have a home.

- For all the complaining I hear about the government, because it means that we have freedom of speech.

- For the parking spot that I find at the end of the lot, because it means I am capable of walking, and that I have been blessed with transportation.

- For my heating bill, because it means I have been kept warm.

- For the lady behind me in church who sings off key, because it means I have freedom of religion and that I can hear.

• For the pile of laundry, because it means my family and I have clothes to wear.

• For weariness and aching muscles at the end of the day, because it means I have been capable of working hard.

• For the alarm that goes off in the morning, because it means that I am alive.

"God brings men into deep waters, not to drown them, but to cleanse them."
—Aughey

"Adversity introduces a man to himself."
—Anonymous

"The difficulties in life are intended to make us better not bitter."
— Anonymous

"People are always blaming their circumstances for what they are. I don't believe in circumstances. The people who get on in this world are the people who get up and look for the circumstances they want, and, if they can't find them, make them."
— George Bernard Shaw

MAIN THOUGHTS AND CHALLENGES

1. Go back to the beginning of this chapter and review your highlighted sentences.

2. Place the highlighted page numbers on this page.

3. Write down the most important highlight, and why it is so important to you.

4. Write down people you know or have heard about who have physical or mental liabilities, and if you know how they overcame their handicaps write it down. This takes some discrete investigation on your part.

5. Finally, write on this page what you think is holding you back from attaining goals, be it physical, psychological or living conditions. Then after thought write down what you can do to overcome.

Chapter 4

BE PERSISTENT AS A SQUIRREL

"The power to shape the future is earned through persistence"

—President Calvin Coolidge

People can be a pain in the neck sometimes, but I have found early on in my career that you can't do business without them. Thank God for the good people, and fortunately there are many of them. Socrates said, "No evil can befall a good man in this life or the next." So why be concerned about the business you've lost or the friends or loves you lost? Simply learn to be persistent, and new and exciting things will come your way. This is proven in this book that is in your hands now, and by everyday life going on around you in this wonderful world.

One of the great lessons about persistence took place many years ago in Briggs Stadium in Detroit, Michigan. If you are a baseball fan you no doubt have heard the name Ty Cobb. You know that name because he was one of the first players inducted into the Baseball Hall of Fame in Cooperstown, New York, and in his time was considered the best there was to play America's national sport. At one time Ty Cobb held more hitting and base-stealing records than anyone else in the game, but perhaps what many fans do not know is that he was a dismal failure in his first season with the Augusta, Georgia team he played for. He was so bad that after hitting a sorrowful .237, and playing in only 41 games, management finally told him that he had no talent and gave him his walking papers. Ty wrote his father, telling him of his decision to give up and get into another profession and his father told him not to come home until he had given baseball his best effort. He decided not to give up, and determined that he would be the best or nothing at all, and that is exactly what happened, because several years later Ty Cobb was considered the best in baseball.

Today I learned a valuable lesson. Three weeks ago I filled up the bird feeder outside with some of the feed I give my parakeet. Guess what animal first came to feed. For all you squirrel lovers out there, you know how persistent they can be when they want to get at food. Well, this little rascal would get on the feeder, and I would walk outside and chase him away. Guess what? He would come back 10 minutes later, sometimes from a different direction. I would chase him away, but he just kept coming back. Suddenly it dawned on me that God was teaching me a lesson. When you have a goal, keep at it. I am now letting him feed for a few minutes and then chasing him away so there is enough for the birds, but mainly because I want him to constantly remind me how important persistence is. There he is again. Gosh, how I love that little rascal. He is just sitting there daring me to chase him away. He is saying go ahead chase me away, I will be back. "Determine that the thing shall and can be done, and we will find the way." —A. Lincoln
It reminds me about a funny story Cavett Roberts, a very successful real estate investor and public speaker, told to an audience in the 1960's. He was in a meeting and the board was considering promoting a man in the company to VP. One of the board members voted not to promote the man in question because he was a confirmed alcoholic. Another board member chimed in, "Well, at least he is not a quitter."

Of all the qualities needed to make for a success, persistence is one of the hardest to acquire. Think about it for a second. Life is grand when things are going your way, but when you hit that snag in the road, it suddenly seems the words impossible, or too difficult pop up and especially from the negative thinkers. They will chime in with, "see I told you so." Or they will say, "Why don't you give up this foolishness and use your common sense." The list goes on and on. But don't listen to them. Take the positive route and use the failure as a learning experience. Remember that life is a learning experience and no road was ever paved straight and true. Every road has curves and hills and valleys to traverse to get to the final destination. Go to your library when you have a major setback and read the biographies of famous people. You will find out that each and every one faced a setback, but they did not take their eyes off the goal. Remember as Hannah More said, "Obstacles are those frightful things we see when we take our eyes off the goal." Think of Thomas Edison and the many experiments he went through to develop the light bulb. Plus he spent over $40,000 in research and development before he finally came up with the vacuum and carbon filament that produced the long lasting light bulb. That was in the 1870's. Persistence is when your hands and feet keep working, even though your head says it can't be done.

Why do people quit? There are many reasons why. Should you quit sometimes? In an earlier chapter I alluded to the fact that there is one time that you should change direction on a goal. Contrary to what you might think, I believe there are times you should. I don't consider it quitting, but rather realizing that the goal is too damaging. You must take into consideration the end result. Is what you are trying to accomplish too damaging to the ones you love or yourself? If you have found you are in a field where the majority of people are charlatans and outright crooks you must re-evaluate your position. If it is apparent the only way to make money and be successful in the field is to be like one of them you must listen to your conscience. You must never try to cheat people, because you will be found out sooner or later and then you will have to live with the consequences. So, is it prudent to quit? Yes! When the question of integrity and honesty are in doubt and you did not realize it at first, you should then re-prioritize your goals. That brings up another question. Did you do the proper research at first before you set your ultimate goal? Your life goal should be well thought out and planned. Unfortunately, I am guilty of that error. Am I suffering the consequences? Yes! But I will not succumb to negativity, because I know the **three-word motto**. Now I have the correct goal: of that I am positive, and that goal is to get this book into your hands.

I keep watching and learning from my little friend the squirrel, and I decided to put grease on the roof of the bird feeder to test him or her. At first he jumped on the roof and slid off. It was comical, but he came back and tried again and again. Suddenly, he figured out how to cling onto the area on the side that was not greased. Presto! Now he is getting the food again. I have decided to put more grease on the roof and sides to see how he figures it out. I have no doubt that he will figure it out in time, because he is patient and analytical. He sits on the branch and analyzes which direction to jump from to be able to cling on to the least greasy spot. What a great lesson God teaches us through the animals he created.

It is amazing how people stay in business while making basic mistakes, like not proofreading their own agreement. This is what I deal with on a daily basis. However, my job is not to criticize them. I have to be a diplomat if I want to keep and attract business. [A diplomat is one who tells you to go to hell and makes you look forward to the trip]. And overcoming the little and big irritations in life is what makes life exciting and a daily challenge.

I am used to failure as well as success. We all should be. That is the difference between the winners and losers in this sometimes wonderful, wacky world. There are some people born with a silver spoon in their mouth. But they have faced failures too. **No one goes through life untested-no pressure, no diamonds.**

We all have sad times in our lives, but why dwell on them. We can't change the past. In one of his letters to the Philippians, Saint Paul stated, "Forgetting those things which are behind and reaching forward unto those things which are before, we press toward the mark." -Phil. 3:13- I am sure Paul meant the goal.

It kind of reminds me of the jokes Bob Hope told about Zsa Zsa Gabor. Bob said, "She only marries on Fridays, so if it doesn't work out at least the whole weekend is not ruined." I guess her goal was to marry more men than any other woman in history. Ah, women! God's wonderful gift to men. And by the way, my personal feeling is that we men should appreciate that gift, and treat them like ladies, and pamper them and treat our lady like a princess. The world would be a better place if more men thought that way. Many a great man accomplished his goals thanks to a great lady backing him. Henry Ford's wife had the utmost confidence in him and pushed him to continue after bankers turned him down when he sought financial backing. Dr. Norman Vincent Peale's wife, Ruth, was his guiding light. He always listened to her guidance, because he knew she had great sagacity. They were on vacation in Switzerland, and while sitting on a bench overlooking the majestic beauty of the Matterhorn Mountains; Dr. Peale complained that he didn't think he could overcome the many problems of his ministry. Mrs. Peale took him by the shoulders and told him that he was the ultimate Positive Thinker, and through persistence and faith he would overcome the problems. Needless to say, he did!

My father tried acting in the silent movies sometime around 1917 and it is ironic that he wound up behind a camera instead of in front of one. But while he did not continue as an actor, he was a great cameraman. He was awarded a huge trophy for his camera work and always submitted more stories per day than most of the other cameramen on the beat. Dad was part of history, and was a confirmed Positive Thinker. He did not cry because of his failure as an actor. He simply squared his shoulders and took a different direction. He was there at Lakewood right after the Hindenburg went down, and there are many rumors about the Hindenburg pertaining to lightning and sabotage. Dad told me he was convinced that one of the crew hated Hitler and set up a time bomb, but that it exploded prematurely. There are some newspaper articles written with that angle, and a movie was based on that theory starring George C. Scott.

Dad sneaked out several parts of the Hindenburg in his tripod case. There was strict security, but Dad was a smooth talker, and he had distracted the police. While they were walking in the opposite direction he grabbed several parts from the wreckage. Dad was also convinced the military knew that the Japanese were going to invade Hawaii on December 7, 1941. I read a newspaper article Dad gave me, which states that Movietone News sent a motion picture cameraman to Hawaii several days before the attack. The bureau chief, Tony Muto, received a tip and the rest is history. My personal opinion is that we knew beforehand, but simply botched it. Luckily this country was full of Positive Thinkers or we might never have won the war.

Dad was one of the still photographers at the first Miss America contest in 1921, and in that contest there were only eight contestants. I still have the picture of the eight contestants, and another picture of the photographers in a group shot. The first Miss America was Margaret Gorman, from Washington, D.C. The pageant lasted an hour and Margaret won a seashell. Dad eventually talked the pageant director into giving him her crown since she did not want it. She never went to another pageant even though she was invited as a special guest through the years until she died. When I started the World Positive Thinkers Club I sent her the induction documents to the club. The second Miss America was, Mary Taylor, and she was the only Miss America to win twice. Dad said that she was picked by all the photographers to win the third time, but the pageant directors discovered that based on the pageant by-laws the crown would have to be retired if she won again. Dad had that winner's crown in his collection too, which recently sold for a hefty sum.

Also on the positive side, he was a fighter. He taught me not to take guff from people if they cornered you and to never give up. For that I thank him. He was a fighter, and many times I heard him arguing on the phone with his boss in New York. I sometimes wonder why Dad was not fired, but Dad was steward of the local photographers union, had many friends in high places and was a very ambitious worker. He constantly was scooping other cameramen and getting the best shots. Other cameramen would follow him around on a story because he had a nose for the action. He was persistent in his quest for the right photo shots. He taught me that being a diplomat was very important if I wanted to succeed in my profession. And while he was hard on me and impatient when I went on stories with him, he always sweet-talked the police or any other official when he needed a shot. He never let the fact that he only had an eighth grade education due to family circumstances at the turn of the century stop him from getting the job done. But he was a respecter of authority.

One time when the Queen of England arrived at the North Philadelphia train station all the photographers were trying to get her off the train to take pictures. Finally after dad arrived the other photographers asked him to get her to come out. Dad had a reputation of getting things done, so he walked up to the train window where she was sitting and yelled out, "Hey Queenie, how about giving us a break, and come out for some pictures so we can earn our pay for the day? We won't hurt you." He then shut up and looked at her. They say the silence was deafening with them both staring at each other. Then Dad winked at her, and she stood up and walked outside to the train railing for the pictures.

My brother told me the same thing happened when the King of England came to Philadelphia, except that Dad didn't wink this time. Dad's reputation had preceded him this time, so the King also cooperated.

These two stories taught me valuable lessons. Always shut up when you go for the close, and stay positive and don't let people bully you regardless of their station in life. Positive Thinkers have self-confidence and are not concerned about a person's station in life. Dad never cowered from a confrontation when he was convinced he was right. Be a respecter but not a coward.

Dad lost every thing he had in the early forties due to a scheming person, who was "out to get him." I remember being put out on the street with nothing but the clothes on our bodies, (I lived in an orphanage earlier) but Dad was a fighter and suicide was not a word to be found in his dictionary. He put it all together and seven years later we moved into a brand new home twenty miles to the west.

This was a valuable lesson for me as a child, because I was eventually living with my grandparents in Narberth, Pennsylvania, after we were tossed out in the street. I had to fend for myself against the children who made fun of the only child in the neighborhood who came from divorced parents, and I was goaded into defending our family's honor. I even had to face the humility of not being invited to the next door child's birthday party, because of my circumstances, but my grandmother told me not to be concerned about uncaring people. Eventually the other kids in the neighborhood came to respect me, even though I was the smallest and won very few fights. But, I never backed down from a fight. The Positive Thinker never lets his circumstances deter him or her and always wins through persistence.

Now I always try to talk myself out of trouble, but because I have earned the Black Belt in Karate I will not cower if I am backed into a corner. We all need to stand up for our rights when honor is on the line. I am a big believer in diplomacy, and have responded to insults from clients by staying diplomatic. That way I keep their respect and business. Remember: the good diplomat tells you to go to hell and makes you look forward to the trip. But don't get me wrong, I will not allow myself to be bullied unreasonably and neither should you. A Positive Thinker never allows himself to be bullied unreasonably. He wins through diplomacy, and positive thinking, and persistence, but he keeps his respect. Remember an earlier quote: "It is better to die on your feet than to live on your knees."

One of my Karate students taught me a valuable lesson about persistence, and to this day I think of him whenever I face a mountainous obstacle. I have never met a person as shy as Ed Brown, and what is so amazing is that he sold Fuller brushes door to door. When he first lined up with the other students for a basic front kick he looked ready until he tried to kick, and let me tell you, I have never seen a more uncoordinated person in my life. All I can remember thinking was, "What did I get myself into?" But Ed was persistent, and little by little Ed got better. His speed and technique improved with a little tutoring on my part, and eventually his power was awesome. He eventually earned the brown belt, which is no small feat. As a matter of fact in pre-World War II, in Japan, two Karate green belts testing for their brown belt had to fight each other and the winner won the brown. The only obstacle was that he had to kill his opponent to earn it. I was so proud of Ed that I think of him every time I overcome an obstacle, and if he happens to read this book I sure hope he contacts me. He proved that you can do anything deemed impossible.

Are you willing to be persistent enough to achieve your goal that you will be willing to eat onion sandwiches? That is what "Ole Blue Eyes" put up with in his quest for stardom. Early in his career, around 1939, Frank Sinatra was the singer in the Harry James Band, and they were booked at the classy Victor Hugo club. While they were playing All or Nothing at All the manager approached the stage waving his hands. He started complaining that Harry James' trumpet was too loud and that Frank's singing was, "Just plain lousy." He then followed up by saying; "The two of you couldn't draw flies as an attraction." To add insult to injury the manager refused to pay the band, leaving them flat broke and no food for Frank and his pregnant wife Nancy to eat. So for two days they had nothing to eat but onion sandwiches. [And I talk about nothing but peanut butter and jelly.] Needless to say, the Victor Hugo club eventually closed and the Harry James band went on to stardom. Slowly but surely Frank Sinatra's career took off as his fans the "bobby soxers" went wild over Frank. Frank through his persistence, when his career was again on the skids landed a part in the movie, From Here To Eternity, staring Burt Lancaster, Deborah Kerr, Montgomery Cliff, and many other stars. Frank's persistence paid off, winning him an academy award for best supporting actor in that movie. Frank has passed away and he had his critics, but they can't accuse him of negativity and of not knowing the **three-word motto**. To further prove the point you might want to see the movie, Rudy. It is a true story about a young boy who had a dream all his life to play football for Notre Dame. The major obstacle was that he was very small. He was laughed at and his teammates physically punished him unmercifully. The administrators and coach tried to discourage him for fear he would suffer serious injury. If you want inspiration, go see the movie, and if you are facing an obstacle or circumstances you think are impossible to overcome you will go away inspired. Rudy, as the social engineers say was, "vertically challenged," but his heart had no size limit due to his persistence and knowledge of the **three-word motto**.

One of my favorite old-time singing cowboys was so afraid of speaking in front of an audience he would literally perspire and get the shakes. He refused to make speeches to groups, yet he had no problem singing or acting in front of a group. As a young man he earned a dollar a week plowing corn in Portsmouth, Ohio and during the depression picked peaches in the California fruit orchards pictured in the poignant movie, *The Grapes of Wrath*. Roy Rogers never gave up his desire to speak and after practicing for hours and hours, and with the realization that persistence will overcome he eventually overcame his fear. He learned to relax through the great faith of his wife, Dale Evans, and his faith in himself and God. Even though the winners have failed at one time they have the attitude: "Well I failed already, so now I have nothing to lose; so I might as well relax and give it my best shot next time."

Who would have thought a story about four talking rabbits would turn out to sell over twenty million books. Beatrix Potter tried for years to get a publisher interested in her children's tale and finally had to resort to printing, *The Tale of Peter Rabbit* with private funds. Through her persistence Flopsy, Mopsy, Cottontail and Peter became a sensation in 1901. The book has been printed in 13 languages as well as in Braille.

When told by an admirer, I'd give my right arm if I could sing like you," Marian Anderson replied, "Would you give eight hours practice a day?"

Winners do not blame their circumstances; stay focused through persistence and know the **three-word motto**.

"No one can make you feel inferior without your consent."
— Eleanor Roosevelt

MAIN THOUGHTS AND CHALLENGES

1. Go back to the beginning of this chapter and review the highlighted sentences.

2. Place the highlighted page numbers on this page.

3. Write down the most important highlight on this page.

4. Write on your sheet times that you can remember where persistence paid off for you.

5. Now write down times that you remember when a family member or friend won through persistence.

6. Write down on this page an instance that you are aware of that someone famous won through persistence, i.e. Lance Armstrong.

Chapter 5

POSITIVE THINKERS ARE HAPPY AND HAVE A GREAT SENSE OF HUMOR

"A good laugh is like sunshine in a house."
—William Makepeace Thackery

The White House can be a very serious place to live, but not for one of our greatest Presidents. His children's and his laughter filled the halls. The children, of whom there were six, had their numerous pets running around loose. The children had dogs, cats, badgers, rabbits, macaw, and a pony. This great Positive Thinker played football on the White House lawn with his children. He even engaged in pillow fights with them. Teddy Roosevelt enthusiastically wrote. "I don't think any family enjoyed the White House more than we have." And Teddy never took himself too seriously.

He said of his daughter, Alice, "I can be President or I can keep Alice straight, but I can not do both." Perhaps that task falls into the one-percent impossible category.

Our 16th president, Abraham Lincoln was vilified like no other president before or after him, yet he was able to maintain a keen sense of humor. He was called an ape, a baboon, a traitor, a monster, an idiot, a bully, a lunatic and many other names not worth repeating. A particular newspaper in New York constantly referred to him as "that hideous baboon at the other end of the avenue." Lincoln answered these vitriolic, obtuse statements by stating, "If I were to try to read, much less answer all the attacks on me, this shop might as well be closed for any other business. I do the very best I know how-the very best I can; and I mean to keep on doing it to the end. If the end brings me out all right, what is said against me won't amount to anything. If the end brings me out wrong, ten angels swearing I was right won't make any difference."

Lincoln's ultimate goal was to become president, but after being in the White House for a short time he stated that he only found "ashes and blood." Yet in spite of it all he kept his great sense of humor, and is considered the first humorist to occupy the Oval Office. One well known pundit, Bill Green, claimed, "Lincoln could make a cat laugh." Lincoln was famous for his story-telling. And during the Civil War, London's *Saturday Review* exclaimed to its readers: "One advantage the Americans have is the possession of a president who is not only the First Magistrate, but the Chief Joker of the Land." Lincoln called laughter "the joyous, beautiful, universal evergreen of life." He felt it was important to rely on amusing stories to put people at ease, and he once said, "Humor was an emollient that saves me much friction and distress." He even made fun of himself once when the great orator, Senator Steven Douglas said that Lincoln was two faced during one of their debates. Lincoln replied: "I leave it to my audience. If I had another face, do you think I would wear this one?" The audience roared and Douglas turned to an aid and said, "I just lost the election."

One of his endearing qualities was that he had the courage of his convictions and he remained steadfast during the Civil war holding tight to his main objectives. He refused to compromise in his stand to preserve the Union and abolish slavery. And yet through the ravages and terrible bloodshed of the Civil war, Lincoln was still able to keep his sense of humor as he repeated one particular story to his friends as often as the possibility allowed. It seemed two Quaker ladies were discussing Lincoln and Jefferson Davis, the president of the Confederate states. The first lady said, "I think Jefferson will succeed." The second lady asked why, whereby the first lady replied. "Because Jefferson is a praying man." "And so is Abraham a praying man," replied the second lady. "Yes, but the Lord will think Abraham is joking," retorted the first. Another time during the Civil War, during which he went through many incompetent generals he learned that the Confederates had captured a Union general and 12 army mules. In true Lincoln character he joked. "How unfortunate, those mules cost us two-hundred dollars apiece."

"The best way to cheer yourself up is to cheer everyone else up."
—Mark Twain

Through all the pain and suffering Lincoln went through he always thought of the people first. On the fateful night of April 14, 1865, Lincoln was not really interested in seeing the play, *Our American Cousin*, because he had already seen it. But because it had been advertised that he would attend the play he didn't want to disappoint the people. As he was leaving for the play he turned to the White House guard Colonel William H. Crook and said, "Goodbye." This innocuous statement puzzled Crook, because ordinarily Lincoln said, "Good-night."

Some people might think presidents are always serious, yet many including Bill Clinton hired joke writers along with their speechwriters. Senator Bob Dole rated the American presidents as humorists in what he calls his "unscientific poll." The first ten are rated as follows: 1. Abraham Lincoln 2. Ronald Reagan 3. Franklin D. Roosevelt 4. Theodore Roosevelt 5. Calvin Coolidge 6. John F. Kennedy 7. Harry Truman 8. Lyndon Johnson 9. Herbert Hoover 10. Woodrow Wilson.

There is an old saying that goes: if you are not happy in your job you are paying too big a price and when you go to work smiling it is no longer a chore. You must love what you are doing, and many a person has changed careers, because he was unhappy in that profession. Cary Middlecoff, the great golfer was a dentist first. Robin Cook is a prolific writer, pouring out book after best selling book, yet he is a graduate of Columbia University Medical School. USA Weekend wrote of him, "The man who invented high-tech horror." Grandma Moses started painting when most people occupy graves. They all became happier doing what they always wanted to do.

If you want to know how important laughter is, you should ask a very close and talented friend of mine. She wrote her thesis for her Masters degree about laughter, and to this day is one of the happiest people with the most beautiful smile you will ever see. Were you to sit down and chat with her, you would never guess that she is eighty-six years young. As a matter of fact the publisher of the *Saturday Review* of Literature wrote about the importance of laughter pertaining to terminal illness. You might want to look up the article.

You may not believe this, but my high school teachers can confirm that I did not care much for my history or English courses at all, and yet I have not asked anyone for help in writing this book that gives me so much joy. I am happier writing this book than any other time in my life, because I know it will in turn make you happy. When I pass from this wonderful world I don't even need my name on a gravestone. All it has to say on the smooth granite is, "He came to earth to help and make people happy." My claim to fame in high school is that in the yearbook it stated that I was "BMOC," (big man on campus). Yet I would rather it have been written "FMOC," (funniest man on campus). I took great delight in making people laugh, and I still do. To prove that, you should ask a good lady friend of mine, Patty Jolliff, from Slater, Missouri, what happened to her in the ladies undergarment department in Wal-Mart in Marshall, Missouri one day. I looked at her and said, "Oh Patty here are those training bras you are looking to try on." The other shoppers in the department took one look at Patty with her size 36D chest and burst out laughing. Patty was red faced, but joined in the laughter.

"Laughter heals a lot of hurts."
—Madelein L'Engel

When you decide to change careers you must go all out. You must decide to change your self-image and be the best in your new field. It will keep you focused on your new career and convince you that you made the right choice to be happy.

Use your God given talents to do what you were meant to do. It takes courage to give up a lucrative position, but you must follow your intuition and take that chance. If you are not using your God given talents to follow your dream you are traveling third class instead of first class. You deserve the best!

My grandmother said I had spunk and kept her laughing. The Italian words for a happy heart are *cuor contento*. The Italians call a happy person and one who never seems to fret, does not fly off the handle and does not seem to carry the weight of the world on their shoulders a *cuor contento*. I loved to laugh and it was my escape, even though I didn't realize it back then.

I have a penchant for pulling practical jokes on people, and April Fools Day has always been one of my favorite dates even to this day when I convinced my good friend and confidant recently that she had a flat tire. And I'll never forget the time 20 years ago when a neighbor pulled into his driveway. It was late in the afternoon and he and his wife had just opened the car doors to go into the house. I called over to him and congratulated him on the fact that they apparently were buying new furniture for their house. He asked me what I meant, and I said that it was obvious since a big truck was there earlier loading all their furniture. "What?" he yelled, and ran to the back door. He put the key in the door and just as he opened it I yelled, "April fools." It was a classic moment, as he stopped dead in his tracks and slowly turned around. His mouth was wide open and his wife and I roared with laughter. He shook his head and joined in the laughter.

Sports were always important, and they dominated my activities, especially baseball. My new hero became, Bobby Shantz, a 5'7", 137 pound pitcher for the old Philadelphia Athletics. I have played golf with Bobby; have broken bread many times with him and he loves a good laugh. He had some really funny stories to tell about the ballplayers he played with in the major leagues. [Let me say here and now that my real hero has always been Jesus Christ, and I am convinced he loved a good laugh].

I listened to the radio any chance I could when Bobby was pitching in old Connie Mack Stadium in North Philadelphia. I wanted to be a pitcher in the big leagues in the worst way and when we chose sides for sandlot ball, I was among the first chosen. Even though I rarely pitched I used his name, as all the kids pretended to be their hero's. Bobby is the ultimate Positive Thinker, and was an inspiration to my eventually becoming a pitcher in Junior High School, being scouted by the Pittsburgh Pirates and offered a partial scholarship while in high school. I had my chance in the majors, but that is a story for another time.

Baseball is filled with past clowns of baseball, like Lefty Gomez of the New York Yankees, who pitched in the 1930's and 1940's. Lefty occasionally rode a motorcycle from the bullpen to the pitchers mound, and refused to pitch when an airplane flew over the stadium. His handle eventually became "Goofy Gomez." I had dinner with Lefty in Atlantic City back in the mid 1980s along with the famous Hall of Fame umpire, 5'7" Jocko Conlan, who played second base for the Chicago White Sox and was an umpire from 1941 to 1965. Also present was Pee Wee Reese, the famous shortstop from the old Brooklyn Dodgers, and Happy Chandler, former Governor of Kentucky and former commissioner of baseball. I never laughed so hard at stories; it was one funny story after another and you just knew that these men loved the game. These men just reeked of a positive attitude and they did not have one bad word to say about anybody. Their playing careers in the majors were elongated because they had fun and they knew the **three-**

word motto. "The happiest people seem to be those who have no particular reason for being happy except that they are so." —W. R. Inge

The professional sports leagues are filled with practical jokers and clowns. There is a lot of pressure to win and many players fill the locker rooms with pranks to help take off the enormous pressure that faces the professional ranks of athletes. Ken Griffey Jr. once made a bet with his manager, Lou Piniella, and the loser had to buy the winner a steak dinner. Ken lost the bet and he told Lou he would give him his steak dinner in a few days. Several days later Lou walked into his office and there was a real live cow standing there. And the players also play pranks on their relatives, as Seattle Mariners Jay Bunkers wife found out. He puts clear plastic wrap over her toilet seat and shoves baby powder in her hair dryer. The locker rooms are filled with laughter, and the players make big money, enabling the pranks to be very expensive.

Not only did I win the championship for my age group in ping-pong at age 12, but I won the doubles championship in horseshoes as well. Ironically, my doubles partner in horseshoes lost the ping-pong championship to me. My winning this simple game of ping pong may not seem too significant to you, but it set the stage for my cycle of having a craving to win, winning attitude and refusing to quit. And I always, always loved a good time as I do now. It is fun to have fun. And guess what? It is proven having fun keeps you healthier and young. I am living proof of that philosophy because I have only been in the hospital once for a sinus operation and no one ever guesses my correct age. By the way, Champions come in all ages, young and old. Joy Foster at age eight in 1958, was the youngest ever to win an international table tennis tournament, by winning the Jamaican singles and doubles tournament.

When you are a child you aren't as aware of the good things in life as perhaps the child who is born into wealth. So, while we had just the bare necessities I was too happy go lucky to be concerned, let alone be aware of how little we really had. I only had two pairs of shoes, two shirts, and two pairs of pants. Don't ask how many pairs of underwear or socks I possessed.

My brother, Larry was a heck of a ping pong player and one of my goals in life was to beat him at ping pong. I never could as a child, but after coming out of the Army we had a match. Larry was doubles champion in Germany and I was doubles champion in Korea, so this was a really big match. I did beat him because he is mostly a defensive player and I had sharpened my offensive skills while in Korea. Larry has a great sense of humor and he laughed when I beat him, and said, "Well, my little brother finally figured out how to beat me." I also tell you this to further demonstrate that you can attain your goals in life if you really want them bad enough. You will attain them if you think positive, think hard and work smart and have faith in yourself, and doubt whom you will, but never yourself. But most of all – you will need the **three-word motto**.

I keep remembering Job from the bible and his plight. And there is always the old story of, [Chapter 8] "I complained because I had no shoes, until I met a man who had no feet." The Positive Thinker never complains in public about his or her plight. They smile a lot, because they enjoy life and look forward to its many surprises.

We should understand that we go through life constantly facing obstacles. These obstacles can be financial burden; physical pain and suffering; and mental pain. How we handle these sufferings tests our mettle. The old saying is - pain is inevitable, and suffering is optional. "The greater the obstacle, the greater the glory of overcoming it." —Moliere

I remember a long time ago seeing a bunch of little children in wheelchairs on the top landing of the Art Museum in Philadelphia having a ball. These unfortunate children were wheelchair bound, but they were having fun and laughing as though nothing was wrong. Now that was a group of Positive Thinkers. I made up my mind that day that I would always look at the good side of life and always try to make other people smile and laugh. And speaking of wheelchairs: I have a young friend in Canada who was crushed under her horse after it stumbled and fell. She was not expected to live, and after many months in the hospital and many painful operations she was wheeled out in a wheelchair. This little girl also had some other bad experiences as well, before the accident. She became very bitter and cynical about how life picked on her. She was very mistrusting of adults as is the case with many teens with emotional scars. Many hate everyone in authority, so they will, because of mistrust, not get close to anyone. Someone close to them might have hurt them and so they will not leave themselves open to hurt again. They go on the attack to keep away any more rejection. They tend to drive away the very people who can be of great help to them, and that is exactly what she tried with me at first. But I refused to let her have the advantage so I gave her tough love and understanding. I knew she was hurting emotionally and physically and was lashing out in anger against the "system," not me personally. In essence it was an experiment with me. I wanted to prove to her and myself that positive thinking and laughter will work in her instance. I also knew that many years ago, Professor William James asserted, "The deepest principle in human nature is the craving to be appreciated." I also knew that Dr. John Dewy, one of the most notable American philosophers and a pioneer in educational theory and method, and author of the well known book, *Reconstruction in Philosophy*, said, "The deepest urge in human nature is the desire to be important."

And so, I started pumping positive thinking ideas into her head. At first she refused to listen, but at least she would talk with me, and I would always leave her with a positive quote or thought. After a time I asked her to try an experiment with me, to which she agreed, after coaxing her to promise she would. From the tone of her voice I knew she hardly ever smiled, as she was constantly in pain. I asked her to smile every day when she walked into the classroom and to smile at someone in the lunchroom. At first she rebelled, but I reminded her of her promise, so she reluctantly agreed to do it.

Two months later she became a friendlier young lady who hardly ever complains about her pain except to get positive input from me that it will go away. We enjoy our chats now and her voice has taken on a happy tone. We chat on the Internet and Internet phone and now she sends smile faces and positive responses. I have even put her in the community room I opened called, "Positive Input room." Yes, positive thinking works!

Dr. John A. Schindlers definition of happiness is, "A state of mind in which our thinking is pleasant a good share of the time." The well known Russian psychologist, K. Kekcheyev, found that after testing people with pleasant thoughts they could see better, taste, smell and hear better and have better feel when they touched things. Our senses improve with pleasant thoughts as proved by Dr. William Bates.

Do you have to walk around with a smile on your face all the time? No, but I highly recommend that you do not walk around with a scowl, because people will avoid you. Professor William James, who is considered the dean of American psychologists said, "The attitude of unhappiness is not only painful, it is mean and ugly." Professor James went on to say, "What can be more base and unworthy than the pining, puling, mumping mood, no matter by what outward ills it may have engendered? What is more injurious to others? What less helpful as a way out of a difficulty? It but fastens and perpetuates the trouble which occasioned it and it increases the total evil of the situation." Professor James also said, "Much of what we call evil is due entirely to the way men take the phenomenon. It can so often be converted into a bracing and tonic good by a simple change of the sufferer's inner attitude from one of fear to one of fight; its sting can so often depart and turn into a relish when, after vainly seeking to shun it, we agree to face about and bear it cheerfully; that a man is simply bound in honor, with reverence to many of the facts that seem at first to disconcert his peace, to adopt this way of escape. Refuse to admit their badness; despise their power; ignore their presence; turn your attention the other way; and so far as you yourself are concerned at any rate, though the facts may still exist, their evil character exists no longer. Since you make them evil or good by your own thoughts about them, it is the ruling of your thoughts which proves to be your principal concern."

The famous attorney Clarence Darrow demonstrated a classic example of as Professor James states, "a simple change of the sufferer's attitude from one of fear to one of fight." Darrow tried to secure a mortgage for $2,000.00, when the wife of the lender said, "Don't be a fool—he will never make enough money to pay it off." Darrow suddenly became angry and set out to become a success. His self-worth was not threatened because he did not have a weak ego. He was not self-centered as he had a healthy ego and self-esteem. While he was angry he let the remarks, "pass over," and he took positive action. He refused to let the remarks fester. He simply set out to prove that lady wrong, and be a success so that bad experience would never happen again.

It has been proven that happiness is a state of mind and happy people are healthier than unhappy people. Don't form the opinion that it would be selfish or wrong to be happy. We deserve happiness, not sorrow. Even while sorrow comes every person's way it does not have to lead to continued misery. We simply have to face the fact that problems pop up once in a while, and after we overcome that problem, another will take its place in time. So we stay happy in between the problems. And by the way, my philosophy is to stay focused and happy during the problem. I say, "OK little problem, do your best; give it your best shot. I am not going to let you get me down." All Positive Thinkers think this way.

The late Bob Hope (considered by many as the most popular entertainer of the 20th century) always kept a smile on his face, and what a smile it was. Bob loved people and never let problems get him down. Bob had a great sense of humor and everyone, even an ogre loves to watch a good comedian perform. He once said, "When we recall the past, we usually find that it is the simplest things not the great occasions-that in retrospect give off the greatest glow of happiness." You can confront most unhappy people and they will refuse to admit they do not have a good sense of humor. Who wants to admit to that? However, sometimes I have run into unhappy people and I ask them why they don't smile. With great conviction they say, "I hate to smile. I have nothing to smile about." What a pathetic state to live in!

In the late 1960s, sales motivator Fred Herman spoke to an audience on how important it is to smile often. He told about a day he was chatting with his son in the early morning and his son asked him how he felt. Fred responded by saying that he felt great. His son looked at him long and hard and then replied with a shocker by saying, "Then why don't you notify your face." Every once in a while I meet a real sourpuss and I ask them the same question. I never respond though, because I know it will hurt their feelings if I respond like Fred's son. But I walk away and get a chuckle knowing I could say it.

Abraham Lincoln once said, "Most people are about as happy as they make up their mind to be." You can acquire all the wealth and possessions, but as Doris Mortman stated, "Until you make peace with whom you are, you'll never be content with what you have." Psychologist, Dr. Matthew N. Chappel said, "Happiness is purely internal. It is produced, not by objects, but by ideas, thoughts, and attitudes which can be developed and constructed by the individual's own activities, irrespective of the environment."

Once you realize that unhappiness, like happiness, is a habit and can be changed you can become happy. One of the keys is, unhappiness results from an unhappy event and is a blow or an affront to our self-esteem. We missed the plane so we are angry. You became stuck in traffic due to construction. Your appointment did not show up so you are angry. What is happening is you are allowing outward events to dictate your feelings. Suppose you had a con artist steal your life savings and you say, "How can I possibly be happy?" The key is: keep your own opinions of the situation out of the equation. Yes, the money was stolen, but it is your opinion that you are ruined. The sage, Epictetus, said, "Men are disturbed not by the things that happen, but by their opinion of the things that happen." Listen to what Robert Louis Stevenson said, "The habit of being happy enables one to be freed, or largely freed, from the domination of outward conditions."

Psychologist H. L. Hollingsworth said, "Happiness requires problems, plus a mental attitude that is ready to meet distress with action toward a solution."

It is funny how life throws a curve to test your mettle. Marcus Seneca, the great philosopher stated, "Gold is tried by fire, brave men by adversity." I have had so many obstacles thrown in front of me that I am used to them and just say, "OK, little obstacle, let me see how long it takes to overcome you." I look at it as a challenge. And do you know what else, dear reader? You may think I am nutty, but this is fun. I get enjoyment overcoming obstacles. Now don't get me wrong. I do not actively go looking for them, but I know they are there, so when they come they do not surprise me. I do not initially enjoy them. You would have to be slightly off balance to enjoy that consternation, but to know that you can overcome any obstacle by having complete confidence in yourself and abilities is very comforting. And by the way, I sleep like a baby at night. When I put my head on the pillow I start the 23rd Psalm and never finish it. Usually, halfway through it, I am asleep.

So I go into my positive mode and am relaxed, and I know the **three-word motto**. I read the Bible most mornings and it is very calming and reassuring to me. I particularly like the story of Job and the heartbreaking obstacles he had to overcome. He lost all his children in one fell swoop. Next, he lost all his thousands of livestock stolen by bandits, and finally, boils from head to foot afflicted him. But he did overcome with faith in God and himself. He later became the father of the same amount of children he lost, and doubled his original livestock, and I think God put this story in the bible to give us hope.

I consider myself a professional problem solver, and some time ago went on the Internet and into the chat rooms. As soon as I went on with my nickname, Mr. Positive, people started writing my name on the screen. They would write that they liked my attitude and could I help them with some positive thinking. I will not allow myself to try to act like a psychiatrist or psychologist or get involved. So all I would do was listen, give them positive input statements and tell them they need tools to overcome the negativity by reading positive thinking reading material. I always recommend Dr. Norman Vincent Peales book. *The Power of Positive Thinking,* or *Zig Ziglars, See You at the Top* or to watch the Oprah Winfrey show. Oprah is a breath of fresh air, and is living proof of how a person can overcome their terrible past and be happy and focused. Yes, she has controversy on her show, but the results are positive and everyone has fun. Dr. Peale was a pundit, but he had a great sense of humor and kept his audience in stitches during most of his talks, and Zig has such a positive outlook in life with his down home mannerism and smile.

The Internet is exciting as well, because I met people from all over the world. A former nurse was working in the ICU when her cousin came in with serious wounds. While they were trying to put him under, he suddenly sprang up and started beating on her chest, collapsing her heart. She is now bed ridden and is disabled, and has lost a $36.00 an hour job. The doctors advised her that she would be bedridden for life, so sadly it was very difficult for her to relate to positive thinking. She was very bitter and I could only give her tough love by telling her to stop feeling sorry for herself, and told her the story of Joni Eareckson Toda. Joni was paralyzed from the neck down in a diving accident, but she places a paintbrush in her mouth and creates beautiful paintings. I have seen a picture of her and she has a beautiful smile. She does not talk about what she no longer has, but instead of what she has by the grace of God and her faith in herself. Every picture I see of Joni is with a big Smile on her lovely face. She is a best selling author and a member of the World Positive Thinkers Club.

One of the great success stories is about World Positive Thinkers Club member Lance Armstrong, who had cancer in five areas of his body. Lance is a Positive Thinker and with positive thinking and medical help overcame his disease. But he was considered damaged goods and no group would allow him on their bicycle racing team. Finally the young, inexperienced U.S. Postal team took a chance on Lance with a small stipend. In 1999, he entered the world's most prestigious race, the annual Tour de France, which is over 1200 miles long. The racing of his heart must have been over 200 beats a minute, because he was in for the race of his life. That special day he was to start to prove the skeptics wrong again, as all Positive Thinkers are wont to do. [Unlike the skeptic, a Positive Thinker is one, who when he sees the handwriting on the wall, does not claim it as a forgery]. This is not your standard bike race, but it is considered by many as the most grueling athletic event in the world, and is not for the faint hearted.

I only wish I could have been there to see this giant of a Positive Thinker cross the finish line in first place. What an inspiration he is to all the people in the world who are continually advised not to try the impossible. The shame of it all is that Lance was accused of using performance enhancement drugs and he had to face the humility of taking daily drug tests to prove his own ability. Another clear-cut example of a Positive Thinker overcoming all odds. Lance knows the **three-word motto**. He said, "If you ever get a second chance in life, you've got to go all the way." Lance received a second chance and won the Tour de France the next year as well.

I hope you are sitting down right now, because Lance Armstrong proved the skeptics wrong, not once, not twice, but he proved it always pays to be a Positive Thinker. In the Tour de France in 2001 Lance was in 23rd position at the beginning of the mountain stages and blew past the competition to win the most prestigious and grueling race on the planet for a third time in a row. Lance proved again that there is no such word as impossible. If you talk with Lance, you will see he has a great outlook on life and a good sense of humor. I am so proud of this perfect example of, "The Positive Thinker achieves the impossible." Lance was in first place by 2 ½ minutes with 123 miles to go and won his fourth straight Tour de France, and I am convinced he will enter next year to tie the record of six consecutive wins set by Miguel Indurian of Spain. When he ties that record my personal opinion is that this giant of a Positive Thinker will go on to attempt to set a new record of seven consecutive wins in the Tour de France. I read Lances book, *It is not about the bike*, and I recommend it highly.

Oh yes, **Lance Armstrong knows the three-word motto**! Right now I sit here with a feeling of tremendous joy and excitement, knowing that Lance Armstrong won his fifth Tour de France in a row, tying the record with Spain's Miguel Indurian. I can't tell you how excited I am. Lance accomplished this in spite of falling twice in the grueling race, winning by a mere 61 seconds. The date is Sunday July 27, 2003, and Lance has proved conclusively that positive thinking can overcome the toughest obstacles and cynics. Will he race next year to try to win a record five in a row? He says he will, and if he stays healthy and focused his chances are positively breathtaking, and I believe he will win six. Not only is he a Positive Thinker, but also Lance has a great sense of humor and an engaging smile. This is one happy day for Lance Armstrong, America, and Positive Thinkers worldwide, and this writer! Now how am I going to top this latest exciting news?

Well dear reader, it is a year later and I just topped it as Lance achieved the impossible by winning six straight titles. Will he try for seven in a row? I am betting on it!

Let me write that I have taken the time to learn stories and jokes and polish the delivery in which I tell the stories or jokes. The joy I feel making people happy is a rush and pleasure, and many people have told me I should be a stand up comedian. My favorite schtick is teasing people while acting like a junior Don Rickles. I love a good clean joke and have a file full of them. People who get ulcers need to lighten up, because it has been medically proven you can get ulcers because of constant worrying and friction. The late Cardinal Krol of Philadelphia was once asked by a reporter if he got ulcers from the strain of his position. He replied in a typical Positive Thinkers fashion, "I don't get them, I give them."

I entered the ninth grade and my life was never to be the same, because something happened to me physically and mentally. I cannot explain it in a pragmatic way except to say that I became like a person possessed in the sports arena. I was outstanding on defense on the football team and on the basketball team. While short, I made the first team in basketball until I had a back injury. I remember going up for a rebound against, John 'Twinkletoes' Tunnell. He came down on my foot as I tried to go up again for the rebound and I remember a little pain. A week later I woke up with terrible pain in my back and couldn't straighten up. My brother thought I was faking injury to get out of chores, so no one would do anything until a few days later the tears from pain convinced my parents to take me to have x-rays. My stepmother took me to a clinic and the nurse told me to take off my clothes and put on a white gown. Unfortunately, I did not hear her tell me to put on the gown, and walked into the hall buck-naked. To this day I still laugh, when I think of the nurse with a red face, screaming for me to get the gown on.

The x-rays were taken and it showed that I had a slipped disc. I remember the doctor telling my stepmother and me that I would never play sports again. The only thing he wanted me to do was swim and stay away from all other exercise, but in those days not many pools were around where I could rehabilitate. So I had to wear a back brace and take pain pills. Can you imagine a young boy who loved sports suddenly finding out that he would never play sports? What a negative thinker that doctor must have been. He was well meaning I am sure, but a negative thinker regardless.

Well, my stepmother, who had a great sense of humor and positive attitude, consoled me. She could not be angry with the doctor for being so negative and it reminds me of a quote of Ralph Waldo Emerson's, "Of cheerfulness or a good temper—the more it is spent, the more of it remains." I vowed to prove the doctor wrong but I was forbidden to play sports by my parents. So what does a normal young boy do when he loves something? He sneaks around. So I would go to basketball practice and watch, but the coach would not let me practice due to the back injury.

As the basketball season ended I looked forward to the baseball season even though I was forbidden to play sports. I had a plan, and the plan was to stay after school and tell my parents that I was being tutored. The only problem was that I had to keep my grades up to prove I was being tutored, so I had a friend help me with my studying.

During one gym class the gym teacher told the whole ninth grade that anyone who could hit the softball over the left field fence would receive 'A' for the grade period. I remember the class groaning and complaining that it was impossible to clear the fence with a softball. Mr. Metzger, the gym teacher, just smiled and kept pitching to the kids as one by one they never even got close. As I stepped up to the plate for my turn, Mr. Metzger told me to sit down because of my bad back, but I begged him to let me swing the bat. I will never forget that day for the rest of my life, because no one in the school history ever cleared that fence. I can still see myself swinging the bat and the ball sailing towards the fence. There was a quiet hush as the ball left my bat and then a sudden yelling as the ball approached the fence. "It is going to clear. It is going to make it," everyone yelled. The ball cleared the fence by a good 20 feet and my feet never touched the ground as I rounded the bases, while the class yelled and cheered. Mr. Metzger stood on the pitcher's mound shaking his head in disbelief, and then a huge smile crossed his face. This was to teach me a big lesson in life, as I moved through the years. I never forgot the ball sailing over the fence that looked a mile away. What was that lesson? The lesson I learned was succinctly this: there is no such word as impossible. *The Positive Thinker sees the invisible, feels the intangible and achieves the impossible.*

Shakespeare said,"Our doubts are traitors and make us lose the good we oft might win by fearing to attempt."So, at least attempt to hit the ball over the fence.

So now the baseball season started, and here I was in the thick of things trying out for pitcher with a bad back. But did I make the team? You bet! As a matter of fact I made starting pitcher. And not only that, but I was the leading hitter on the team.

The uniforms were old and hot, so you really perspired and itched wearing the heavy wool uniforms. But we didn't think about those things; we just wanted to play. And play we did, as I mowed the opposing teams down with a slider, a blazing fastball and a change of pace pitch. My hero, Bobby Shantz, kept giving me inspiration as he was still pitching in the big leagues. I could see his winning smile and it inspired me, because while I believed he was the greatest, I also knew he was having fun winning. "Happiness is not mostly pleasure; it is mostly victory." —Harry Emerson Fosdick

One day later in my life while he and I were playing golf, Bobby told me that when he was traded to the New York Yankees during the days of Yogi Berra, Mickey Mantle and Roger Maris, et al., he would have walked from Kansas City to New York if that was one of the requirements. And win he did, as he produced one of the two lowest earned run averages as a pitcher in the American League one year with the Yankees. Bobby told me he had more fun in those few years with the Yankees than in his whole career, except the year he won Most Valuable Player in the American League in 1952. He said the Yankee players knew they were the best and had a ball proving it. Now that is not cockiness, but self-assuredness, which comes from confidence in one's abilities and of course self-respect.

Winning is fun, as those Yankees proved and winners have very few frown lines in their foreheads. One of the great Yankees was Yogi Berra, and today there are "Yogi-isms. For example: someone asked Yogi what time it was and he quipped, "Do you mean right now?" He still has a great sense of humor. Unfortunately, some of the critics have called him ignorant, but if I were inducted into the Baseball Hall of Fame, and had a best selling book, like Yogi, I wouldn't mind their insults either.

One of the greatest inventors the world has ever known, Professor Elmer Gates of the Smithsonian Institution, in Washington, D.C, had a "happy thought" philosophy. Professor Gates said, "Let a person who wants to improve himself summon those finer feelings of benevolence and usefulness, which are called up only now and then. Let him make this a regular exercise like swinging dumbbells. Let him gradually increase the time devoted to those physical gymnastics, and at the end of the month he will find the change in himself surprising. The alteration will be apparent in his actions and thoughts. Morally speaking, the man will be a great improvement of his former self."

One million Americans succumb to many forms of cardiovascular disease every year and around 62 million Americans face a heart-related problem such as high blood pressure. "Laughter pumps up heart health," says Dr. Michael Miller, director of the Center for preventive Cardiology at the University of Maryland School of Medicine. Dr. Miller examined 20 volunteers, to find out how blood vessels react when the volunteers viewed movies that were humorous or stressful, and found that 19 of the 20 had increased blood flow when they laughed and in 14 of the 20 the blood flow decreased when they tensed when viewing the stressful scenes.

"Laughter increases the production of 'killer cells' that go after virally infected cells and tumor cells," reported Lee Burk, an associate research professor for pathology and human anatomy at the Loma Linda University School of Medicine in Loma Linda, California after conducting studies showing that laughter improves the immune system by reproducing adrenaline.

In the early 1960s Norman Cousins, former editor of *Saturday Review* magazine found that laughter is the best medicine when he was faced with a debilitating form of arthritis. He decided to start watching funny movies on a regular basis and chronicled his findings and experience in his best selling book, *'Anatomy of an Illness,'* after discovering that his pain subsided.

I personally love to have a good laugh as often as possible and have found most people love to be around a happy person. So I make it a point to stay loose and find humor in situations, and I make sure that anyone who has interaction with me enjoys that time. When I am in an environment where I feel negative vibes I will be cheerful and kid with the people and if they ignore me or show hostility of some sort after I try to "lighten up" the situation I make the decision to "move on."

Dr. Maxwell Maltz, gives this following advice to help you become a happier person. He suggests you repeat these statements to yourself daily.

1. I will be as cheerful as possible.
2. I will try to feel and act a little friendlier toward other people.
3. I am going to be a little less critical and a little more tolerant of other people,

their faults, failings and mistakes. I will place the best possible interpretation upon their actions.
4. Insofar as possible, I am going to act as if success was inevitable, and I already am the sort of personality I want to be. I will practice "acting like" and "feeling like" this new personality.
5. I will not let my own opinions color facts in a pessimistic or negative way.
6. I will practice smiling at least three times during the day.
7. Regardless of what happens, I will react as calmly and as intelligently as possible.
8. I will ignore completely and close my mind to all those pessimistic and negative "facts" which I can do nothing to change."

Dr. Maltz, highly recommends that you must act out the above habitual ways of acting for at least 21 days. If you miss one day you must start over.

"Man is meant for happiness and the happiness is in him,
in the satisfaction of the daily needs of his existence."
—Leo Tolstoy

A day without laughter is a day wasted."
—Charlie Chaplin

"Be happy. It is a way of being wise."
—Colette

"We are only on earth once, so enjoy it while here."
—Will Rogers

"Why would you not want to make people laugh?"
—Bob Newhart

MAIN THOUGHT AND CHALLENGES

1. Go back to the beginning of chapter six and review your highlighted sentences.
2. Place the highlighted page number on this page.
3. Write down the most important highlight and why it is so important to you.
4. Write down names of people that you know who are fun to be around.
5. Do you consider yourself fun to be around-yes or no.
6. If you do not consider yourself fun to be around write down what you intend to do to change that.

Chapter 6

DON'T BE SATISFIED WITH AVERAGE

"I am only an average man but by George, I work harder at it than the average man."
—President Theodore Roosevelt

First off, you have to decide who you are and who you want to be. If you consider yourself average, and/or your peers consider you average and you are satisfied with that, you will have a hard time accomplishing great things. The question is, do you want to accomplish great things? Let me be frank with you here and now. You have come this far in the book, so that proves you want to be better than average. Now the skeptics will say, 'What is wrong with average?' The answer is: nothing, absolutely nothing! We need the average people to do their share of helping to achieve progress. But, average people mainly contribute; they do not forge progress until they start new companies, or break records, or discover new medicines or nutrients for disease or discover new products to make life easier for mankind. Average ministers do not convert many to Christianity. The Billy Grahams of the world do that. And Billy Graham is not average. Average speakers do not motivate, but the Zig Ziglars of the world do.

Charles Barkley, one of the greatest players in basketball history played well above his average basketball height. Charles despite his height of 6'6" was one of the better rebounders in the league as well as a prolific scorer. He once said, "God gave a lot of players in the NBA talent. I don't want to be one of them. I want to be a step above." And he showed that he was not just your average human being when it came to being kind to people. Charles got the phone number of an elderly lady, who called a Philadelphia radio talk show to vilify Charles for his behavior on the court. He called her and invited her to a game and even sent a limo to pick her up. "I just wanted her to know that the mean, aggressive guy who's on the court, who only wants to win, is not the same person off the court" said Sir Charles.

One thing is perfectly clear, and that is that average people do rise to greatness, as you will also read in Chapter ten.

Let me expound. Look at a fingerprint, which has been said in the past by experts, is the most perfect means of identification. However, with the advances in technology the eye is said to be another perfect means of identification. Suddenly DNA identification came along, which tops them all for perfect identification. There are absolutely no two fingerprints that are exactly alike, just as there are no two eye scans or DNA exactly alike. Take it a step further. We all think differently, and no two people think exactly alike. If that were not true then one of the two that thought alike would not be necessary. For example: it is relative when we think about taste. You may take salt on your eggs and I take none, but we both taste the eggs as being as salty as we desire it. How about the color green? What color do you visualize when you see green? Is it dark or light? When I see green on a painting I have a hard time deciding if it is blue or green with certain shades.

If you were to ask a person who is average if they think they are average, they will say that they are. But when you ask them what average means, they will just stare at you and say they don't know. Is that someone you want working to help you build your new company? After the company is built they will be considered an asset, but they will not be much help to you while you are forging new frontiers, other than performing legwork. After the company is built then you will need more of the clerks and those type people. Just remember though, average people have raised to greatness too. Many presidents of companies have come from the mailroom or other lower positions. So the old adage is still true. Always treat your employees with respect, because they might become your boss someday.

The point is there is no such creature as "average." There are just levels of competence. And all men and women can rise above their level if they really want to. A classic example of that is the small, young African American boy, who after hearing a speech by Charlie Pennock, America's greatest runner at that time, ran up to the podium and shouted to Charlie that he was going to be the greatest runner in the world some day. Charlie encouraged this poor little boy, who lived on the other side of the tracks, and as a matter of fact he did become the world's greatest runner. In the 1936, Olympics in Germany, Jesse Owens won four gold medals, one of which was in the 200-meter dash, making him the fastest man in the world. He broke the world record, by running it in 20.7 seconds. So there you have it. It all boils down to goals and the **three-word motto**.

One of the leading chemical engineers in the country, Harold Wilson, of the huge DuPont Company said, "Knowledge is that acquired information which includes both your professional learning and your understanding of people. Nothing will inspire people's confidence and respect in you more quickly than your demonstration of that knowledge and your ability to put it to work to get results. You cannot conceal a lack of knowledge about your job. You cannot bluff people about that, at least, for very long."

The people with inferiority feelings just want to blend into the maddening crowd and appear faceless. Some, as a matter of fact, would love it if they could become invisible. I remember a movie years ago about an invisible man. One of my friends casually mentioned that he would love to be invisible, so no one could require him to do anything and he would be left alone. We all think of that once in a while, but that is not reality, so the next best thing is to have times by ourselves. Make sure you have at least 21 minutes of quiet time alone each day to reflect and focus on the positive things you did that day. And only focus on the positive. You can take a few minutes later to think about the things that went wrong, but with the intention of making sure they do not happen again. You must realize that self-recrimination is not healthy. Once you come up with the solution to correct the mistakes, move on. Do not dwell on the negative. You cannot un-ring a rung bell. Make the decision to do better next time. Then do better!

Let me throw another scenario at you - two men go into the Army at the same time and serve on the same battlefield in the same war. They both have the same duties, and yet one becomes a hero, and the other turns tail and becomes a coward. It proves then that no amount of training such as the Army gives will force all persons to think and act exactly alike at all times.

A classic example of that is Audie Murphy. Audie was an average soldier in World War II as an infantryman. As a matter of fact, he stood around 5'6" tall. He had never done anything especially unusual and was just your average soldier. But one day tanks, followed by infantry pinned down his company. Audie took on the squad of tanks and literally wiped them out one by one. He jumped on each tank and threw in hand grenades, and then machine-gunned most of the infantry following the tanks. He was wounded in the leg and continued to perform heroically. This little guy was nine feet tall that day, and because of the heroics of this average soldier, the company was saved. Audie won the highest award America gives in war time-the Congressional Medal of Honor. Only 440 Congressional Medals of Honor were awarded in WWII, 250 of them posthumously. Audie eventually took on Hollywood and became a box office success. This again proves the average person can rise to greatness.

Speaking of nine feet tall, I think of Goliath, the hero of the Philistine Army in the days of King Saul. The opposing armies stood on both sides of a ravine. Each day Goliath came out in the morning and dared any Israeli soldier to take him on one on one. Not one Israeli soldier took up the challenge, as they each thought it was impossible to defeat Goliath. Then, an average little shepherd boy by the name of David, son of Jesse, heard of the challenge and the way Goliath was insulting and blaspheming the living God of the Israelites. David told King Saul that he would meet Goliath, and the King put his armor on David. But David was not used to armor, so he took it off and went out to meet Goliath with nothing but a sling and seven smooth stones. Goliath, according to the King James Version of the Old Testament, was six and one half cubits tall. A cubit equals the length from the elbow to the end of the middle finger, which is approximately 18 inches. If you multiple 18 times 6 you come up with 108 inches, plus another 9 inches. That total is 117 inches divided by 12" equals 9' 7 ½". That is nine feet seven and a half inches. He must have weighed over 400 pounds and his armor would be used on a small tank today. He wore a helmet with only one little open spot between the eyes, and that is the exact spot David hit with the flat stone he slung at Goliath with his sling. The giant who was thought impossible to overcome one on one by all the soldiers in the Israelite Army was defeated by an average shepherd boy, who took a stand for God and his country, just as Audie Murphy did over two thousand years later. Both were average people who rose to greatness.

If as a high school student you had feelings of inferiority, don't let that stop you from learning how to overcome them, as many before you have done. Listen to what Ernie Nevers, football Hall of Fame tailback, and picked as one of the backs on the All Pro squad of the 1920's, said. "As a youngster I was very shy. I was scared to death of people. But football gave me an outlet for my emotions. You get the chance to go man-to-man and see if you can stand up against the best they can throw at you. On a football field I was just a different person."

Bill Glass, former defensive end for the Cleveland Browns, and motivational speaker said, "In this century people in ordinary jobs are cut off from what they are doing. They sit behind their desks and don't have any real relationship to what else is going on. They are struggling against things they can't see. There is a day-to-day routine, but never any immediate crisis situation that has to be solved in a split second. But in football, it all builds up to a peak performance for two-and-a-half-hours on Sunday. There is a clearly defined objective, an obvious opponent. You have to be emotionally and physically ready for that crisis. And if you triumph it's clear right away. Football is so exciting, because it's an intensified slice of life." Seymore Feshback, professor of psychology at the University of California at Los Angeles said, "In a middle class society, inhibitions and control on one's emotional and physical expression are problems. Delayed gratification of these needs can cause tensions and anxieties. In contrast, it seems likely that the spontaneity and release experienced by the football player is enjoyable and satisfying." Dub Jones, All-Pro halfback from 1946 to 1955, said it so succinctly, "The beauty of the game of football is that so often you are called upon to do something beyond your capabilities- and you do it." Jim Marshall, Hall of Fame defensive end for the Minnesota Vikings said, "A man who is a professional has had to play with a great deal of pain at one time or another. Such a man has a lot of pride about what he can do within himself, of the great sacrifice he can make. It helps him feel that he is a strong specimen, that he can tolerate that which the ordinary man can't tolerate mentally and physically." By the way, Jim holds the record for most fumble recoveries, but in 1964 he picked up a fumble and that play went down in history as one of the great blunders in professional sports. Somehow he became turned around and as he scooped up the football he then headed for his own goal line scoring a safety for the San Francisco 49ers. The average athlete would have gotten down on himself and played poorly the rest of the game. But not Marshall, because it inspired him to play even harder. George Mira fumbled the ball when Jim sacked him later in the game, whereby Carl Eller picked it up and ran it in for the winning touchdown. There you have it! Regardless of the sport, challenge, or competition, ordinary men and women excel. Those type people know the **three-word motto**.

Dr. Norman Vincent Peale, my mentor, who wrote more than 15 books on Positive Thinking, starting with the best seller, "*The Power of Positive Thinking*," admitted to having inferiority feelings as a young boy and man. But he had the sense to read of great people and took the advice of one of his professors in college who assured him that he was not average. Dr. Peale was my mentor and his peers and readers consider him the second greatest Positive Thinker after Christ. I know personally that Dr. Peale knew the **three-word motto**.

During President Woodrow Wilson's tenure as President of the United States, he had failed to get Congress to agree to his dream to become a part of the League of Nations. He suffered a heart attack because of the great disappointment and stress. One of his trusted advisors was Napoleon Hill, who was at Wilson's bedside when Wilson was dying. Wilson looked at Napoleon and said, "Those men on Capital Hill have killed me." Napoleon looked long and hard at this great President and then said, "Mr. President, ultimately nothing matters." Of course, unbeknownst to him at that time, President Wilson had laid the groundwork for America to enter the United Nations.

"Out of the dust we have been formed and into the dust we return." On the lighter side: we came into this world with nothing, so lawyers and doctors feel it is their duty to send us out the same way.

What is one of the things that changes average people into winners? They develop the "winning feeling!" The winners know that they must set goals and those goals must be set in terms of end results. You supply the goal, but your automatic creative mechanism, takes over and guides you towards the goal, much like a guided missile. You must have goals, for no harbor is the right harbor for a ship without a rudder. After the winner sets the goal, he or she then sits calmly with their eyes closed, and concentrates until they see the end result. You must dream and become obsessed about it.

When you set goals do not at first attempt to achieve the impossible. You must set small goals that can be accomplished. It is like a good boxing manager. He starts his fighter off with easy opponents to give him a success pattern. Gradually he works up to the fighters who have been in the fight game for a while. You have to be your own manager when it comes to goals, so you must think them out carefully. Eventually, you go for the "big one." Just remember to set weekly, monthly, yearly, five-year, and lifetime goals. You will not have any feeling like that of when you meet a goal you have set. It is a feeling of euphoria. If you do not meet a goal simply shake your head and reset it and go after it with more passion.

The great psychologist Pavlov, told a group of students who asked for his last bit of advice while on his deathbed, that they were to have, "passion and gradualness."

Every major league player dreams of being in a World Series, and every pitcher dreams of pitching a "perfect" game, and particularly in a World Series. But for every pitcher that is all it has been: nothing more than a dream. The negative thinking critics said that it was impossible for many reasons; one in particular being the tremendous amount of pressure in a World Series. It was felt impossible except for one average pitcher. In game five of the 1956 World Series, he was pitted against Sal Maglie of the Brooklyn Dodgers. The Dodgers had beaten the Yankees the year before in the World Series in seven games, but that day, 64,519 fans were about to watch the "impossible" accomplished. The game was scoreless until the Yankees Mickey Mantle, of the Yankees, hit a two run home run in the fourth. Dale Mitchell for the Dodgers, ended the game by striking out and history was made, as Don became the first and only pitcher in World Series History to pitch a perfect game. Almost 60 years later that feat has still not been duplicated. The stadium erupted like an atom bomb and Don Larson was mobbed by his teammates. During an interview Don admitted that he had a strange feeling the night before, and the following day an average pitcher make history that has never been repeated.

We can talk about "below average" people too. Take the case of Tom. Tom was born with half a right foot and a withered right arm. Growing up the children made fun of Tom, as children have a tendency to do, but Tom simply ignored them as he had other things in mind.

Tom grew up and his childhood tormentors got a chance to see Tom attempt to make history, because now Tom was the place kicker for the professional New Orleans Saints football team. But the ridicule did not stop as Tom lined up to attempt an unheard of 63- yard field goal in the closing seconds of a game on November 8, 1970, against the Detroit Lions. The announcer started laughing and deriding the Saints for making such a stupid move. Many of the 66,000 fans started leaving as the Lions called a time out to try to rattle Tom. They did not have a clue about this below average person's determination; his belief in himself and his great heart. The fans that stayed started laughing and yelling at Tom, and Tom and his coach were the only ones in the stadium who felt he had a chance to make the longest field goal in the history of professional football. Perhaps if they had read the record books they would have seen that a college player dropkicked a field goal from the same distance many years earlier. And so the laughter continued while Tom's teammates shook their heads in derision.

I know Tom; have talked with him and he is a member of the World Positive Thinkers Club. He did not care what the critics thought or said, because this below average man physically did not believe in the word impossible.

I remember listening to the game and I will never forget it. The center made a perfect snap to the holder and Tom swiftly moved toward the ball with perfect precision. His half foot made contact with the ball and it sailed towards the uprights and suddenly there was a hush throughout the stadium. The announcer suddenly turned positive as he excitedly yelled, "I don't believe it, I don't believe it, it has a chance!" Of course it had a chance!

As the ball sailed through the uprights the announcer started screaming, "He made it, he made it, I don't believe it, I don't believe it!" and the remaining fans erupted with screams and laughter. They were patting each other on the backs, jumping up and down, for they had just witnessed history being made and the impossible being overcome. The fans that were out of the stadium were rushing back to the stadium to find out what happened. Pour souls! If only they had been Positive Thinkers they would have seen a below average man named, Tom Dempsey set a world record. I personally know that Tom knows the **three-word motto**.

And, as if that were not enough to silence the critics, Jason Elam of the Denver Broncos booted a sixty-three yard field goal 28 years later on October 25, 1998.

Do you know who Vonetta Flowers is? Vonetta is the first American in 46 years, along with her teammate Jill Bakken to win an Olympic medal in bobsledding. She accomplished this "impossible" feat in the 2002 Salt Lake City Winter Olympics. The men couldn't do it but the women could. This average, but lovely lady, Vonetta Flowers, is also the first African American to win a Gold medal in the history of the Winter Olympics. What a thrill to be the first to accomplish greatness, and what a thrill to rise above being average as Vonetta proved you can do. Vonetta is another Positive Thinker.

Once the Positive Thinker visualizes it, they know for certain that it already is accomplished. They then just have to go through the motions to really physically complete it. The next step is to write the goal in bold letters on three 3 X 5 cards and place them strategically. Then the cards are placed on your bathroom mirror, refrigerator and your desk at work or car dash. From this point on your, "homing device" takes over, and, as long as you concentrate on the cards, and visualize your goal every day, it is assured of happening. I talk about this in detail in another chapter; because you need to be reminded as often as possible as to how important this is to be a winner as well.

Remember to highlight the things in this book that you feel you need to remember. The two big things that separate the average from the great are first, goals, and second the three-word-motto, which you will learn shortly. The great Irish writer and patriot, Maud Gonne said, *"I will fight until I die against the tyranny of small ambitions."*

MAIN THOUGHTS AND CHALLENGES

1. Go back over the beginning of this chapter and review the highlighted sentences.

2. Place the highlighted page numbers on this page.

3. Write down the most important highlight and why it is so important to you.

4. Write down "yes or no" as to what you believe you are in regard to being an average person and why.

5. If you consider yourself average, write down what do you intend to do to change that image of yourself?

Chapter 7

THE GREAT COME BACKS

"The difficult we do immediately,
the impossible takes a little longer"
–Hap Arnold, General

"The opera isn't over till the fat lady sings"
–Dick Motta

That quote was made in regards to a sporting event, and the "fat lady" was a great singer by the name of Kate Smith. Kate was a chubby, popular singer in the 40's, 50's, 60's and 70's, with the voice of a songbird. She opened the Philadelphia Flyers Hockey games by singing "*God Bless America*." The Flyers considered her a good luck charm, and insisted she open their games with her singing. They went on to hockey greatness, winning two World Championships in the early 70's, and one of their trademarks was their ability to comeback after being behind. One athlete was asked if his team had a chance of winning after being so far behind. He responded, "It ain't over till the fat lady sings. He was referring to Kate. His team went on to make a comeback and win the game. Dick Motta said it first when he was coaching the Washington Bullets in the 1970's. He used to say, "The opera isn't over till the fat lady sings." Yogi Berra had a take off of it when he used to say, "It ain't over till it's over."

I have to tell you a funny story relating to Kate. My stepmother was a wonderful, Positive Thinking lady, and she had a parakeet named Peety that she trained to talk. He was amazing with a great vocabulary, saying things like, "Peety is a pretty boy." One day my stepmother was watching Kate Smith singing on the television, and of course the song was, "*God Bless America*." My father walked in from work and started talking while Kate was singing, whereby my stepmother shouted, "Be quiet, Kate is singing *God Bless America*, you damn fool." From the perch on the window we heard a little squeaky voice sing out, "*God bless America* you damn fool." We all looked at each other and burst out laughing. I have sent that story to a certain magazine for their humor stories twice, and they refuse to believe it is a real story, so they will not print it.

Mario Lemiux, in 1992, led the Pittsburgh Penguins to their second straight National Hockey League Stanley Cup Title. However, in 1993, Mario underwent radiation treatment for Hodgkin's disease, causing him to miss 24 games that season. In spite of that he still won the scoring title in 1995-96 season and was named Most Valuable Player of the league that year. He retired and was already inducted into the Hockey Hall of Fame when he made a comeback in 2000 to help the Penguins avoid bankruptcy. In just 43 games he scored an unheard of 35 goals and 76 points that year.

Several comebacks come to mind from my earlier days. I was a big Philadelphia Athletics baseball team fan, and it seemed that whenever the New York Yankees came to town they would beat the A's no matter how far behind they were. This was after Connie Mack the owner and manager had dismantled his great team due to financial problems. In one game the Yankees were down by 11 runs in the ninth inning and went on to score 12 in the ninth to win, as they held the A's to no runs in their half of the ninth inning. And it seems the Yankees have a penchant for making great comebacks, as they did in the 1996 World Series against the Atlanta Braves. The Yankees were down 6 to 0 going into the eighth inning, when suddenly they scored three runs. But against the great pitching Atlanta had that year the skeptics still thought the Yankees would not comeback to win the game. All they did was hold Atlanta to no runs the rest of the game, and win the game in the tenth inning to make for one of the greatest comebacks in the history of sports.

Another significant comeback took place right after I was married. We had moved to an apartment and I was watching the Dallas Cowboys play the San Francisco 49'ers. Dallas was behind something like 38 to 10 with two minutes to play in the game, so I decided that it was time to go outside and wash our two cars. About 20 minutes later I came in and there was bedlam and screaming on the television. I asked my wife what was going on and she said that there was a lot of commotion going on and Dallas was coming back. I remember her saying, "I didn't think you would be interested, so I didn't bother to tell you." As I looked at the screen I shook my head in disbelief as the announcer was yelling that Dallas had come back to win the game. One of the greatest comebacks in sports history and I missed it. Did that ever teach me that, "It ain't over till it's over."

Bernard King, averaged 22.5 point's a game for five teams and was named Comeback Player in the 1980-81 season averaging 21.9 points a game. This was after missing the 1979-80 season with a knee injury. In 1984-85 he led the NBA in scoring again after overcoming an alcohol problem. His knee was injured again and he missed the 1985-86 season-he was traded and his average shot to 28.4 points a game. Another injury forced him out for the 1991-92 season, but he would not quit and came back in 1997 to play in 32 games.

Every Professional sports league has a Comeback Player of the Year award, because sports are so demanding. The different leagues want to show appreciation for athletes who have shown the greatest desire and ability to come back from adversity.

Another football game in 1993 that comes to mind became the greatest playoff comeback. Houston was playing Buffalo and was ahead by thirty-two points with only a few minutes to play. To make a long story short, Buffalo came back and won in the final minutes, winning 41 to 38. "It ain't over till it's over."

I think of Greg Louganis, the great Olympic diver, who banged his head on the diving board causing a big gash. He put on a great comeback; performed the perfect dive and won the gold medal in diving in the 1985 Olympics.

One of the greatest comebacks in the history of the sporting world is the superstar heroics of Michael Jordan. Michael was the big factor in winning championships for the Chicago Bull's basketball team and then he retired. But he felt he had much to offer the game as a manager and player, so in the 2001-2002 season Michael started for the Washington Wizards and scored 34 points in a recent game. In one game that season Michael scored 50 points, and that after the negative thinking critics said he was washed up. You can be assured that Michael Jordan knows the **three-word motto**.

Lisa Hartel of Denmark won a silver medal in the dressage equestrian event in the 1952 Olympics, eight years after losing full use of her legs when she contracted polio during pregnancy.

Koroly Takacs of Hungary was one of the world's greatest pistol shooters and an Olympic favorite to win in his event in 1938. But in World War II his right hand was blown off in a grenade accident. He decided to learn how to shoot left-handed, and quieted the skeptics by winning the gold medal in the 1948 Olympics.

Rafer Johnson had the bottom of his right foot ripped off in a cotton mill accident in Kingsburg, Tennessee. The doctors told him he would never walk again without a limp, but he refused to believe them and gingerly put pressure on the foot. Soon he was walking, and the right foot eventually became his take off foot in track and field events. Rafer Johnson went on to win gold medals in the 1960 Olympics, setting world and Olympic records.

One of the best "comeback artists" was Johnny Unitas, the great quarterback of the Baltimore Colts, before they moved to Indianapolis, Indiana. Johnny was known as the, "Comeback Kid." Professional football coaches at that time were polled as to what opposing quarterback they did not want to face if their team was ahead. They all agreed to a man that they did not want to face Johnny. All Unitas did was set a record that stands to this day, by throwing touchdowns in forty-seven straight games from 1957 to 1960. I used to have breakfast with Johnny and I know he knew the **three-word motto**. The latest quarterback named by the recent coaches was the great John Elway, who helped win two Championships for the Denver Bronco football team. But according to some football experts the greatest comeback quarterback was Joe Montana, who was the top rated passer in the NFL five times, and led the San Francisco 49rs to four Super Bowls. I used to have breakfast with Johnny, and you can bet the mortgage that these great quarterbacks know the **three-word motto**.

One of my favorite quarterbacks was, Roger Stauback, who played for the Naval Academy and then for the Dallas Cowboys. I watched him in many comebacks. He was nicknamed, "Roger the Dodger," for his ability to escape from opposing lineman. In the annual Army Navy game I was standing with my father in the roving photographer's area, and Navy was behind. Roger was scrambling and he was being tackled by one of the Army defenders. As he was going down he unbelievably side-armed a pass to his end that set up a first down and Navy went on to win the game. Roger graduated from the Naval Academy, where he won the Heisman Trophy as the best college football player in the nation. He then served in the Navy for five years. After his Navy hitch he played for the Dallas Cowboys who drafted him in the tenth round, as no other team thought he could comeback after five years away from football. All Roger did was lead the Cowboys to two championships in 1972 and 1977, and Roger is a member of the World Positive Thinkers Club.

The Positive Thinker never believes he is beaten, and most believe they are not behind anyway. The attitude is: we are on the upswing and will win, as we are just giving our competitor a head start. They know the **three-word motto** and, "It ain't over till it's over." Perhaps you remember the "Hail Mary" pass Doug Flutie threw in the closing seconds to win a game for Boston College. I don't recall the year, but I remember the play.

Some years back my friend; Patty Jolliff's father was crushed between two trucks while laying the artificial grass on the pitcher's mound in the then new Arrowhead Stadium, in Kansas City, Missouri. The doctor's emphatically told him he would never walk again as the pelvis was crushed. Patty's father has passed away now, but he was a Positive Thinker, because less than a year after the accident he was walking and returned to work. Don't tell me that miracles do not happen!

Today is a very significant day. This is the third day after terrorists attacked the United States. The lives of every American will be changed forever now as happened on December 7, 1941. On Tuesday, September 11, 2001 four passenger jets were hijacked, and three slammed into the two World Trade buildings and the Pentagon, causing the loss of thousands of lives and jobs, and billions of dollars. On December 7, 1941, "A day that will live in infamy," we were "sneak" attacked by the Japanese, and lost over two thousand lives. It was a heinous crime, because of the Japanese government's delay in relaying their country's declaration of war to the Japanese ambassadors until after the attack. America through its determination and positive attitude was able to eventually comeback to defeat the Axis powers, and I am convinced that we will win the war against terrorists. We still have a steely determination and this great country is filled with many Positive Thinkers.

After that attack in 1941 many in Japan felt America could never comeback from such a mortal blow to our navy. They felt we would be demoralized, but Admiral Yamamoto, who went to college in America, thought differently. He stated that because his country had perpetrated the sneak attack the Japanese had awakened a, "Sleeping Giant," and in his opinion, all the Japanese could do was delay the inevitable. America put on the greatest comeback in the history of warfare due to the determination of Positive Thinkers, who knew we would eventually win the war. I personally feel that even though we have a very different type war now, we will by our resolve, determination and positive thinking put on a great comeback again. Our twin towers in New York are lying in helpless heaps where they once magnificently stood, but I have no doubt that New York will resolve to re-build them. (As of this date, architectural drawings are in place for the new center). That will be another great comeback. Even though the skeptics will say that it is too dangerous and costly, our Positive Thinkers will overcome the obstacles they will face. The skeptics a few years ago said America had lost the will again to comeback from adversity. That came from some of America's top leaders. The skeptics after the taliban attacked said that we would never defeat them, as the Russians had tried and failed. Time after time the negative thinkers have to eat crow, because right now it is March 24, and we have eradicated much of the taliban. They are hiding in their little holes, shivering, listening to the diabolical bin laden (caps purposely left out) and his sick zealots. But they are not quitters because they have a goal to destroy America, so they will strike where they can.

Speaking of New York, I think of one of the biggest real estate tycoons of all time. He was on top of the world. The standing joke was, he owned most of New York and half of Atlantic City, New Jersey. Then suddenly his world came crashing down. He was facing bankruptcy and even his beautiful wife left him. He was faced with mounting debt and foreclosures, and the banks refused him further credit.

What did he do through all this? He simply did not worry about it and sharpened his golf game. His attitude was one of complete confidence and Donald Trump did comeback. Did Donald Trump worry about the critics and negative thinkers? Not on your life! He is now listed with over $1 billion in assets, and wrote a book about his great roadblock and how he overcame it. His comeback was never a nebulous venture in his mind, even though the skeptics laughed and wrote him off. A true Positive Thinker never listens to the skeptics, because he knows there are no statues erected to them.

Another of the great corporate comebacks occurred when, Gil Amelio, took over the helm of failing National Semiconductor. The financial experts had written the company off and it was headed for the corporate graveyard of many multi-million dollar giants. Gil turned the company around and also turned around failing Apple Computer.

Perhaps one of the biggest comebacks in the history of the corporate world took place after one of the giants was headed toward bankruptcy, while losing millions of dollars every month. A new man took the helm, and marched into Washington, D.C. to ask the biggest employer in the world for a loan of $1.2 billion. Meeting after meeting took place and many financial experts said he was wasting his time. But this man had a vision and did not want thousands of people out of work, which would have a strong adverse effect on the U.S economy. Lee Iaccoca convinced the United States Government to loan millions of taxpayer funds to bail out Chrysler Motors. Chrysler Motors paid its debt and became solvent again, thanks to a Positive Thinker, who knows the **three-word motto**. And by the way, Lee is a true patriotic American, as he was the chairman of the Statue of Liberty—Ellis Island Centennial Commission, putting in four years of hard work. He raised $305 million dollars by February 1996, to restore the Statue of Liberty and Ellis Island. Lee and his team beat the original goal of $230 million by $75 million.

Another favorite story of mine is about a deceased member of the World Positive Thinkers Club. His father and grandfather never made it to the big leagues, so they were determined that this average boy would. Everyday they had him practice for five hours batting left-handed and then right-handed. He eventually made it to the major leagues after a scary injury while chasing a ball, coming close to colliding with the legendary, Joe DiMaggio, which almost caused his leg to be amputated. He was a bust in the majors his first time up, striking out five times in a row in a double-header. But determination and faith in himself and God gave him a second chance and in a game in Griffith Stadium in Washington, D.C., Mickey Mantle came back to hit a ball 565 feet and out of the stadium. This average boy was inducted into the Baseball Hall of Fame in Cooperstown, New York. Luckily, he played with Yogi Berra, the man who said, "It ain't over till it's over."

Who was Walker Smith? One of the greatest comebacks of all time took place in the boxing ring, in Chicago, Illinois. The washed up champion, according to the critics, was a 17-5 underdog to the champion, Bobo Olson. After all, Walker Smith, eleven months earlier had looked flat footed and ordinary against Tiger Jones. The "smart" money said the twice champion, Walker

Smith, could never make it back. It had never happened before that a two-time champion had come back and became champion for the third time.

But that night was different. Walker Smith, at 35 years old, won the first round 10 to 9 and in the second round flattened Bobo Olson, to win the middleweight title for an unprecedented third time. He proved that a winner is a symbol of what the human will can do under terrible duress. Walker Smith (Sugar Ray Robinson) proved that you never can tell who the winner is until the fat lady sings, because the winners like Sugar Ray are true Positive Thinkers.

One of the recent comebacks happened in the city where the twin towers formerly stood. New Yorkers are well known for their ability to comeback. After the great snowstorm that crippled the city in 1888, many said the city would not get back to its original state for months. In a few short weeks New York bounced back, as it will now after the horrible events that negative cowards perpetrated on September 11, 2001.

This time it happened on the baseball diamond, as the New York Yankees in the 2001 World Series were down to their last out in the last inning, two runs behind. No team had ever bounced back from so deep a hole. However, a Positive Thinker was at bat that night with two strikes on him, and the fans were ready to exit the great, "House that Ruth built." Scott Brosius never remembers his feet touching the ground or bases, as he made that historic run around the infield after blasting a homer to win the game. And to top it off, as if the impossible can't be accomplished twice in a row, the Yankees came back the next night to accomplish the same exact feat. Granted, they did not win the World Series, as ironically the Arizona Diamond Backs were in a similar position and about to lose the 7th game. And then along came a Positive Thinker named Louis Gonzalex. He only faced the best closer in baseball, and dropped a loop single over the infield to win the game and the World Series. I have to believe several-million baseball fans suffered from vertigo after such an exciting series.

In December, of 2001, the Chicago Bears were behind 21 to 7 with one minute left in regulation. Obviously the Bears were not the Bears of old, always losing games in that situation, because they scored with 28 seconds left in the game. Chicago took a gamble with an on-sides kick, recovered the ball and then scored on an unbelievable "Hail Mary" pass, scoring again, forcing overtime. You guessed it. They went on to win the game, when the experts picked them to lose. Nope, "It ain't over till it's over."

Another of the great comebacks occurred during the 2002 Winter Olympic Games. Chris Klug lived through liver transplant surgery. During his event a boot buckle broke and he repaired it with duct tape. By improvising and not giving up Chris won the Bronze Medal in the parallel giant slalom snowboarding event.

Chris had the help of one family and with that help and the will to live he overcame tremendous odds. Olympic triumph was about more than sports. "I thought I was going to die waiting," Klug said of the days before his liver donor was found 19 months earlier. Leisa Flood, the mother who made the choice to donate her 13-year old son's organs in July 2000 was overwhelmed when she heard of Klug's victory. "I'm so grateful we were given the opportunity to help him," Flood said from her home in Idaho. "It makes me feel good." And this is another example of not listening to the naysayer's who said it was impossible to comeback after such an operation.

One of the greatest individual comebacks in the business world happened in Detroit, Michigan. One day, Joe Girard, had to face his wife with the sad news that his construction business had failed. To make matters worse, his wife informed him that there was not enough food to feed the children. Just then, there was a knock on the door by a bill collector. Joe hid behind the dining room door while his wife pleaded for more time. In that humiliating moment Joe made a decision to get a job selling cars to put food on the table for his family. He marched down to the local Chevrolet dealer and convinced the sales manager to hire him on commission. This was during the slowest time of the year-right before Christmas. Joe convinced the sales manager to advance him enough to buy groceries for the family and then proceeded to sell his first car to a man who only came in off the street to get warm. And presto! Joe went on to become the greatest salesman in the world, according to the Guinness World Book of records. He proceeded to be the top salesman for General Motors year after year, out-producing the next two biggest producers combined.

Joe was lucky some might say. Joe believes he was lucky too, except he practiced how to be lucky. He had the right attitude and he knew that to be lucky he had to go out and make preparation meet opportunity.

Martin Seligman, professor of psychology at the University of Pennsylvania, says that to cultivate the right attitude you must believe that good things will happen to you. "If you perceive life's setbacks as business as usual, you won't bother behaving in positive ways that can change your situation." Joe Girard thought positively and consequently he was hired during a bad time of the year in the Automobile business. Professor Seligman goes on to say, "If you believe you're fortunate much of the time, you're likely to exhibit behavior that makes people more responsive to you." That day there was no way the sales manager could turn Joe down for a job. And the minute the customer walked in the door just to get warm he was sold in Joes mind.

Ellen Langer, professor of psychology at Harvard says, "People who seem lucky are appealing because they are effective and happy. "We are drawn to them because we feel safe around them, we hope they will help us succeed, and maybe their luck will rub off on us." I am firmly convinced that luck is preparation meeting opportunity.

Joe did not stay at home and sulk and feel sorry for his predicament as negative thinkers usually do. John Krumboltz, professor of education and psychology at Stanford University said, "You won't improve your luck by sitting at home. You have to embrace random events that happen to you and see their potential for improving your luck." One important facet to "luck" is that you make your "luck" if you are open to new experiences. Joe kept an open mind and believed in himself, and became the greatest salesman in the world. It was a great pleasure to induct Joe into the World Positive Thinkers Club and I am positive Joe knows the **three-word motto**.

J.C. Penny built a great empire with his stores, but found himself penniless in his old age. He knew he had done it all before, and so with renewed determination and complete faith in his abilities and God he rebuilt his fortune and operated more stores than before he found himself without a penny. J. C. Penny had formed the "habit of success," so it was automatic that he would comeback and succeed again. Penny said, "I would never have amounted to anything were it not for adversity. I was forced to come up the hard way."

Do you remember what happened in the 1980 Winter Olympics at Lake Placid, New York, in the wild world of ice hockey? Let me refresh your memory with some interesting facts. The American team did not have a chance to win a medal, or so the experts spouted. After all, in an earlier match against the powerful Soviet team they were clubbed by a score of 10 to 3. Even their coach, Herb Brooks, said they did not have the talent alone to win, and that the common man does not go anywhere.

In the opening round the American team came back with 27 seconds left and salvaged a tie with the talented Swedish team. The Americans went on to defeat Czechoslovakia 7 to 3, and then defeat Norway and Romania. Then they performed another "impossible" feat by beating the heavily favored German team 4 to 2, coming from behind again. Now it was on to face the powerful Russian team that had a future hall of famer in goalie Vladislav Tretiak. The Soviet captain, Boris Mikhailov, was considered by hockey fans as the Gordie Howe of Gorkey Street. Again the skeptics said the American team had no chance, and it appeared the skeptics might be right as the Americans fell behind early on in the match. But with one second left in the first period the Americans tied the game. Then in the final period they fell behind again 3 to 2 with twenty minutes left. Unbelievably, with 8:39 of the final period left they tied the game, and eighty-one seconds later Eruzione beat the new Soviet goalie with a screen shot to go ahead. The noise in the arena was deafening as the American crowd leapt to their feet and cheered. When it was all over the players were jumping all over each other and pounding each other's backs, as the crowd roared their approval and waved American flags furiously. Now the American team, that virtually no one gave a ghost of a chance to even win a bronze medal was about to meet the powerful Finland team. Yes, they did come back again from a score of 2 to 1, by scoring three goals in the final period; completing a miracle and thereby astounding the world. You can be sure the American team took Positive Thinking seriously, and proved once again, "It ain't over till the fat lady sings."

This chapter should end with a bang! As long as I live I will feel I witnessed the greatest comeback in sports history, by watching the Boston Red Sox perform another "impossible" come back after falling behind the New York Yankees three games to none in the 2004 A.L. playoffs. Boston came back and won four straight games to accomplish another impossible feat, and that is a feat that had never been accomplished in the over 100-year history of professional baseball. I remember hearing sports casters and other prognosticators claiming that it was an impossible task. Time and time again it is proven that, "It's not over till the fat lady sings."

"They conquer who believe they can."
—Ralph Waldo Emerson

"It's hard to make a comeback when you haven't been anywhere"
—Yogi Berra

MAIN THOUGHTS AND CHALLENGES

1. Go back to the beginning of this chapter and review the highlighted sentences.

2. Place the highlighted page numbers on this page.

3. Write down the most important highlight and why it is so important to you.

4. Write on your sheet comebacks that you are aware of including your own.

5. When time permits do some research and then write the comebacks on this sheet.

Chapter 8

ORDINARY PEOPLE CAN BECOME EXTRAORDINARY

"There are no great men.
Just great challenges which ordinary men, out of necessity,
are forced by circumstances to meet"
–Admiral William F. "Bull" Halsey

The American Heritage Dictionary defines ordinary as: **"Usual, normal, average in rank, ability or merit; commonplace."** One of the most ordinary people who ever wore shoe leather did weekly sketches for his barber for twenty-five cents or a haircut. He attended high school but never graduated. He enlisted as a Red Cross driver in World War I, and then returned to Kansas City and worked as an ordinary artist with an advertising company. This ordinary man formed a company with his brother Roy and together they produced a comedy series. In 1928 Walt Disney used sound along with cartoons and produced the 'Steamboat Willie' movie, staring Mickey Mouse; the first sound cartoon, thus making movie history.

Walt went on to dream of a park where children and their parents both could go and enjoy fun together, and in 1955 Disneyland opened on 180 acres of land at Anaheim, California. In 1971 another park opened in Orlando, Florida, on 28,000 acres, as well as a park in France in 1992. This ordinary man won over 100 prizes for his films, including the Oscar 29 times, and President Lyndon Johnson awarded him the Presidential Medal of Freedom in 1964. Walt once said, "All the adversity I've had in my life, all my troubles and obstacles, have strengthened me ... You may not realize it when it happens, but a kick in the teeth may be the best thing in the world for you." It was said of him, "He was an ordinary man, who had extraordinary talent for making people feel good."

Vic Pocker, an ordinary Hungarian, came to America penniless and unable to speak a word of English. His first job was as a welder and he saved his money and went to night school to learn English. Vic lost everything during the depression, but he made a decision not to cry over spilled milk and started his own welding shop in 1932. That little welding shop grew to become a million-dollar company, because Vic was another true Positive Thinker.

Years ago, Dr. Norman Vincent Peale stated that when he and a group started the inspirational magazine, Guideposts, they needed money desperately. The company was successful in that it was growing, but it was on shaky footing financially and was about to fold. Dr. Peale felt the enterprise was too important to give up on, but he knew that if the directors did not come up with ideas to raise money it was curtains for the enterprise. The board sat around a meeting table with gloom and doom and especially negativity in their voices and thoughts. Dr. Peale had invited a lady named Tessie, because he figured since she had donated once, perhaps, as he put it, "Lightning would strike twice. But she put the board in further misery by stating that she was not going to donate another nickel." She asked them if they knew what money was for and they said it was to pay all the bills. Tessie said, "If I pay these bills you will soon have more bills." She said, "Money has no inherent value within itself, it is only a tool by which a creative person builds something. Now if you get creative, you will get all the money you need." "How do we do that?" the board asked. Tessie said, "You need to close your eyes and visualize the bills no longer on the spindle." So the board closed their eyes for many minutes, and actually visualized the bills disappearing, but to their surprise when they opened their eyes the bills were still there. But the board had suddenly come alive and ideas started being thrown out on the table. Some were good and others were not, but that day started them on the way to financial success. Guideposts became the most successful and widely read non-profit magazine in the world with articles all about ordinary people overcoming difficulty. Dr. Peale was my mentor and I assure you he knew the **three-word motto**.

"It is fortune not wisdom that rules man's life."
—Cicero

"O fortune, fortune! All men call thee fickle."
— Shakespeare
Romeo and Juliet. Act 3 Sc.5

East Harlem in New York City is one of the toughest neighborhoods in the nation. Accomplished violinist, Roberta Demetris, took a teaching position in the school district in the music program, and soon afterward started a program called Opus 118 for children to learn the violin. Naturally, the negative thinkers said she could never teach these under privileged children the violin. Roberta did not listen to them, because she had faith in her ability and theirs as well. She knew you could do anything you set your mind to, but many of these children were unruly and considered not intelligent enough to learn an instrument. Roberta taught these under privileged children that this was an important program for use later in life, and that they would feel better about themselves while learning this difficult instrument. She knew that ordinary people could become extraordinary.

The program was a success, and when the state tried to take funding away from the program, Roberta formed a parents group to petition the state. Their actions succeeded; the program was saved, and has been extremely successful. Over one thousand students have taken Roberta's course and there is a waiting list to get in the program. Roberta felt that you must stand for something worthwhile, or you will fall for anything not worthwhile. Good advice from another Positive Thinker.

What does this all mean to you and me? It is succinctly this. We are molded by our thoughts, not our circumstances. We become either successful or a failure based on our thought process. Success has nothing to do with whether or not we are ordinary. It means we need to dream and wish, and then put the dreams and wishes on paper and read them daily. We need to make up our minds exactly what it is we want; commit the **three-word motto** to memory, and then never change the goal until we succeed, no matter what the obstacle, except in only one instance, which I will write about later in this book. Most importantly, we need the **three-word motto**. And we must all pay some sort of price for glory, or to achieve our goals. There was even a movie titled, *"What price glory."*

Dr. Maxwell Maltz discovered, as I wrote earlier, that many people's personalities changed after plastic surgery. Not every one of these patients changed, but enough that Dr. Maltz realized that "self-image" represented, "a breakthrough in psychology and the field of creative personality." Dr. Maltz was not the only plastic surgeon who realized personalities changed after plastic surgery. One of his colleagues discovered it, but was reluctant to publish the findings for fear of being accused of exaggerating or trying to start a cult. Dr. Maltz realized that once a person's face is changed, so is his or her future in many cases. Dr. Maltz also came to the conclusion that after plastic surgery it takes 21 days for a patient to get used to the change in his features. After a limb is amputated, there is what is known as the "phantom limb" syndrome. The patient actually feels the limb still attached. When you purchase a new home, Dr. Maltz asserts, "It takes three weeks before it seems like a new home." This holds true when you have decided to become a Positive Thinker. It takes at least three weeks for it to sink in that you really want to get rid of your negativity, and are in fact on the path to conquering that negative image. Of course this only holds true if you start to get rid of the negative input, such as certain television, too much news, or too many newspapers, and all other negative input. For example: when a friend or relative spouts negativity you must counter with, "I can understand how you feel, but I choose to be positive; let's talk positive now."

The key to your thinking is your self-image. Everything you do is consistent with your self-image. How do you feel about yourself? Do you see a winner or a loser in the mirror? If you think you are a victim of your circumstances you will always be pointing the finger at society and other people. (Remember, however, that when you point the finger at someone, or something, there are three times as many fingers pointing back in your own direction). You will find circumstances to verify your opinions of the situations you find yourself in. The wallflower at the dance invariably thinks nobody wants to dance with him or her. The truth is nobody wants to dance with someone who has a scowl on his or her face, denoting a moribund attitude. People want to dance with the person with a smile. Positive Thinkers like to be around happy people. Even ordinary people like to be around Positive Thinkers! Positive thinking is contagious. Be a carrier, and don't be stingy: spread it around.

I have had people say to me that they have tried positive thinking before and that it does not work. Well of course it will not work if you only give it a few days or a half-hearted try. Remember that it takes three weeks for the positive process to fully take hold, and you must know and practice the **three-word motto**.

The trouble is they thought to themselves they would get the job, or the business venture would be fruitful, but they never changed the real image they had of themselves. You have to believe you can change your thinking as to who you really are. Next you have to make up your mind to change. You have to start changing your self-conception. It may seem silly, but you have to say to yourself, well darn it, if he or she can do it why can't I? Say to yourself, I am going to be such and such, and then you have to start acting the part you have decided to become. You must always think positive if negative thoughts from within or from others come to you. If you fail a test, do not say, "I am a failure." Say, "OK, I failed the test, so what? I will pass the next one."

Not only do you have to change the mental self-image, but you have to change the physical image too. If you are going to change your self-image you need to change your appearance too. You can go out and get a nice haircut or have your style changed by a good stylist. Buy a few nice clothes that emit success. Get your car detailed. Get your house in order. In other words, you have a complete makeover. You have to make yourself acceptable to "numero uno." Don't try to be a particular movie star. Don't try to be anyone else but the new you. You may know someone you admire and it is OK to say, I like that person's attitude and looks. But to try to act like that person is asking for big trouble. Mary McBride tried to be an Irish comedian on radio. When she acted like she was-a plain country girl from Missouri she acclaimed stardom. Gene Autry tried to dress differently, and said he was from New York, and people laughed at him. As soon as he played the guitar and sang cowboy ballads he became the most popular cowboy in the world. Charlie Chaplin's first director insisted on Charlie imitating a popular German comedian of that day. Once he acted like himself Charlie became famous.

Simply decide how you want to act and what your goals are and then say to yourself, "I am as good as the next guy and if he or she can do it so can I." Your new self- image must be one of reality. You must ignore the possibility of negative comments. Do not listen to the negative people. They simply want to drag others down to their level of insecurity. You must forget the past. You can't change it; it is over and done with. In his letter to the Philippians 3:13, St. Paul said, "Forgetting those things which are behind and reaching forth to those things which are before, I press toward the mark." Doug Ivestor wrote, "Never let your memories be greater than your dreams." And remember that we continue to make mistakes. Nobody, but nobody is perfect who resides on this great planet. President Teddy Roosevelt once said, "If I could just be right seventy five percent of the time that would be the fondest of my dreams." If one of the greatest leaders the world has ever had the good fortune to know could only feel seventy-five percent correctness is the top, then who are we to think we will be right one hundred percent of the time. Just don't try reinventing the wheel. Oh by the way, have you been highlighting? If not, as Gomer Pyle used to say on his humorous television show, "Shame, shame, Shame."

When you have decided what your new self-image is to be you must now form a mental picture of that person. You have to understand the mechanics of the subconscious mind. The subconscious mind is not a mind at all. It is a mechanism, a goal-striving mechanism. The mind uses and directs this system, which is contrived of the brain and nervous system. However, this system needs goals to direct it. It needs input just like a computer needs input. Once this input is determined, it acts accordingly. If you put in negative input, the mind acts accordingly, and the same with positive input. In other words, it waits for our imagination to form the mental pictures so it can react. In his book The Computer and the Brain, Dr. John von Newmann says that the human brain possesses the attributes of both the analogue and the digital computer. The servomechanisms your brain possesses automatically "steer" to a goal. Do not confuse yourself and think you are a machine. You possess a machine that you have the ability to use. The human brain works much like a guided missile. It first seeks a target, whether the target is known or not. It then uses its sensors to keep it on the right course. When it gets off course (negative feedback), it corrects itself. You will notice that a missile zigzags toward the target. That is a series of corrections from the negative feedback that sends a signal to the rudder to compensate until it finally locks on the target. Dr. Norbert Weiner was a pioneer in World War II, who was mainly responsible for developing the guidance systems in torpedoes and he became convinced that the human brain works in a similar fashion. In other words, after you select the goal and set in motion the actions necessary to accomplish it, the servomechanism in your brain takes over, and guides you to the end result. The really beautiful thing is that once the brain triggers the servomechanism, it is remembered for future use. The servomechanism then repeats the successful action in the future.

You have to close your eyes and visualize yourself accomplishing, just like Loretta Switt, who I wrote about in the first chapter. Loretta actually visualized herself as an actress while still a small child. Throughout this book there are stories like hers, and like Bruce Jenner, the great Olympic Decathlon champion. All the winners actually visualize success before accomplishing it, and later in this book I will tell you about a little boy I coached who was the worst player on the team. By mentally picturing the end result he, as you will read, achieved unbelievable results.

A scientist known throughout the world, who preferred to remain anonymous, wrote. "Up to my fiftieth year I was an unhappy, ineffective man. None of the works on which my reputation rests were published. I lived in a constant sense of gloom and failure. Perhaps my most painful symptom was a blinding headache that recurred usually two days of the week, during which I could do nothing."

"I had read some of the literature of New Thought, which at the time appeared to be bunkum, and some statement of William James on the directing of attention to what is good and useful and ignoring the rest. One saying of this stuck in my mind, 'We might have to give up our philosophy of evil, but what is that in comparison with gaining a life of goodness?' or words to that effect. Hitherto these doctrines had seemed to me only mystical theories, but realizing that my soul was sick and growing worse and that my life was intolerable, I determined to put them to the proof. I decided to limit the period of conscious effort to one month, as I thought this time long enough to prove its value or its worthlessness to me. During this month I resolved to impose certain restrictions on my thoughts. If I thought of the past, I would try to let my mind dwell only on its happy, pleasing incidents, the bright days of my childhood, the inspiration of my teachers and the slow revelation of my life work. In thinking of the present, I would deliberately turn my attention to its desirable elements, my home, the opportunities my solitude gave me to work, and so on, and I resolved to make the utmost use of these opportunities and to ignore the fact that they seemed to lead to nothing.

In thinking of the future I determined to regard every worthy and possible ambition as within my grasp. Ridiculous as this seemed at the time, in view of what has come to me since, I see that the only defect of my plan was that it aimed too low and did not include enough."

"The outward changes of my life, resulting from my change of thought have surprised me more than the inward changes, yet they spring from the latter. There were certain eminent men, for example, whose recognition I deeply craved. The foremost of those wrote, out of a clear sky, and invited me to become his assistant. My works have all been published, and a foundation has been created to publish all that I may write in the future. The men with whom I have worked have been helpful and cooperative toward me chiefly on account of my changed disposition. Formerly they would not have endured me ... As I look back over all these changes, it seems to me that in some blind way I stumbled on a path of life and set forces to working for me which before were against me." -By the way, the great scientist's headaches disappeared within a week after embarking on his new attitude-The great creator made every living thing with a built in guidance device to help reach its goal. For animals it is finding food, procreation, and shelter and avoiding enemies. Animals do not need emotional and spiritual satisfaction like humans. But they do have a success instinct that guides them to food, even after they have been chased out of the nest. The animal's goals are set in advance, whereby man has the good fortune to be blessed with creative imagination, and can formulate and direct his success mechanism by using his great imagination.

Steve Cauthen, the youngest jockey to win a Triple Crown, at age 17, in 1978, (an almost impossible feat to accomplish for a jockey, or for a horse for that matter), rode a bale of hay around the barn when he was nine years old pretending he was racing in the Kentucky Derby, the Preakness and the Belmont. Winning the Triple Crown is so hard, that up to today there has not been a winner since 1978 when Steve rode Affirmed to that elusive title. And by the way, Steve was also the first to win all of the international thoroughbred races. Steve knows that Positive thinking does work.

Forming a mental picture gives you a chance to practice this new self-image you have decided on, just like Steve Cauthen on that bale of hay. When you paint that picture in your mind and close your eyes and visualize, after a while it absolutely becomes real. It does not happen over night, so you must have patience. "Great acts take time."-Cardinal Newman- I hope you have been highlighting.

Many experiments have taken place to prove this theory. In one controlled experiment, Research Quarterly reported that three groups were tested practicing free throws with a basketball. The first group was scored on the first day. Then for 20 days they practiced their free throws for 20 minutes. At the end of the 20 days, they improved by 24 percent. The second group did not practice for the 20 days and there was no improvement. The third group practiced in their imagination and improved by 23 percent. In football there is "skull practice." In boxing there is "shadow boxing." In Karate, there is what is called a Kata, whereby moves are put together against imaginary opponents. These Kata's have many moves that are put together and can take up many minutes to perform. To the unskilled and skeptics they can look silly, but they have practical use when used against a live opponent or opponents, and Jackie Chan the great martial artist and actor still practices his Kata's.

When interviewing for a job, the good employment agencies coach you to practice for the interview. They will give you a list of usual questions and then tell you to practice with a friend or family member, and/or in front of a mirror and tape recorder before the actual interview. Every actor and actress rehearses tirelessly before a show. In the movies there are takes before the director yells, "print it." One of the worlds most recognized authorities on teaching piano, C. G. Kop, taught his students to practice a new composition in their minds first. The composition should be memorized first before ever playing it on the piano keys. Ask any successful person if they formed a mental picture of the success they sought, and each one will admit that they formed a mental picture of the end result long before they started on the journey to the goal. Every great athlete will tell you that he or she visualizes the end result before going out on the playing field. Does visualizing the end result work? Perhaps you might learn from the great high jumper, Dwight Stones, of Long Beach, California. Dwight set a world record of 7' 7 ¼", and attributes it to psychic projection or imagining, which many other winners swear by. Dwight claims that he could see himself clearing the bar two steps before he left the ground. This is a basic faith principal that when coupled with goals and the **three-word motto** you can't help but succeed.

And you, like them, must practice this new self-image you seek. Dr. Albert E. Wiggam called this mental picture, "the strongest force within you." Do not believe the critics, when they say you can't be this or that. The great singer Caruso was told by his singing teacher that his voice sounded like wind in the shutters. Had Caruso given up, the world would not have had the happy experience of hearing his beautiful voice years later. As I wrote in a previous chapter, Jimmy Durante was told his nose was too big for show business. Jimmy made that large nose his trademark, and would jut out his chin to make it appear larger and the audiences would roar with laughter. Larry King was fired by his editor for being too chummy with his subjects. He is now one of the greatest interviewers of famous people. J. K. Rowling, the talented author of the highly successful Harry Potter books and movies was a secretary and her boss fired her for writing on company time. Burt Reynolds was told he could not act and became the number one box office draw for five consecutive years. Elvis Presley was told to go back to driving a truck after he first sang in a studio. Steve Jobs, the founder of Apple Computer was booted out in 1986 and in 1996 he was back at the helm.

John Curtin is the Prime Minister who led Australia through the dark days of World War Two. Many believe he was Australia's savior ... and our greatest leader. Curtin was born in the Victorian gold mining town of Creswick in 1885.

Life was tough as illness forced his father to give up work as a policeman, and seek jobs managing hotels. With money tight, John left school at the age of thirteen to find a job. He moved to Melbourne where he worked as a newspaper copy boy, but he made up for his short formal education by reading books ... sparking an interest in politics, and the rest is history.

A very important point for you to fix in your mind is that you should not create a monster. By that, I mean, you should not try to create a self-image that is all-powerful, egotistic and arrogant. That simply will be a cover up of insecurity feelings, and it will transmit itself to those around you. You must not aim for "superiority." It will do nothing but frustrate you. The one thing is not to compete with another personality. There are no two people exactly alike. Abraham Lincoln once said, "God must have loved the common people for he made so many of them." Many common folk have been raised to greatness, because they believed they would. Another part to the equation is some people exaggerate the task at hand, thinking it is harder than they are capable of doing. For example: I have a lady friend who until I met her always worried. She was very shy and continually said she could not do certain things. This is an educated lady, but she continues to say she can't do certain things. She claimed that she was just average and was a no body. She is a very religious person and I told her that God does not produce nobodies. She listened and with positive input she is now coming around, and I fervently believe she will have a much more positive self-image of herself in a few more weeks. I will continue to pump positive input into her and get her to read positive input books. She promised to buy *Zig Ziglars, See You at the Top*. She admits that at the end of the day she is stressed and needs a massage to relax her. The next best thing is to relax and massage your mind. At times she feels overwhelmed, and would stay up at night and watch the 11:00 late night (negative) news with the excuse she needed to see the weather. Then she would toss and turn all night. Now she waits until the time the weather is usually on, and she sleeps better not having pumped negativity into her brain. I feel one of her problems is that she is fearful of the results and too careful. A clear-cut example is that she is afraid to fly. Yet Christ said, "Take no thought for the morrow,"

Professor William James in 1899 said, "Man is too tense, too concerned for results, too anxious, and there is a better way. You must understand a basic principal of our self-image. As a man believes in his heart, so shall he be. If we wish our trains of ideation and volition to be copious and varied and effective, we must form the habit of freeing them from the inhibited influence of reflection upon them, of egoistic preoccupation about their results. Such a habit like other habits can be formed. Prudence and duty and self-regard, emotions of ambition and emotions of anxiety, have, of course, a needful part to play in our lives. But confine them as far as possible to the occasions when you are making your general resolutions and deciding on your plans of campaign, and keep them out of the details. When once a decision is reached and execution is the order of the day, dismiss absolutely all responsibility and care about the outcome. Unclamp, in a word, your intellectual and practical machinery, and let it run free: and the service it will do you will be twice as good."

You must analyze the situation, and ask yourself this important question. Is my belief about myself real or imagined? Is it based on actual fact, or an assumption, or a false conclusion? You must really get into the "nitty-gritty" here and come to a conclusion. If you don't, then you need to work until you do make sense of the facts. You will find that your self-image is erroneous unless it is that of a person who sees him or herself as a successful person.

If you want to help improve your self image read a life story of someone who has reached the top in your profession or someone you admire, and imagine you are just like that person. You must set aside at least twenty-one minutes a day imaging yourself achieving and enjoying your goal. [Highlight that sentence] This is extremely important, and it is worth repeating. You must set aside at least twenty-one minutes a day imagining yourself achieving and enjoying your goal. The best time for this is right before bedtime, because it will make you sleep better.

Notice that all winners are not necessarily young and good looking, and if you think about it, all the academy award winners are not the "beautiful people" all the time. A few years ago, Jessica Tandy, at the ripe age of 80 won the best actress award in the stirring movie, Driving Miss Daisy. She has since passed away now, but Jessica had a good self-image, and she knew the **three-word motto**.

Some studies have indicated that some of the "beautiful people" seem to be less adjusted and not as happy as one would think. Shakespeare, in his play Hamlet, has Polonius say, "And this above all, to thine own self be true." Next time you are around a Positive Thinker/winner, notice his or her demeanor. You will notice that they smile a lot, and that smile is a caring smile. These people appear to have a glow about them. It is important to feel good about yourself. In the January 1959, issue of a major magazine, T. F. James wrote the results of research done by certain doctors and psychologists. "Understanding the psychology of self can mean the difference between success and failure, love and hate, bitterness and happiness. The discovery of the real self can rescue a crumbling marriage, recreate a faltering career, and transform victims of personality failure. On another plane, discovering your real self means the difference between freedom and the compulsions of conformity."

Let's set the record straight at this point. Throughout the book I talk about, "success." This is not implying anything to do with prestige, but rather creative accomplishment. Your goal is to be successful, not necessarily to be "a success." "To do for the world more than the world does for you-that is success." -Henry Ford- Ford proved that philosophy time and time again, as it is not very well known that he was a philanthropist, as well as a great innovator in manufacturing. One story in particular comes to mind about his paying all the hospital bills for surgery to correct a club foot on a little boy whose parents could not even afford to buy the boy shoes. He then had his assistant buy shoes for the whole family, and would not allow the assistant to tell that Ford had paid for the shoes and surgery.

Earlier in the book I wrote the following statement from Teddy Roosevelt. I believe so strongly in his words that I felt it important to give them to you again. It is worth highlighting. Theodore Roosevelt, our great 26th president stated, "The credit belongs to the man who is in the arena. Whose face is marred by sweat and dust and blood; who strives valiantly; who errs and comes up short again and again. Who knows the great enthusiasms; the great devotions; and spends himself in a worthy cause, who at best, knows the triumph of high achievement; and at the worst, if he fails, at least fails while daring greatly, so that his place shall never be with those cold and timid souls who know neither victory or defeat."

Teddy was put on the ticket as Vice President to get rid of him, but when McKinley was assassinated Teddy became President. That caused Senator Mark Hanna, to exclaim, "That damn cowboy is in the White House." Despite Teddy's reversals in life he went on to become one of our greatest Presidents and won the Nobel Prize for peace for settling the Russian-Japanese wars. He was sickly as a child with terrible asthma, but built up his body and became a champion boxer in college occasionally sparing with the great heavyweight champion, John L. Sullivan. Teddy staged one of the great comebacks from being sickly and almost dying to becoming one of our greatest Presidents, because he was also one of the great Positive Thinkers.

In 1969, Colonel Kris Mineau was flying two and a half times faster than the speed of sound in his F-4 fighter/bomber when the controls froze, while he was in an upside down position heading for an outside loop. He had no choice but to pull the seat ejection handle, but the mechanism refused to respond. Suddenly, he was only five hundred feet from the ground when the canopy separated from the F-4 and he was ejected. The problem he faced was that he needed at least two to three thousand feet for the chute to be effective and land safely. So in essence he technically needed three seconds for the chute to open. The chute miraculously opened in one half a second. Unfortunately, he was heading to the ground much faster than if he had the two to three thousand feet required to slow him down. Kris lived, but he suffered two broken arms, two broken legs, and many internal injuries. Luckily, he had no head or neck injuries.

Kris spent many months in the hospital in surgery and traction and finally was flown in a full body cast to Florida, due to medical reasons. After over three years and ten operations he was considered clinically healed by the doctors and after a year and a half of wearing braces, he was assigned to a desk job.

Kris was considered washed up, but he was determined to make a comeback, so he badgered his superiors and went to see the flight surgeon to start the process to be evaluated as sound for flying. Because of his time off and the seriousness of his injuries, he had to go through many tests, both physically and mentally. The tests he had to take were similar to the ones astronauts take, because he had been written off as a hopeless case. In January of 1975, Kris received his new orders to fly based on the Surgeon General's decision and ironically, he was given a takeoff time of 4:30 P.M. The accident had occurred exactly six years to the day and hour before his new takeoff time. To deepen the irony, he discovered that his new airplane was number 898, which was the number on the plane he crashed in six years earlier. This time this amazing positive thinker flew without incident, and he knows how important Positive thinking is.

I am convinced that these kinds of things happen for and with Positive Thinkers, because Positive Thinkers make things happen positively. I would go so far as to say that Positive Thinkers make miracles happen. And at the very least, they achieve the impossible.

What do you do when your world is shattered? What do you do when you lose both your legs and suddenly your profession is no longer a viable option? You are close to death and are given very little hope of living, and if you do live, the quality of life you will face is tenuous at best. What do you do? Do you sit back and say, "Well this is it; life is not worth living anymore. I've had it. There is no hope of restoring my life to the precious joy and fulfillment I enjoyed."

Here is what an ordinary man did in that exact circumstance. In 1993 Sergeant First Class Dana Bowman, an aerial demonstration parachutist with the United States Army parachute team, traveling 150 mph, collided in midair with his team-mate during the teams training exercise in Yuma, Arizona. His partner died due to injury complications and Sergeant Bowman lost both his legs. Six days after the accident Sergeant Bowman attended his partner's funeral against his doctor's orders. Two months later, he ordered the reluctant doctors to remove two inches of his leg that had become infected. He insisted that he would be fitted with prosthetic limbs against the doctor's recommendations. He even helped design the limbs, and to top it off, nine months later, he skydived to the reenlistment table in a field, thus becoming the first double amputee to reenlist in the US Army, thereby turning a terrible tragedy into a positive triumph. At no time during his nightmare did he believe he would not recover and go back to his normal life. He became assistant director of Media Relations for the Golden Nights diving team. He snow skis, scuba dives, hot air balloons and dances to country-western music. Sergeant Bowman has been on many television shows and has been featured in Sports Illustrated, Readers Digest, People and many other publications. He was awarded the Veteran of the Year for 1995-96, and Barbara Bush beat him out for the prestigious Jefferson Award. An award has been named after him, which is for the help of others and the will to never quit. He was Grand Marshal with Christopher Reeve, (Superman) for the Fourth of July parade in 1996, in Atlanta, and parachuted into the stadium for the Para-Olympics on August 15th of that year.

"Oh, he had special help," the cynics and negative thinkers will say, but I called Sergeant Bowman in 1995 to induct him into the World Positive Thinkers Club, and he told me that the doctors and his commanding officers fought him at every turn. He was practically ordered to stay an invalid for the rest of his life. His faith in himself and God made it possible for him to fight the negative thinkers and keep his steely determination to make a comeback. I talked again with Dana in November of 2007 and I can assure you he knows the **three-word motto**.

I feel for the handicapped walking the streets or moving about in wheelchairs, and wish I could help every one of them. But do you know what? Many of them do not want our help. They feel they are ordinary just like you and me. The positive thinking, physically disabled don't want our sympathy. They do not want doors opened for them. They want equal opportunity. They want us to know that they can be just as capable as most of us. Naturally they are limited in some respects, but don't tell Sergeant Bowman that. He is another of the ordinary people, who is labeled a, "Comeback Kid." Sergeant Bowman is a perfect example of people who dare to risk as exemplified by what you just read. And it also reminds me of the quote by Sam Ewing, when he said, "Nothing is as embarrassing as watching someone doing something that you said couldn't be done."

Here is a little quiz for you. What ordinary man wrote, "Among the things that he passed on to me were the belief that all men and women, regardless of their color or religion, are created equal and that individuals determine their own destiny; that is, largely their own ambition and hard work that determine their fate in life."

The same mans father said of his ordinary son, who was born in a flat above a local bank in Illinois, "he looks like a fat little Dutchman. But who knows, he might grow up to be President some day." That mans father was a shoe salesman, and his son lost a job as clerk for Montgomery Ward starting at $12.50 a week after graduating from college. His first desire after college was to be a radio announcer, so he hitchhiked to Chicago, but no station wanted an inexperienced kid during the depression. So he was rejected at every station he applied to, and hitchhiked back to his small town flat broke. This ordinary man learned from his mother the value of prayer, and how to have dreams, and believe he could make them come true, and by dreaming and knowing the **three-word motto** he landed a job in a small radio station in Iowa. The rest is history.

That sentence was a quote from the autobiography of an ordinary man who became the fortieth President of the United States, Ronald Reagan, one of the greatest Positive Thinking Presidents this country has ever had the good fortune to have at the helm. He literally changed America into a Positive Thinking nation after years of downward negative spiraling of the economy, military unprepared ness, and poor morale. President Reagan had many defeats along the way and had his share of critics, but along with his many other accomplishments he was instrumental in the tearing down of the Berlin Wall, which all the cynics said would never happen.

Do you know who said? "No matter what your background, no matter how low your station in life, there must be no limit on your ability to reach for the stars, to go as far as your God-given talents will take you. Trust the people; believe every human being is capable of greatness, capable of self government ... only when people are free to worship, create, and build, only when they are given a stake in deciding their destiny and benefiting from their own risks, only then do societies become dynamic, prosperous, progressive and free." If you had said Ronald Reagan you would have been right again. No matter your politics, you have to admit his profound words are good philosophy.

One of the problems President Reagan faced when he took office was a "malaise" in America. There was a feeling of loss of faith in itself. We were told that America was past its prime. We were told such bunk as, we had to get used to less, and the American people were responsible for the problems we faced. We were told we would have to lower our expectations. Unbelievably, we were told by the so-called skeptics (I call them quitters), that America would never be prosperous or have a bright future as it once had. Can you believe that was the permeating philosophy in this great land? This was the land that became the most powerful nation on the face of the earth. This was the land that became the most prosperous country ever conceived. This was the land that forged the greatest military in history. Now negative thinkers were telling us that we had had it as a nation. This was coming from losers and the negative influence filtered to the press who unfortunately seeing a story, picked it up and ran with it causing a tidal wave of negativism. President Reagan found nothing wrong with the American people. He disagreed with those who spouted that we had to be satisfied with less. He believed that we had to recapture our pride in our country and ourselves. It didn't happen overnight, but it did happen.

I remember being at a sales meeting in the mid 1980's in San Diego, California, where a Colonel in one of the Armed Services gave us a speech. Being a former serviceman I asked him how he felt about America's readiness now that we had a new President. He asked to speak off the record and told me that we were woefully unprepared both mentally and militarily by the time Ronald Reagan took office. However, President Reagan's enthusiasm and positive thinking turned things around for the military and we were now on top again. Another blow against negative thinking!

President Reagan went about finding out what went wrong and then went about putting America back on the correct course. And America came back with a roar, thanks to an ordinary son of a shoe salesman who became President, and President was a member of the World Positive thinkers club and I am sure he knew the **three-word motto**.

There are many instances of ordinary people taking a written test and then exceeding by miles physically what the test showed they could not accomplish. One such instance happened during World War II with First Lieutenant Bill Cullerton, from Chicago, Illinois. He passed the written test by the minimum of seventy and the counselor told him, "There's no way you are going to make it." That was just the challenge Lieutenant Cullerton needed, as this ordinary combat pilot finished the war as the second highest scoring ace of his fighter group. The moral of the story is demonstrated time and time again: You can be embarrassed later on if you tell someone they can't do something.

The world is divided into two types of people: those who are skeptical of others until the others prove themselves, and those who presume that other people are good and decent until proven otherwise.

"My mother said to me, "If you become a soldier you'll be a general; if you become a monk you'll end up as the pope.
" Instead, I became a painter and wound up Picasso."
—Pablo Picasso

MAIN THOUGHTS AND CHALLENGES

1. Go back over this chapter and review your highlighted sentences.

2. Write the highlighted page numbers on this page.

3. Write down the most important highlighted sentence on your sheet.

4. Write down a goal that you would now like to achieve within the next 30 days. If you do not achieve that you must start over again until you achieve the goal on a monthly basis.

5. Write on this page, "I am not an ordinary person." Highlight it.

Chapter 9

DON'T ITCH FOR SOMETHING YOU ARE NOT WILLING TO SCRATCH FOR

"I have a simple philosophy. Fill what's full. Scratch where it itches."

–Alice Roosevelt Longworth

Are you willing to scratch for what you desire in life? Are you willing to scratch the itch in order to achieve your goals? If you do not have goals to achieve to make your mark then I say to you, you are among those cold and timid souls that President Teddy Roosevelt spoke about. Have I been too harsh here? I don't believe I have, because I have great faith in humans. I want more than anything to give you hope and ambition to achieve more than you thought you possibly could, and to reach for the stars knowing that nothing will stand in your way. A good boss tries to fire up his employees, rather than have to fire them. Since you purchased this book, and are keeping an open mind, you are on your way to being a permanent Positive Thinker, and, discovering the exciting **three-word motto**. By the way, have you been highlighting up to this point? No, it is not nagging, but simply reminding and encouraging you to reach higher.

Today you have to be different; you have to stand out in a crowd; you have to be willing to take a chance; you have to be willing to put it all on the line if you really want to succeed in a big way. Or as a famous singer, Loretta Lynn, who struggled to the top said, "You have to be first, best or different." One of my favorite movies is about her struggle in life titled, Coal Miner's Daughter, starring Sissy Spacek, and Tommy Lee Jones.

Just like the great Roman leader, Julius Caesar, who burned the ships after his troops landed on foreign soil in what is now England. They now had to defeat the enemy so they could use the enemy's ships to get back home. Now that is motivation, wouldn't you agree? His troops went on to victory and so will you, once you learn the **three-word motto**.

What is the difference between the great musical groups and the ones who last about a year? Johnny Carson said, "Out of every 100 musical groups that start, only one or two will be around after one or two years. The reason for that is that they are not willing to pay the price to learn more than four or five songs. They sound great for those few songs, but they don't take the time to learn a complete repertoire of numbers. So they can't get past the second encore, and no one wants to hire anyone who is limited." "Try going out on a limb; that is where the fruit is." ––—Anonymous

What does the man who earns $70,000 a year know that the man who earns $25,000 doesn't know when they both have the same amount of formal schooling? He knows several things. He knows that wisdom consists in knowing what to do with what you know. He knows that school is never out for the pro. He reads everything he can get his hands on. He takes extra courses at night. He knows that knowledge is power, but imagination is the switch. He joins clubs and volunteers his time, getting to know and help people, thereby making connections, known as networking. He knows that it is the old story of, it is not just what you know, but it is whom you know. He is willing to scratch. And he knows the **three-word motto**.

A classic example of that is an old friend who is a former self-defense student of mine, Paul Pennypacker, former Chief of Police of the Tredyffrin Police department in Berwyn, Pennsylvania, one of the most respected police departments in the nation. When I met Paul, he was a patrolman on a small force. Paul took all the schools the police had to offer. He worked his way up to Lieutenant and was finally promoted over men who had been there longer. These policemen were knowledgeable, but did not have the schooling or ambition that Paul possessed. Paul was willing to go the extra mile and his goal was set on being chief. He knew that to become chief he would have to stand out head and shoulders above all the rest, and Paul never forgets his roots. My son completed his college internship with Paul's police force and told me that all the men and women highly respect Paul. He goes to bat for his men and gets them extra education if they want it, and every time I see

Paul he has a smile on his face. He was willing to scratch, and he is a member of the World Positive Thinkers Club.

Did you ever wonder why some companies are number-one in their industry and eventually fall to number two, and eventually number three, then suddenly they are filing for bankruptcy? One of the reasons is they forget what got them there in the first place. They forget their roots. They hire new blood, which has different philosophies than that of the founders of the company. A classic example of that is a large retailer that was the biggest with the most in their price range. Then a strange thing happened. Wal-Mart came along. Wal-Mart did a ton of advertising and this retailer pulled back on advertising. They changed their inventory ordering system and instituted other procedures that were not akin to their industry. The retailer in question kept hiring new chief executives and other high executives, and they all instituted new changes. They just filed for bankruptcy, and even though Wal-Mart founder Sam Walton died his company stuck with the basics. Sam Walton was a Positive Thinker and turned his great company into the largest retailer in America. There is no doubt in my mind that Sam knew the importance of Positive Thinking.

Another reason Companies fail is they do not keep up with the latest technology. They feel they are in such a powerful position, that they will stay there. A classic example was Baldwin Steam Locomotive Works, in Philadelphia, Pennsylvania. Their executives were warned that diesel fuel was the fuel of the future. It was cleaner, cheaper and easier to burn. Diesel fuel does not leave off the tremendous soot that coal shoots into the air. And steam locomotives require a tremendous amount of water for cooling. Maintenance is higher for steam locomotives as well. Baldwin executives were told to convert their equipment to manufacturing diesel locomotives or they would be out of business in a few years. They did not listen to their engineers, because they were not willing to pay the price and they refused to enter the future. The industry had an itch to improve but Baldwin was not willing to scratch. When I was a small child I loved to go to the coal yards in Narberth, Pennsylvania, and watch the locomotives steam into the coal yard to load up with coal. A strange thing happened. As I grew older, I noticed the steam locomotives were no longer pulling into the station. Gone was the smoke. The constant chug-chug was replaced by a powerful humming sound. To me the romance was gone, and eventually so was Baldwin Steam Locomotive works. To enter the future you have to be willing to scratch.

Another thing that happens to the person headed for success is that when he gets hired he does not just do his or her job. He or she makes it known to the right people that he or she is reliable, and can be depended on to do his or her job and do it well. They acquire the reputation of being able to get the job done, whether it is the job they were hired for or other job requirements. It is like the old story I heard years ago. "A message to Garcia." During the Spanish-American War in 1898, President McKinley needed to get a message to General Garcia, the leader of the Cuban rebels, hidden deep in the jungle in Cuba. One man stood up and told the President he knew who could deliver the message. It was Lt. Andrew Summers Rowan. Rowan knew that the outcome depended on getting the message through and that a lot of American lives would be saved. He did not know where Garcia was, but he told the President not to worry, as he would get the message through. He knew that if America were to win the war earlier, thus saving many lives, that someone had to scratch harder to satisfy the itch. Lt. Rowan strapped the oilskin pouch to his chest and landed off the coast of Cuba in an open boat. Three weeks later he emerged on the other end of the island having delivered the message and many American lives were saved.

Don't say, "I was not hired to do that, let someone else do it." "I can't take the time, it's not that important." "Why do you need that information?" "You will never find Garcia in that jungle." "Can't you do it yourself?"

Don't be like the employees as purported to be taken from actual federal-employee evaluations.

- "Since my last report, this employee has reached rock bottom and has started to dig."
- "Works well under constant supervision and when cornered like a rat in a trap."
- "Sets low personal standards and consistently fails to achieve them."
- "This employee is depriving a village somewhere of an idiot."

The Positive Thinker goes the extra mile. Being dependable does not always require blind obedience, and the smart boss knows that he must be open to suggestions from his subordinates. If he is not open then he is too ego centered and will someday be replaced, by someone who knows he is expendable. I had a boss just like that once. He was formerly a salesman and worked his way to sales manager and then became plant manager. There was no way you could reason with this man. It was his way or the highway and he became arrogant and insulting to all around him. I lost a huge order, because he would not listen to me when I told him the customer said we had the business as long as we did not ask for his present price. He asked the customer for the price and the customer threw us out the door. Then he did the unpardonable. He became such a big shot and a know it all that he bought supplies from sources other than his own company. He also felt he had the authority to send workers who were painting the factory or repaving the parking lot to his house to get free work. It wasn't much longer when the "big boys," from the home office pulled a surprise audit and fired him. He became greedy and was not willing to remember his roots. He took the "don't itch for something you are not willing to scratch for," overboard. Do your scratching in a way that does not hurt others.

One hundred of the most successful entrepreneurs who started their own companies were interviewed and it was found that they failed in business an average of seven times before becoming successful. Some failed twice and some failed 20 times, but the average is seven times. They all admitted to a man that they were willing to risk it all to be successful. You can be assured that if you give up after one try you haven't a clue as to how to succeed in life. It is said that money talks, all it says to some business people is "Goodbye." So stick to the fight when you are hardest hit!

People need to read the basic books, such as, *Think and Grow Rich,* by Napoleon Hill. I am only writing based on my research and being associated with the successful people as Napoleon did. His book became a best seller. Earl Nightengale is one of the most respected names in the motivational world and he gives great input in his material as to winning and success. His definition of success is, "Success is the progressive realization of a worthy ideal." In other words, keep on scratching.

Some years ago I watched a movie directed in 1946 by William Wyler about returning veterans from World War II. In that movie, *The Best Years of Our Lives,* there were two great actors, Dana Andrews and Frederick March, the great actress, Myrna Loy, and a third actor who I had never heard of before. The movie was very moving, (the brilliant Academy Award winning actress, Bette Davis claimed it was the best movie ever made) because it showed the hardships men faced when returning from a kind of hell. This unknown actor gave a moving performance, and at one point in the movie I was choked up. "Gosh, what a great piece of acting," I said to myself. I wondered how much time he had spent learning to use the hooks that were now his hands. In those days there were no special effects computers to make up for certain hard moves or sequences. So I was impressed with this unknown actor's ability to portray the part perfectly as an amputee, and I wondered how they made those hooks work. I asked myself, how did they make it look like he was an amputee?

Harold Russell, this unknown actor, won an Academy Award for best supporting actor for his performance in that stirring movie, and another Oscar for bringing hope to the down trodden, as well as national acclaim for his courage in overcoming a serious handicap. I learned he really was an amputee, who had lost both hands in World War II, but Harold never gave up on himself while other amputees would sit around feeling sorry for themselves. In an article he wrote, "There is something in most people that won't let them take defeat lying down. Call it anything you like, but to me it is faith-faith in God and myself, faith that I can rise from every serious setback. Every person is licked without this."

Harold was willing to help scratch the itch America possessed to win the war. He fought for his country and lost both hands in the process, but Harold refused to give up by sitting around feeling sorry for him-self. Oh yes, Harold knew how to stay Positive.

The great philosophers, Emerson, Thoreau, and William James, did more to change the thought process of Americans than any persons. They combined to create the attitude of the American, who is not defeated by obstacles. Their teachings are partly responsible for the philosophy of the American spirit, and the thought process that man can overcome the impossible, with unbelievable efficiency. The great Thoreau taught us that to hold a picture of a successful outcome is the secret of achievement. Emerson went on to teach that the human personality "can be touched with divine power and greatness." The philosophy that the greatest factor in any undertaking is, "one's belief about it," is attributed to William James.

The great football coach of the, World Champion, Green Bay Packers, Vince Lombardi, wrote, "You've got to pay the price. Winning is not a sometime thing; it's an all the time thing. You don't win once in a while, you don't do things right once in a while you do them right all the time. Winning is a habit, unfortunately, so is losing. There is no room for second place. There is only one place in my game and that is first place. I have finished second twice in my time at Green Bay and I don't ever want to finish second again. There is a second place bowl game, but it is a game for losers played by losers. It is and always has been an American zeal to be first in everything we do and to win and to win and win. Running a football team is no different from running any other kind of organization-an army, a political party, and a business. The principals are the same. The object is to win-to beat the other guy. Maybe that sounds hard or cruel. I don't think it is." A critic once said of Lombardi, "He possesses minimal football knowledge. Lacks motivation."

Vince went on to say, "It's a reality of life that people are competitive and the most competitive games draw the most competitive people. That's why they are there-to compete. They know the rules and the objectives when they get in the game. The objective is to win-fairly, squarely, decently, by the rules-but to win."

"I don't say these things because I believe in the 'brute' nature of man or that man must be brutalized to be combative. I believe in God, and I believe in human decency. But I firmly believe that man's finest hour-his greatest fulfillment to all he holds dear-is that moment when he has worked his heart out in a good cause and lies exhausted on the field of battle-victorious." Vince was one of the great Positive Thinking coaches.

Charles Lindbergh had a dream. He dreamed of doing something no person had ever accomplished. Lindbergh dreamed of flying solo across the Atlantic Ocean. This was a time when man had barely gotten off the ground, but Lindbergh knew that he had an itch that could not be satisfied unless he was willing to scratch. The first obstacle he had to overcome was the negative thinkers. Naturally he was laughed at, but those negative thinkers forgot that the Wright Brothers were laughed at too.

Lindbergh was a mail carrier and a barnstormer, so he had to do a lot of research. You just don't pick up and do something no one else has accomplished by just dreaming. There is planning, studying, learning, practice, building and financial backing to accomplish. It doesn't happen overnight. Lindbergh had to find the right airplane. That airplane had to have the best motor money could buy. One little problem and he could find himself in the drink.

After many hours of research, Lindbergh settled on a Ryan NYP monoplane with a Wright motor. The wingspan was 46 feet with a fuel capacity of 450 gallons, and the plane was built so that Lindberg could use all the space possible. Naturally the plane had to be tested, so Lindbergh flew it from San Diego to St Louis to New York, establishing a new coast-to-coast speed record in the process.

On the day before Lindbergh was to take off terrible news hit the airwaves. Nungesser and Coli, the French pilots perished trying to fly from Paris to New York. Some of the negative thinkers tried to talk Lindbergh out of his attempt, but Lindbergh had an itch that would not go away. And so, on May 20, 1927, at 7:30AM, Charles Lindbergh, rumbled and bounced down the wet runway to accomplish what man had only dreamed of. If successful, Lindbergh would unite the United States with Europe by air and the world would never be the same. What an awesome challenge he faced.

When Lindbergh landed in Paris 33.5 hours later he was mobbed and his personal world was never to be the same. He became an instant American hero, and enjoyed a ticker tape parade in New York City, but as mentioned before in this book, F. Scott Fitzgerald once said, "Show me a hero and I will write you a tragedy." Lindbergh had his tragedy when his baby was kidnapped and murdered, but Lindbergh was always willing to scratch for the itch he had, and one thing is for sure: Lindbergh knew the **three-word motto**.

Several weeks ago I watched Lindbergh's grandson prepare for a flight that would make history again. All of his family and friends except his wife were against the flight. It was too dangerous they said. You will never complete it they said. And on and on came the excuses just like the ones his grandfather listened to. Luckily, another Lindbergh did not listen to the skeptics, as he flew from New York to France in a single engine plane, exactly seventy-five years to the month later. This scratching Positive Thinker inherited his grandfather's positive thinking genes, and he also knew the **three-word motto**.

Fred Astaire took a screen test and the testing director of MGM in 1933 said, "Can't act! Slightly bald! Can dance a little." Fred scratched and became known as the greatest dancer in the movies. By the way, my personal opinion is that Fred's partner in many of his dance movies, Ginger Rogers, was as good a dancer as Fred, because she had to dance backwards most of the time.

The author of *Little Women,* Louisa May Alcott, was told to get work as a servant or seamstress by her own family. She scratched the itch and wrote a best seller.

Beethoven's teacher called him hopeless. Beethoven scratched his itch.

When Thomas attended school in his early days his teachers said he was too stupid to learn anything. A young reporter asked Thomas how it felt to fail so many times. Thomas Edison who invented the light bulb after thousands of tries, replied, "I never failed once. I invented the light bulb. It just happened to be a 2,000 step process."

On Edmund Hillary's first attempt to climb 29,035-foot Mount Everest in Nepal, China he failed. Several weeks later while speaking to a group he pointed to a picture of Mount Everest and said, "Mount Everest, you beat me the first time, but I'll beat you the next time, because you have grown all you are going to grow… but I'm still growing!" Sir Edmund Hillary was willing to scratch for the itch, and one year later on May 29, 1953 became the first person to conquer Mount Everest, and Hillary could ever conquered Mt. Everest without a pure Positive attitude.

The head of the John Murray Anderson Drama School told one of the great actresses and one of the funniest comedians the world has ever enjoyed watching to try another profession. Lucille Ball became a famous star because she had an itch that would not go away, and she was willing to scratch. I always watched her television show I love Lucy, and Lucille Ball scratched the itch to be a star and she knew the **three-word motto**.

Another of the negative thinkers with no vision had Al expelled, because he claimed Al was, "mentally slow, unsociable, and adrift forever in his foolish dreams." He was even refused admittance to Zurich polytechnic school. If Al had listened to the critics instead of scratching his itch we would never have realized Albert Einstein's *theory of relativity,* as well as all his other great scientific contributions. He once said, "The difference between stupidity and genius is that genius has a limit."

Richard Bach wrote a ten-thousand-word story about a soaring seagull. Eighteen publishers turned it down before Macmillan published *Jonathon Livingston Seagull,* which went on to sell 7,000,000 copies. As an author when you get the itch to be published you must never stop scratching. The published authors know the **three-word motto**, and you can be assured it is not as easy to get published as many people think.

Winny failed the sixth grade, and after a lifetime of defeats and setbacks became the Prime Minister of England at the age of 62. He was defeated again as Prime Minister, but came back a few years later and was elected Prime Minister once more. We know Winny as Winston Churchill, one of the greatest orators of all time. He never gave up the willingness to scratch for the itch. Winners are willing to scratch, and they know the **three-word motto**.

"History has demonstrated that the most notable winners usually encountered heartbreaking obstacles before they triumphed.
They won because they refused to become discouraged by their defeats."
— B.C. Forbes

MAIN THOUGHTS AND CHALLENGES

1. Go back to the beginning of this chapter and review your highlighted sentences.

1. Place the highlighted page numbers on this page.

2. Write down the most important highlight and why it is so important to you.

3. Write down one hobby that you have always wanted to do.

4. Finally write down how you are willing to scratch for this itch you have thought about over time.

Chapter 10

YOUR FAITH IN YOURSELF IS YOUR REAL ATTITUDE

"Let us have faith that right makes might; and in that faith, let us to the end, dare to do our duty as we understand it."

—Abraham Lincoln

Every story I hear or read about overcoming impossible odds is laced with the word faith. A classic example of that is about one of the greatest athletes ever to play in the sports arena. As a matter of fact, many experts are convinced that Babe was one of the greatest all around athletes who ever lived. While many feel Jim Thorpe was the greatest, many others feel it was Babe. In the 1932 Olympics, Babe Zaharis won Gold Medals in the javelin event and the 80-meter hurdles. In twenty years of competition Babe had entered 334 contests in every amateur sport, and won all but two. But in 1952, she was diagnosed with colon cancer. Many people became virtual invalids after a colon cancer operation in those days. Hundreds of letters came from golfing fans that assured her that if she had faith she would overcome, and these fans with colon cancer depended on Babe to prove that colon cancer was recoverable. Because she was the top woman golfer in the world, cancer patients needed her to have faith to overcome to be a spiritual rock for them. Babe had tremendous faith in her ability to overcome and make a comeback after being written off by the negative thinkers. In August of 1953, four months after her operation, she was back on the links in Chicago and came in third. She then continued playing and won the next two tournaments, and came in first in the United States Women's Open, the biggest tournament of the year. She said, "We won it. We are the thousands of people whose faith helped make me strong." Babe knew the **three-word motto**.

Saint Augustine wrote, "Faith is to believe what we do not see; and the reward of this faith is to see what we believe." Mark Twain said, "You can not depend on your eyes when your imagination is out of focus." In Saint Paul's second letter to the Corinthians he writes, "We walk by faith, not by sight." Tolstoy wrote, "Faith is the force of life." "Alas! The fearful unbelief is unbelief in yourself." —Thomas Carlyle

Well there you have it. One of the greatest secrets in overcoming obstacles is St. Paul's seven-word sentence. Do you have faith in yourself? I am convinced you do or you would not have read this far. "If ye have faith as a grain of mustard seed, nothing shall be impossible unto you."—Matthew. 17:20

One of the great joys of my life was my close association with a group of men, who I met with for dinner every year right before Christmas. One of these men was Bobby Shantz, my boyhood hero, whom I have talked about earlier in this book. Dining with us was his catcher in the big leagues, Joe Astroth, who had tied a record for most RBI's (runs batted in) six (6) in a single inning. Another dinner companion connected with baseball was Paul Hill. Paul had one of the largest and most valuable baseball memorabilia collections in the world. Rounding out our group was my best friend, Cornelius (Connie) Hause, a very valuable customer, confidant and baseball fanatic. We met at a different restaurant every year and inevitably we talked about the old days and the new breed of athlete. One of the things we talked about was the attitude of the modern day athlete. For example: Bobby told me one time that he would have played professional baseball for nothing, because he enjoyed playing so much. When he was traded to the New York Yankees in the mid fifties, he said he was so happy; he would have walked from Kansas City to New York just to be able to play with that team comprised of future Hall of Famers, such as Mickey Mantle, Yogi Berra, and Whitey Ford. In 1957, Bobby had the lowest E.R.A. in the American league and pitched in the World Series against the Milwaukee Braves. It is said of the athlete of today that he is spoiled and pampered, and only has faith in the almighty dollar. But fortunately there are still many that put out one hundred and ten percent, and many of these great athletes are not afraid to tell of their faith in themselves and God.

Red Barber, the famous sportscaster and columnist, wrote, "In all my years of announcing sports, I have become deeply impressed with the importance of disposition. Managers, club executives, coaches, and scouts are filled with the sad knowledge of so many physically gifted athletes who did not stand the wear of time and did not arrive at goals they should have reached, because they lacked a good disposition. On the other hand, there are many Major League ball players, who make the grade despite not having all the physical attributes, because they make up their minds that they are going to succeed and they will not accept defeat." They have faith in themselves.

There you have it again! Time after time we hear about people who refuse to accept defeat. They have complete faith in their abilities and refuse to let the doubters rule their lives. They know that they are not as gifted as the "natural" athlete, so they work harder; they take extra batting practice or fielding practice; they stay longer at the golf driving range; they study game films longer. In essence they just work harder to compensate; they have complete faith in themselves and know the **three-word motto**. Professor William James stated that the greatest discovery of the 19th century was the power of the subconscious touched by faith.

Do you aspire to be a scientist? Listen to the words of the famous scientist, Charles Kettering, "Any young man who wants to be a scientist must be willing to fail 99 times before he succeeds once, and suffer no ego damage because of it." Kettering ought to know, as he was the inventor of light generating units for farm houses; originator of Delco Electric Power, and President and General Manager of General Motors Research Corporation.

Earl Nightengale explained success when he stated, "The opposite of success is not failure, it is conformity. It is acting like everyone else." Finally, he stated that all the wise men and philosophers disagreed on all but one thing. They all agreed that, as I wrote in an earlier chapter, *"You become what you think about."* So there you have it in a nutshell. It is not only hard work that makes us successful, but right thinking. But you say, "I need money to make more money or be successful." Read what Daniel Webster wrote about success. "Failure is more often from want of energy than lack of capital." In other words faith!

So one lesson here is that it has been proven that 85 percent of what we worry about never comes to fruition. And yet, people constantly worry about all kinds of things that they can't do anything about anyway. Now don't get me wrong. I am not going to say that I never am concerned about a situation. But to worry is to hammer another nail into the coffin and take a chance of contracting ulcers. Mark Twain said, "I am now an old man and have known many troubles, but most of them never happened." The medical and psychiatric professions have proven that most of our ailments are mentally induced; so it makes sense to live life in a happy go lucky state. Or at best, we should try to think that the outcome would be positive. In other words, the negative thinker gets negative results and the Positive Thinker, if he doesn't always get positive results, at least gets positive results most of the time. He or she has faith!

If I could give any advice to teenagers it would be to study hard in school, and have a dream as to what they really want to be firmly settled in their brains. This dream should be one that there is no doubt about, and they should read everything they can get their hands on about the profession they are sure about. This dream should be a burning obsession with the belief that no obstacle will be big enough to overcome their determination to be successful in any endeavor they embark upon. They also should be given the wise advice to read positive input books like Dr. Norman Vincent Peale's, *The Power of Positive Thinking, Think and Grow Rich,* by Napoleon Hill, *How to win Friends and Influence People,* by Dale Carnegie, and *See You at The Top,* by *Zig Ziglar*. And I humbly add this book. Teenagers should be given positive input everyday in the signs they see and the things they read. They should be taught to know that persistence is the main quality to be successful. "It is the sandpaper that breaks down all resistance and sweeps away all obstacles. It is the ability to move mountains one grain of sand at a time." —Calvin Coolidge. In other words, teenagers and all of us should never give up when we plant a goal in our mind. When we have faith that we will succeed we will. And once we commit the **three-word motto** to memory we are on the road to being successful and happy.

Our problems are all so different, but if we think positive we will eventually overcome them, as long as we believe and smile often. And a very important part of the equation is realizing and accepting the fact that our "actual self" is imperfect. Once you do that you will have an easier time with the mistakes that you are sure to make. The 300 hitter in baseball does not dwell on the seven out of ten times he fails to get on base. The star quarterback will not worry about the interceptions he threw. I have yet to hear about a quarterback who threw 30 passes and completed everyone of them, or a great quarterback who never threw an interception. He knows that he will sit and analyze what he did right as well to avoid throwing another one in the same situation. And if he does throw another interception in that same situation he will shrug his shoulders and simply say. "OK, they got me again, but I will just try harder to be successful." Four-time Prime Minister of England, William Gladstone said, "No man ever became great or good except through many and great mistakes."

When a captain is on the bridge of a large ocean going vessel, he does not allow it to leave port until all the indicators tell him the ship is safe to sail. There are many gauges to tell him and his engineer if a ship needs a replacement part or lubrication. Some people think of these indicators as negative indicators. Turn it around and look at them as positive indicators, telling me that when I take positive corrective action the ship will sail smoothly. While driving a car there are gauges too, but you do not constantly stare at them. You focus on the road ahead and the positive goal of getting to your destination. You have faith that your car will get you to your final destination, unless of course you have one of those lemons we occasionally hear about.

You must think of all the success stories like Oprah Winfrey, Lance Armstrong, Billy Jean King, Jackie Robinson, and thousands of other winners. Oprah's parents separated when she was very young and at the age of nine was abused. She moved in with her father at age fourteen and he insisted on hard work, which eventually won her a scholarship to Tennessee State. Oprah is known as the queen of talk shows is listed as one of the billionaires in the world, and you can tell that she cares about people as well as having a great self-image, with profound faith in her abilities.

I think of Colonel Sanders of Kentucky Chicken fame. He tried to sell his grandmothers chicken recipe to close to one thousand restaurants before one would accept the recipe when he was at the ripe old age of sixty six. Can you imagine the average person continuing after 10 failures? Well, this is what I see today with business people who have come to me to get me to help them find money for their business. I get all kinds of excuses from they have no money to put in themselves, to the market is not right. Why was it many people started new businesses during the Great Depression and succeeded? Why did so many people not commit suicide when they lost everything? Why does a good pitcher turn better when he goes to a new team? Why does a great hockey player lose his touch before he gets too old for the game? Why do businesses fail during good times? It is very simple to answer those questions! We become what we think about. If we think success we become successful. And the opposite is true. If we think failure, we become a failure. And let me take it one more step. It is a matter of faith and confidence. No person ever succeeded who did not have complete faith and confidence in his or her abilities. And that goes back to acting the part of the successful person you have decided to become. I believe this with all my heart and soul. Close your eyes at least once a day and visualize yourself attaining the goal you have set.

"When you're lost in the wild, and you're scared as a child,
And death looks you bang in the eye.
And you're sore as a boil; it's according to Hoyle,
To cock your revolver and . . . . die.
But the code of man, says: "Fight all you can,"
And self-dissolution is barred.
In hunger and woe, oh, it's easy to blow...
It's the hell-served-for-breakfast that's hard.
You're sick of the game! "Well, now, that's a shame.
You're young and you're brave and you're bright.
You've had a raw deal! I know—-but don't squeal.
Buck up, do your damndest, and fight.
It's the plugging away that will win you the day,
So don't be a piker, old pard!
Just draw on your grit; it's so easy to quit:
It's the keeping-your-chin-up that's hard.
It's easy to cry that you're beaten—and die.
It's easy to crawfish and crawl;
But to fight and to fight when hope's out of sight,
Why, that's the best game of them all!"

— *Robert Servko*

All winners have a similar poem or quote to give them encouragement, and if you want to have help in your struggles, you need to read words of wisdom like the above and be able to pump positive input into your brain. Anyone who thinks they can do it alone is making a grave mistake, and the psychiatrists' couches are filled every day with confused patients who tried to do it on their own. In many cases they come away from the couch session still confused. (Some psychiatrists, in my opinion, need help themselves sometimes, as we all do).

I will be the first to admit that I need help in my daily struggles. But all through this heartache and struggle I have called on a power greater than I and accept what He doles out to me. I am not content, but I will not fight His will. I know the **three-word motto**, and so I press on. As our great President, Abraham Lincoln stated so succinctly: "I am a slow walker, but I never walk backwards."

If you want to overcome obstacles learn a lesson from the great inventor, Thomas Edison. He made experiment after experiment searching for a new source of natural rubber in plant matter. After the 50,000th failure, a discouraged assistant said: "Mr. Edison, we have tried 50,000 experiments, and have had no results." "Results!" said Edison enthusiastically. "We have had great results. We now know 50,000 things which won't work!" Fifty thousand failures! I dare you to keep going forward after five. Positive thinkers like Edison have great faith and Stay Positive when surrounded with negativity.

Show me a person who does not have problems, and I will show you a person who is six feet under. What matters is how we handle the problems. Lots of people simply throw in the towel and live the life of a hermit. Others just go through the motions daily and can't wait to get home to their little castle. Others commit suicide. Others withdraw and become mentally incompetent alcoholics or drug addicts.

My father never backed away from a challenge, and I never saw him afraid to take on anyone. He and I did not get along that well until later in my life, but he was an inspiration to me, in that he never showed fear and never gave up in spite of all odds. And he had great faith in his abilities.

I must tell you about an experience that to this day reminds me of the joy of being a respecter of persons who have complete faith in themselves. One of the other Platoon Sergeants in my company in basic training at Ft. Dix, New Jersey, was a short stocky Asian by the name of Sergeant Rae. For some reason you never crossed his path and he seemed to mechanically have a way to make his recruits obey his orders. He was a mystery to me, because he was short and soft-spoken, but when he gave an order you automatically obeyed. As a matter of fact, the other sergeants seemed to have deep respect for him. He walked with great confidence, yet humility and you felt confident he could lead you out of any dangerous situation. It was obvious he had a great self-image and faith.

Many years after I left the Army, I happened to read about a top Sergeant by the name of Sergeant Rae, who was discharged with high honors and the article gave his duty stations. It turned out that this was our Sergeant Rae. To my surprise and delight the article mentioned that he was a sixth degree Black Belt in Karate. By that time, I had my Black Belt, and can remember saying to myself, "No wonder he seemed to command such respect." The impressive thing about it is that he never told us to obey or else, because he was a Black Belt. For some reason you knew you should obey him, even though we did not know he possessed the Black Belt. After reading that article I gained a greater respect for great leaders, like Sgt. Rae, and Generals Patton, MacArthur and Colin Powell. All had/have great faith, were/are Positive Thinkers and they knew/know the **three-word motto**.

A great verse from the bible is: Mark11: 24, "I give you my word, if you are ready to believe that you will receive what you ask for in prayer it will be given you." Matthew 21:22 "You will receive all that you pray for provided you have faith." Finally, in Luke 18:27, it states, "The things that are impossible with man are possible with God." In other-words, it is a matter of faith, believing, trusting, praying, and possibilities. This is necessary even for the non-religious person if he is to achieve his or her goals. The non-religious person prays in another fashion. The Positive Thinker has a card with his or her goal written on it and reads that card three times daily. He or she believes that goal is going to be accomplished and so he or she has complete faith that it will happen and that the impossible will be turned into the possible. That is what makes life so interesting; the millions of stories telling of people overcoming impossible odds. But I am convinced after years of research that goals don't work most of the time without knowledge of the **three-word motto**.

One aspiring writer, who was orphaned, was turned down from job interview after interview. Finally this young man got a job pasting labels on bottles in a rat-infested warehouse; and he slept at night in a dismal attic room with two other "gutter snipes" from the slums. This aspiring writer had faith in himself, and sneaked out at night to mail his first manuscript so nobody would laugh at him. He was repeatedly turned down after each mailing, but one day a manuscript was accepted, and you know the rest of the story about Charles Dickens.

When my son Andrew was six years old, we entered him in T-Ball baseball. He was the outstanding player on the team. I say this not just as a proud father, but he was a natural. His second year of playing I coached the team, whereby the coach underhanded the ball to the batter, and Andrew was a terror at bat and in the field.

I mentioned in an earlier chapter that you would read the following story. One of the players was a below average player who would rarely get his bat on the ball. During our last game we were behind the other team in our final at bat with two men on base, when this little guy came up to bat. All the other players groaned, because they felt there was no way we could win with him at bat. I walked up to this player and calmly asked him what he thought he could do. He replied that he wasn't sure, whereby I said that I knew exactly what he could do. He looked at me as I knelt in front of him to get to his eye level, and I said that he was going to hit the ball and win the game. He said, "Oh no not me." I told him to close his eyes and focus on a picture of him hitting the ball and running around the bases. He closed his eyes and I would not let him open his eyes until he actually visualized the scene. When he finally opened his eyes he smiled and said that he did see it. He got faith. "Now go up there and hit the ball, because you now believe in yourself," I told him. I don't remember how many pitches or the strike count on him, but to this day many years later I can still see him running around the bases with the whole team screaming and a huge smile on his face. His father came up to me after the game and shook my hand until it almost fell off, and told me that his son was going to be a positive thinker from then on. This was a valuable lesson to me, because it confirmed all the positive thinking books I had read and my own philosophy. This was a valuable lesson for Andrew too, because he worked even harder to improve his game.

One of my favorite positive thinking stories revolves around baseball and was told by Dr. Norman Vincent Peale. Josh O'Reilly was the manager of the San Antonio Club of the Texas league and his roster was filled with great players. Seven of these players carried a batting average of over 300, and everybody was convinced this team would have an easy time winning the championship. However the team went into a slump and lost seventeen of the first twenty games. As the season progressed, the players started fighting with each other and accusing each other of being a "jinx" to the team. O'Reilly realized his players were thinking wrong. They didn't expect to get a hit, nor did they expect to win. They simply had no faith in themselves, or each other.

There was a popular preacher named, Schlater, in the neighborhood at the time, who claimed to be a faith healer and seemed to be getting results. O'Reilly asked each player to lend him his two best bats, and told them to stay in the clubhouse until he returned. O'Reilly placed the bats in a wheelbarrow and left. After an hour he returned jubilantly and informed his players that Schlater had blessed the bats and that these bats contained a power that could not be overcome. Naturally, the players were overjoyed and excited.

As it turned out, the very next day the team proceeded to wallop Dallas, getting 37 hits, leading to 20 runs. They then went on to buzz saw their way to the championship, and for years in the southwest players would pay large amounts of money for a "Schlater bat." I know, I know, you are saying, "Come on Ken, nobody falls for that stuff anymore." Oh, yes they do! Professional athletes are well known for their good luck charms and superstitions.

Andrew was now ready for little league baseball and we signed him up for the local league. The problem was there was no coach for his team. He asked me to be the coach but I was reluctant, because I had heard so much about how parents can try to run the team and be upset if their children did not play enough in Little League. I have always refused to get involved in politics and was not interested in putting up with over-aggressive parents, but Andrew talked me into it.

Because the team was put together at the last minute we only had one practice and we lost our first game twenty-one to three. I then had four practices the next week, worked on the basics, and filled this rag tag team with positive thinking. My son and two other boys were the only boys who had ever played organized baseball before, so my work was cut out for me. But we worked hard on the basics. I instilled faith in each of them and won the next game. The team that beat us twenty-one to three played us next and they laughed as we walked on to the field.

I looked at my players and said, "Men, they are in for a big surprise." We went on to win that game twenty-four to nothing. In our first game against them we had committed fifteen errors, but only one this game.

We played in the championship game and lost, but by positive thinking and executing the basics, a group of boys believed in themselves enough to play well above their normal level, because they got faith. "THE POSITIVE

THINKER SEES THE INVISIBLE, FEELS THE INTANGIBLE, AND ACHIEVES THE IMPOSSIBLE."

Edward Bok, the 1921 Pulitzer Prize winning author, said, "It is the young man of little faith that says, "I am nothing." "The first and finest lesson that parents can teach their children is faith and courage."—Smiley Blanton, M.D.

Doubt whom you will, but don't ever dare to doubt yourself.

MAIN THOUGHTS AND CHALLENGES

1. Go back to the beginning of this chapter and review the highlighted sentences.

2. Place the highlighted page numbers on this page.

3. Write down the most important highlight and why it is so important to you.

4. Write down who you know that has tremendous faith in his or her abilities.

5. Would you like to have more faith in your abilities? Yes or no.

6. What will you do to achieve more faith in your abilities?

Chapter 11

WHO IS THE BEST?

"You can be an ordinary athlete by getting away with less than your best. But if you want to be great, you have to give it all you've got—your everything."

—Duke K. Kahanamoku

Because I was so involved in athletics, this chapter is very close to my heart, and as a holder of the Black Belt in Karate I feel I can talk with authority. There is a best in everything. If you do not believe that, then why is there Consumers Reports magazine? Why is there a Nobel Prize? Why is there a Guinness Worlds Record Book? Why are there motion picture Academy awards? Why is there a World Series, or a Super Bowl, a NBA Championship, or a Stanley Cup or the Tour de France? We also have the Kentucky Derby, the Preakness and the Belmont. The PGA has its prestigious tournaments along with the LPGA and College sports. I could go on and on into the Olympics and other sports like tennis or business awards. We could talk about citizen awards, and the war medals. There is also the award for the best motor vehicle produced each year, and in the April 2002, issue of Readers Digest the front cover used the headline, "The Best Used Cars Ever." Whenever Evel Knievel was introduced, the announcer would shout, "The greatest daredevil in the world."

"Wish not to be seen, but to be, the best."
— Aeschylus

Who is the best entertainer in the world? I am not an expert in that arena, but many entertainers have been considered for that honor. I personally think that is up to the fans and the receipts. And each school, be it high school or college has its array of prestigious awards.

Here is the bottom line: people work hard at winning these awards. Why do they? It is simple: people want to be the best. It gives them a great feeling of accomplishment and they revel in the accolades, however humble, or otherwise they might react to the award. The two quotes that come to mind repeatedly in this book are, "The deepest urge in human nature is the desire to be important." -Dr. John Dewy- "The deepest principle in human nature is the craving to be appreciated." —Professor William James

Have you ever been the best in anything? If not, I suggest you ask someone who has been the best, to find out their feelings and why they sought that title.

In Junior High School I was voted the best athlete, along with two others, and I can tell you unequivocally the great feeling of euphoria I felt as I was presented the award. I couldn't stop smiling for at least six weeks. My cheeks developed a permanent wrinkle. That day and the next day were filled with phone calls and slaps on the back. I was on cloud nine for weeks. To this day I will never forget walking up to the stage to accept my award. It was a simple certificate that I have since misplaced, but back then I would not let it out of my sight.

One of my best friends is an artist, and one-year she won best of show for one of her paintings. She was not at the show to accept the award, because she was working, but her best friend stopped by to tell her she had won. Her first reaction was, well she actually screamed so loud she is convinced the scream could be heard for two blocks. She jumped up and down and ran around the room yelling, "You're not lying to me are you? Tell me you are not lying to me," all the time laughing. She remembers that day too. She had worked eight years to win that prestigious award, and she knew she had a "killer" painting. She had worked hard on that painting, and every year when she entered other paintings she failed. But this time she put "me" (herself) in that painting. Her attitude was, "this will either make or break me." That is a key. You have to put yourself into it. You have to bury yourself in the task at hand. You have to be able to risk it all if you want to be the best, as I wrote in a previous chapter.

Sometimes judges make the decision as to who is the best in the Olympic figure skating, or gymnastics, and many other sports. In boxing if there is not a knockout, or if either of the fighters does not give up, the judges make the decision. Sometimes judges or referees, or umpires make bad calls, and we have to live with those calls. That is life, and the real winner does not quit because of a bad call, or like my artist friend does not give up painting. You ignore the decision and just work harder for the next time. "Whoever undertakes to set himself up as a judge of truth and knowledge is shipwrecked by the laughter of the gods." —Albert Einstein

Many of you reading this book have won awards, and you too had that euphoric feeling, however brief it might have been. You have set records. You have proven you are the best or one of the best. You have practiced or studied for hours and hours. You have sweat tears and have perspired. You have stayed up late and risen early to spend hours to study and practice. You have sacrificed going out on a date or watching a movie. You have dieted or gained weight to meet your weight division. You have overcome pain and fatigue. Remember the statement the great coach of the world champion green Bay Packers, Vince Lombardi, wrote on the locker room wall to his players on their way to another Super Bowl, "Fatigue makes cowards of us all."

Have you ever wondered what the definition of a winner is? Doctor Denis Waitley, a national authority on high-performance motivation, who has counseled top sales and management executives and leaders in every field – from Super Bowl and Olympic athletes to Apollo Moon Program astronauts, stated, "Winners in my opinion, are those individuals who in a very natural, free-flowing way seem to consistently get what they want from life by providing valuable services to others. They set and achieve goals that benefit others as well as themselves. You don't have to be lucky to win at life, nor do you have to knock other people down or gain at the expense of others. Happiness is the natural experience of winning your own self-respect, as well as the respect of others. Winning is taking the talent or potential you were born with, and have since developed, and using it fully toward a purpose that makes you feel worthwhile according to your own internal standards."

The great, Vince Lombardi, made a profound statement years ago that the skeptics and social engineers now take offense to. Vince said, "Winning isn't everything, it is the only thing." The social engineers today have programmed our schools to accept a D- as an acceptable grade in school. At one time a C- was acceptable but it was considered below average at best. I can remember students being embarrassed getting a C-. But today some educators claim that we can't be too hard on our children. After all, life is stressful enough, they say. "We have to be sensitive to the obstacles they face and their environment, such as atrocity of homelessness and Aids." American students are losing their drive, because competing is a no-no. "No one should win, to play is good enough," the social engineers say. Really? Tell that to the Lance Armstrongs of the world! Tell that to the rest of the nations who are trying to overtake the United States in military, technological and financial might. Tell that to the other nations of the world whom have banks in terms of assets listed in the top ten, with only one American bank listed now. At one time all top ten were American banks. In this writer's opinion, and I am convinced the opinion of all real winners, that, "no one should win", is the philosophy of losers. Try telling "no one should win" to Jaime Escalante, the mathematics teacher who taught advanced calculus to underprivileged Hispanic children in California. The negative thinkers said that it was too much of a burden; too hard for the poor unfortunate Hispanic children and that it was impossible, (there is that word again) for them to learn. The social engineers said that we were expecting too much from the children. But Jaime proved the negative thinkers wrong. Jamie proved that no matter what race or creed you are, you can succeed. Jaime knows the **three-word motto**.

In another case, a mother from Ohio called the principal of her child's school and wanted to know why the standards were being lowered in the school. The principal explained that kids are taught there are no right or wrong answers-even in subjects like math. Would you want your child to learn that two plus two equals whatever he thinks it can be? "Only the supremely wise and abysmally ignorant do not change." Confusius

Lombardi went on to explain that: "This great country was built on a competitive spirit." That is why the word competitor is such a valued word. Our competitors make us strive for higher goals, thus bringing about better products and services.

As I wrote earlier, there was a time not too long ago in the history of this great country where our leaders said that America had come to a point where it had reached its greatness. They said we had to be satisfied now with the "status-quo." There was nothing left for us to do and we were no longer up to the task, they claimed. (That attitude is reminiscent of Charles Duell, the director of the US patent office in 1898, when he said, "Everything that can be invented has been invented.)" Then came along Ronald Reagan and the country turned around its attitude and began striving for greatness again. Why did that happen? Simply because President Reagan had faith in Americans and in their ability to achieve even greater accomplishments. And so we did, because many winners like Tom Hopkins, of Tom Hopkins/ Champions Unlimited, took over from the losers. Tom is one of the greatest salespeople to wear shoe leather and started his own successful training company. Tom is a winner and a member of the World Positive Thinkers Club. He gives the following philosophy: "I am not judged by the number of times I fail, but by the number of times I succeed, and the number of times I succeed is in direct proportion to the number of times I can fail and keep on trying." Tom's five attitudes toward rejection and failure are:

1. "I never see failure as failure, but only as a learning experience."
2. "I never see failure as failure, but as the negative feedback I need to change course in my direction."
3. "I never see failure as failure, but as the opportunity to develop my sense of humor."
4. "I never see failure as failure, but only as an opportunity to practice my techniques and perfect my performance."
5. "I never see failure as failure, but only as the game I must play to win."

If you think about it, only a few shots on the professional golf tour separate the top money winners from the rest of the tour, and there have been many sudden death playoffs. The baseball-batting champions only get on base 20 or 30 times more than the players who do not make the top ten. In track and field, in the 100 meter dash, for example, the winner is only two-tenths of a second faster than the fourth place finisher. So the best is only a few strokes, a couple of swings, or a few tenths of a second better. In the business field the winners are more persistent, more effective, or have a better positive awareness. The best salesmen make more calls; they close more often; they study and know their product better. The best is not because he or she is more talented, or more educated. Talent is cheap; you can buy it and recruit it, and it abounds. The world has many talented alcoholics, and many educated derelicts that can't relate to others. The best comes in attitudes. And guess what? You can pay for talent and degrees, but you do not have to be concerned about paying for attitude. It is free.

Now for a little controversy! Who was the greatest? Was Mohammed Ali the greatest? Some say Joe Louis was, and still others say Rocky Marciano. There was a computer-generated fight between Rocky Marciano and Mohammed Ali, and Rocky won. Yet some of the experts still think Ali was the best. And one of Ali's greatest attributes was that many times he called the round correctly in which he would win. Some boxing fans will argue vehemently that John L. Sullivan, the bare-knuckled champion, was the best. Others will proclaim Jack Dempsey the greatest. But was Sugar Ray Leonard, one of only two boxers to hold the world championships in five weight divisions the best? The argument will go on for years.

I wrote about Babe Zaharis in Chapter 12, and Grantland Rice, the top writer of his day, wrote that Mildred "Babe" Didrikson Zaharis was the greatest athlete, man or woman. Grantland wrote, "She is the most flawless section of muscle harmony the world of sport has ever known." The Associated Press named Babe the greatest woman athlete of the first half of the Twentieth Century. In 1932 in the Olympics she tossed the javelin 143'4". No one else came close. She won the 80-meter hurdles, setting a world record, and in the high jump tied for the gold. In a jump off she won, but was disqualified for jumping headfirst. She also won the 100-meter dash. After the Olympics she became a baseball player, playing 200 games a year, as well as being a star basketball player. Babe once threw a baseball 296 feet in 1931. Most major league outfield fences are 320 to home plate, and I have never seen a major league player throw home without a bounce from 296 feet. Babe then took up golf and became the greatest woman golfer of her day, winning 12 major tournaments, including three U.S. Opens. She might have won many more tournaments, but unfortunately she died of cancer at the age of 45. She was also an actress, swimmer, diver, marksman, cyclist, skater and an accomplished harmonica player.

There is a town in Pennsylvania named after the man who was named the greatest football player and greatest male athlete of the first half of the Twentieth Century, by the Associated Press. Many others say this Sac and Fox

Indian from Oklahoma was the best athlete of the first half of the twentieth century. Yet, many insist he was the greatest athlete ever, regardless of the time in history. He won the decathlon and pentathlon in the 1912 Olympics in Stockholm, Sweden. That was never accomplished before him and has not been accomplished since. He played in the professional baseball World Series in 1913, and a stirring movie was made about his life staring Burt Lancaster.

Jim Thorp was an American Indian from a poor family, and attended Carlisle College in Pennsylvania, where he set records and helped Pop Warner, one of the greatest coaches ever forge Carlisle into a college powerhouse. It was written of Jim that he was without equal on a playing field. He also played professional football, gaining entry to the Professional Football Hall of Fame. He did everything on the football gridiron. Jim punted, passed, ran, blocked, placed kicked, tackled and drop kicked better than any other player. This poor American Indian was also inducted into the College Football Hall of Fame and the College Track and Field Hall of Fame. Was he the best athlete or was Babe Zaharis? People of that era could argue for days on who was the best, and people today could argue on which athlete in today's era of specialization is the best.

Bob Matthias is only one of two athletes who have won the Gold Medal in the Olympic Decathlon twice. Is he the greatest athlete? You might have your own choice. Perhaps it is Babe Ruth or Hank Aaron or Mark McGwire. Hank Aaron has hit the most home runs totally (742) and Barry Bonds hit the most home runs (73) in a season. Now they are saying no one will pass those marks. But the experts said no one would pass Babe Ruth with his 60 homers in 1927, then Roger Maris, with his 61 in 1961, and then Mark McGwire with 70 in 1998. Now Barry Bonds has clubbed 73 home runs. Bonds did club 755 home runs, but now that mark is tainted with accusations of steroid use. Was the best baseball player ever Ty Cobb, Babe Ruth, Honus Wagner, Hank Aaron, Willie Mays, Mickey Mantle, Ted Williams or Joe Dimaggio, with his 56 straight games with a hit? Could the best athlete possibly be Tom Brady, Mary Lou Retton, Steffi Graff or another great female athlete?

Cy Young has won the most games as a pitcher, winning 511 games, but some experts will argue that others were better pitchers. Some say it was the great Bob Gibson, who pitched for the St. Louis Cardinals. Others say it was Sandy Koufax, whose career was cut short by injury. Still others say Warren Spahn. Was it Nolan Ryan with the record 5,714 strikeouts or the great Walter Johnson who won 417 games with 110 shutouts? Perhaps it was a pitcher not many have heard of named Ed Walsh, with a 1.82 ERA, or maybe even the great Satchel Paige of the old Negro League. Some experts think it was the great Bob Feller, with his fastball clocked at 98.6 mph. (Although many considered his the fastest, it turns out that Mark Koenig, second baseman for the New York Yankees was clocked at 127 mph pitching from the pitchers mound). Ten years from now other athletes will go down as the best. Some say the 1927 Yankees were the best team ever in baseball and yet some argue it was Connie Mack's Philadelphia Athletics in 1929. Perhaps it was Joe Torres' Yankees of 1998, 1999, and 2000, winning the World Series those three straight years.

Was the greatest racehorse Man O' War, the great "Big Red," winning 20 of his 21 starts from 1919 to 1920, setting five American records and running away from the field by 100 lengths once? Man O' War lost his only race in the Sanford Memorial in 1920 due to a poor start and was upset by a horse running in that race with 100-1 odds against him, ironically with the name 'Upset'. Was the greatest Secretariat, also known as "Big Red," winning the Triple Crown in 1973, setting records in the Kentucky Derby and the Belmont Stakes, and also winning that race by an incredible 31 lengths?

Who is considered the best female tennis player? Is it Chris Everett (who was voted the Women's Sports Foundation's greatest athlete of the past 25 years in 1985), or Martina Navriltalova, or Billy Jean King or Margaret Court. Both Martina and Billy Jean won a record 20 Wimbledon titles, and by the way, Martina did it by the age of forty-six and a half in 2003. While we are on tennis: the youngest person to ever enter the prestigious Wimbledon tennis championship was 13-year old Mita Klima of Austria in 1907.

Rodney George "Rod" Laver is a former tennis player from Australia who arguably was the World No. 1 player for seven consecutive years. He is the only tennis player to have twice won all four of tennis' Grand Slam singles titles in the same year — first as an amateur in 1962 and second as a professional in 1969. He is the only male player during the open era to have won a calendar year Grand Slam.

Laver has been rated as the greatest male player of all time by several experts and polls. He was "technically faultless, from his richly varied serve to his feather-light touch on drop volleys plus a backhand drive carrying destructive topspin when needed or controlling slice when the situation demanded it." His left-handed serve was well disguised and wide swinging. His wrist ground strokes on both flanks were hit with topspin, an innovation in the 1960s, as was the attacking topspin lob, which Laver developed into a weapon.

Who do the experts call the best female ice-skater who ever tied on ice skates? Is it Katarina Witt, Peggy Fleming, Michelle Kwan, Tara Lipinski, Kristy Yamaguchi or Sonja Henie. Sonja won gold medals in three different Olympics; was the World Figure Skating Champion 10 straight times, and became a movie star.

Was Annie Oakley the best trick shot artist? Facts speak for themselves sometimes, and all Annie did was shoot 100 percent in trap shooting for thirty-five years. At thirty paces she could split a playing card end on, hit a dime in mid-air or shoot a cigarette from her husbands (Frank Butler) lips.

Who was the best woman track star? Opinion will differ for centuries, but Chi Cheng of China was the first woman to run 100 yards in ten seconds. She also won all 63 races she entered and set five world records.

Could the best athlete now be Lance Armstrong, after winning his seventh straight Tour de France?

Was Picasso the best artist? After all, all he did was sell over 298 paintings worth over $1million each, or was Michelangelo the greatest artist?

One of my favorite sports to watch is golf, and I have watched the greats play what is considered the hardest sport to play. Jack Nicholas came along and won more major matches than anyone else, and I watched him make what were considered impossible putts. Then along came a charismatic man named of all things, "Tiger."

Once while playing with an eight handicap I holed a 30 foot putt, and I consider that luck. Just this year in 2008 I watched Tiger make an impossible sixty foot putt. Tiger Woods at his best would've beaten Jack Nicklaus at his best, and I no longer believe Tiger needs to break Jack's record of 18 major championships to prove the point.

If the 32-year-old Woods stays healthy, he's a lock to get to 19 and beyond, with the smart money on beyond. Tiger posted Jack's records on his childhood walls for a reason. He's planning to do to Nicklaus' No. 18 what Sammy Sosa and Mark McGwire did to Roger Maris' 61 home runs.

Nicklaus never won more in a single season than the seven events he took in 1972 and '73. Woods won nine times in 2000, eight in 2006 and 1999, and seven in 2007.

Entering the season following his 32nd birthday, Nicklaus had claimed nine Grand Slam events, or four fewer than Woods. Entering the season following his 32nd birthday, Nicklaus had won 38 tour events or 23 fewer than Woods.

With his Tiger Slam, Woods held all four Grand Slam trophies at once. Nicklaus never held more than three at the same time — he won the '71 PGA Championship (staged in February that year), the '72 Masters, and the '72 U.S. Open, but was beaten at the '72 British when a dejected Lee Trevino got lucky and holed out what Nicklaus called "a give-up shot.," and Tiger just won the 2008 U.S. Open championship on a bum knee.

So the controversy goes on and on. The point is in my opinion, and many others is it does not matter. They were the best at that time. That is what really matters as to "who was the best." There will be disagreement forever for one simple reason. If we all thought alike there would be many unnecessary people.

Here is another important point. The winners make it happen, losers allow it to happen, and when the final lap is run we are the only real judges in the World Series of our own life, so we should not take seriously what the cynics think. Just know that the winners know the **three-word motto**, and that once you commit it to memory and embed it in your soul you will win your own Super Bowls daily. "Wish not to be seen, but to be, the best." —Aeschylus

The winners always find a way to win-to be the best. For example: let's get off the playing field for a while and talk about energy. Every time there is an energy crisis, the 'best' engineers tackle the problem, and presto; a solution is created. For example using the technology of fusion and water, one sixteenth of an inch of San Francisco Bay powers the Western United States. Liquid hydrogen is now the possible fuel of the future to power our transportation vehicles, besides being the fuel that propelled our spacecraft to the moon. We now take energy from deep thermal rocks near the center of the earth, and the sun as well as the garbage we throw out. On a daily basis, scientists are constantly churning out new ways to make life more convenient and comfortable for the world. If only Charles Duell, the director of the U.S Patent office in 1898 were alive now to see the great inventions and advances dreamed of and created by people with vision. Remember that he said, "Everything that can be invented has been invented."

Earl Nightengale, the great salesman and motivator told about a time when he visited the Great Barrier Reef, which covers 1800 miles from Australia to New Guinea. The coral polyps on the inside of the reef seem lifeless and colorless, but the coral on the outside of the reef, where the tide and waves move constantly, are bright and beautiful colors abound. There is a reason for the difference. The coral on the inside face no challenge for growth and survival, while the coral on the outside face the power of the waves, thereby growing.

By the way, Australia has 16000 miles of coastline and 11,000 beaches-the most in the world.

Marcus Seneca stated it so succinctly when he said, "Gold is tried by fire, brave men by adversity." So there you have it. We grow and blossom with adversity and obstacles, just like the coral reef. If you are a watcher and not a doer you eventually wither. If you look at adversity as a natural growing process, then it is properly used to develop immunity against depression and anxiety, and the results of stress.

The Positive Thinkers never let adversity overcome them. They continue to face adversity and obstacles with their chins up and their backs straight and they never run from a challenge or an obstacle. Sometimes they appear cocky to the cynic, but that is really self-confidence, and they all know the **three-word motto**. The true winners never get caught up in their own self-importance, like the man who was fired by his father-in-law. The son-in-law said, "Who are you going to find to fill the vacancy?" The father-in-law shot back, "Don't flatter yourself. You aren't leaving a vacancy."

If you can't be a pine on the top of the hill, be a scrub in the valley-but be
The best little scrub on the side of the hill; be a bush if you can't be a tree.
If you can't be a bush, be a bit of the grass, and some highway happier make.
If you can't be a muskie, then just be a bass-but the liveliest bass in the lake!
We all can't be captains; we've got to be crew. There's something for all of us here.
There's big work to do and there's lesser to do, and the task we must do is the near.
If you can't be a highway, then just be a trail, if you can't be the sun, be a star;
It isn't by size that you win or you fail-Be the best of what ever you are!

"It's a funny thing about life; if you refuse to accept anything but the best, you very often get it."
— W. Somerset Maugham

MAIN THOUGHTS AND CHALLENGES

1. Again, go back to the beginning of this chapter and review your highlighted sentences.

2. Write the highlighted page numbers on this page.

3. Put down the most important highlight and why it is so important to you.

4. Write down who you think is the best in a particular field of endeavor.

A. Sports B. Business C. Government D. Religion E. Any other field of endeavor you are interested in.

5. Write you opinion as to why that particular person is the best.

6. Do you want to be the best or one of the best in your field? Yes or no, and why.

Chapter 12

ARE WOMEN BETTER POSITIVE THINKERS THAN MEN?

*"The world and all things in it are valuable;
but the most valuable of all is a virtuous woman."*
—Mohammed

During my research for this book I discovered many interesting facts that surprised and delighted me. At first I had a hard time believing these definitive pieces of information, but as I continued to research, and look back on personal experiences it started to make sense. Of course when I was much younger it would not have made sense, but my research has been as a more mature and more pragmatic person.

I was raised in an era where the women stayed home and took care of the home and family. My grandmother always stayed home, as most women did. She would be up early to make breakfast for the men in her family and then after they went off to work, she did the housework. She then prepared supper, as almost everything in that day and age was homemade and therefore took a while to prepare and cook. To this day I can visualize her slaving over a hot stove in the summertime, with beads of perspiration pouring down her lovely face. During a brief recess, she would sit and crochet beautiful chair arm guards or a tablecloth. She was so methodical and skillful, and as I think of her now, she was mostly stoic. She always had supper ready for the family on time and she and only she would clean up, unless my Uncle Frank was there to help. How insignificant I used to think her chores were. But now as I think about it, my grandmother and all women were and are the glue that keeps the family strong and bonded.

Women, as sensible men have happily discovered, are and have always been more than housekeepers and cooks. They are and have always been the shining lamp that brightens a home or place of business. Women are the oil that keeps the machinery running. And in a majority of cases these beautiful Positive Thinkers are the machinery itself. They have been taken advantage of, and thank God they now have a bigger say pertaining to policies in not only business, but government as well. Women have come a long way in this country since President Grover Cleveland in 1905 emphatically stated, "Sensible and intelligent women do not want to vote."

I do not want to expound on the inequities women have faced throughout history, because for the most part they have more than made up for them. There are still cases, however, like the taliban, (cap purposely left out), in Afghanistan, where women were and are still treated as lower class citizens. We could do several chapters on that subject, but this chapter is to expound on the successes and the way women have made a difference and helped shape history. More than anything, I prefer to stay focused on the positive, because that is what this book is supposed to be about.

I personally, in my years of researching for this book, have come to the conclusion that women are Gods beautiful gift to men, and we should do all we can to appreciate that gift. Now that statement might ruffle a few feathers on both sides, but I am entitled to my opinion too. My plan here is not to keep the fires of controversy burning, but rather report the facts as I happily discovered them. I have formed my personal opinion as to who is the better Positive Thinker, but I will let you figure that out. Let me add though, that in my opinion after all my research, women have overcome more barriers than men ever dreamed of facing.

I personally love to pamper my lady and treat her as a Princess on occasion, and I have been known to bring my lady breakfast in bed and treat her to half hour-long back and foot rubs. For me, she is a beautiful creature to behold and I love to tease women and kid with them. After all, I am a Libra!

While my wife and I were not destined to stay together, I feel that she is a very competent lady. We did not get along very well, because unfortunately our opinions and personalities clashed, and she thought pampering was silly, but to this day I will defend the fact that she is, in my opinion, the best nurse ever born. She is the most devoted person to a profession I have ever met. I say that even though I have not seen her for over seven years. But,

I know she would not change. She is a gracious hostess as well and always believed her children deserved the best. She is a perfectionist, and in her profession that is extremely important, because she works in life and death situations. One little mistake can cost a life. She is typical of women Positive Thinkers. They know what they want and believe in themselves.

Women played a very important part in the Civil war, not as combatants, but as spies and nurses. Let me go one step further. During the American Civil War, the Surgeon General of the Union Army was a very talented, resourceful, well-respected doctor. It was discovered to the absolute amazement of everybody concerned that the Surgeon General turned out to be a woman, during "his" autopsy.

The following was stated about the following pertaining to the civil war: "In some of the more recent studies of the subject it has been strongly suggested that the prime reason for the defeat of the Confederacy was a decline in, or loss of, the will to fight. There is certain merit in the point, though the more remarkable fact, considering the course of the conflict, is that the will to fight remained so strong so long."

"For that, the women of the confederacy were in large measure responsible. Not every woman could be classed as a "heroine of Dixie," but it was commonly observed at the time by friend and foe alike, and has repeatedly noted since, that among the women of the South that the spirit of resistance flamed highest. The harder part of war is the woman's part."

"Though their Southern patriotism was intense, for the women devotion to the family came first-always—and none of them would knowingly and willingly have chosen a course of war that reversed this order of devotion. At the very start-just after the Act of Secession was passed-a woman of South Carolina stated, "What do I care for patriotism? My husband is my country. What is my country to me if he be killed?" "As they faced the grim reality of a long and bitter struggle, this came more and more the secret or avowed question of their deeply troubled hearts."

During the Civil War, Southern and Northern women acted as very competent spies. Many put their lives on the line and some were captured. Several of these brave women on the side of the Confederates were the charming Belle Boyd, and the dangerous, Rose O'Neal Greenhow. For the Union, there was the brilliant Emma E. Edmonds, who successfully passed herself off as a black man. The course of the war was changed many times due to the bravery of these intrepid women, and they knew the **three-word motto**.

Every war has its share of women heroes. We can talk about Joan of Arc, and Florence Nightengale. The list goes on and on. Throughout history there have been many other women besides those during our Civil War, who have saved their nation from disaster or being annihilated. One of these women saved her nation during the time of Xerxes, who ruled from 486-465 B.C over 127 provinces, stretching from India to Cush. This is a thrilling story of how Esther saved the Jewish nation when she put her life on the line and ignored the royal decree. Even though she was Queen, she could not appear in the presence of the King without his invitation, yet in order to save her people she appeared before the King and said, "If my life be taken so be it." The King was stunned by her daring and agreed to listen to her plea. Esther was intelligent enough not to blurt out what the problem was, but rather invited the King, and Haman, the possible future destroyer of her race, to a banquet the next night. She knew she needed to relax the King and the evil Haman first. The next day the King and Haman went to dine with Esther, and the King told Esther that he would grant her request even if it meant giving her half the kingdom. Even though Esther now "had" Haman, she still acted with cunning and diplomacy. As a Positive Thinker, Esther knew she still had to keep herself and the King relaxed before she told him of the plot to kill her and her people. She also knew she had to heighten the drama by not telling the King on his first visit, so she begged him to come with Haman a second time and she would then make her plea. This naturally aroused the Kings' curiosity to greater heights and put Haman completely off guard. [I hope I never tangle with an Esther]. The next night the King and Haman arrived to a sumptuous feast and after small talk, Esther then told the King of Hamans plot. The Jewish nation was saved and the villain Haman went to the gallows, which ironically was erected by Haman for Esther's Uncle Mordecai.

I make no apologies for bringing the Bible into this book. There are millions of Bible believers in this wonderful world, who can, through historical and scientific evidence, prove the validity of these stories. There are other great stories about Biblical women who saved their nations or performed other heroic or unselfish acts, like the widow, Ruth, who refused to let her elderly mother-in-law, Naomi, fend for herself. Her mother-in-law begged Ruth and Orpah not to go with her to her hometown to support her, but to take care of themselves. Ruth refused to allow her mother-in-law to fend for herself, and because of that unselfish act she later became the wife of Boaz, a wealthy and honorable man.

Ruth was indicative of devotion to another person, and there are many more stories showing devotion to a cause or a friend or relative. One in particular is a wife's devotion to her husband's memory. For 57 years Elizabeth worked tirelessly to clear her husband's reputation after he lost his life in a decisive battle.

After he died he left her in debt to the tune of $13,000, because of his poor decisions in the stock market. Elizabeth was left with several hundred dollars after the smoke cleared, and she was forced to move to New York to take a job as a secretary. During her life with her husband she was the driving force during his sterling career, and while he wanted to quit the Army and become a businessman, she kept him on course. Even though she faced hardships (that none of us can even imagine) while living as an Army wife, she stayed with him and never complained.

After the fiasco on those rolling hills someone had to be the scapegoat and along with the top Army brass even President Grant accused her husband of causing the slaughter. But Elizabeth became a writer and tirelessly worked to clear her husband's reputation, until finally after dozens of years President Taft and she unveiled a statue of her husband sitting on a horse, which stands to this day in Monroe, Michigan. This wonderful lady died a few days before her ninety-first birthday, and even in death she proved her devotion. On her gravestone it is written, "Wife of George Armstrong Custer." You can bet the mortgage that Elizabeth Custer knew the **three-word motto**.

Who was the first real woman hero of the Twentieth Century? There are many diverse opinions. Amelia Earhart was born on July 24, 1897, in Atchison, Kansas, and during the Great War, she worked unselfishly as a nurse in Canada and then as a social worker in Boston. In 1928 she became the first woman to fly across the Atlantic as a passenger. Amelia opened the door for women by flying solo across the Atlantic in May of 1932, and in 1935 she completed a solo flight from Hawaii to California. She was in the forefront of opening commercial aviation for women. Because of her efforts, airplane passenger companies hired women as stewardesses to show men how safe it was to fly. After all, if a woman was not afraid to fly, why should a man be afraid?

One of the great mysteries of the 1900's is: what ever became of Amelia? In 1937, Amelia and her copilot,. Commander Fred J. Noonan, took off from Miami for a flight around the world in a twin-engine Lockheed. Search teams from the U.S Navy and Army searched in vain for her missing plane, which disappeared in the South Pacific. Was she really a spy for the U.S government, hired to spy on the Japanese war preparations? Was she shot down and killed by the Japanese? Perhaps we will never know what happened to this brave trailblazer, who knew the **three-word motto**. You might be interested in reading her husband's biography of her titled, Soaring Wings, published in 1939.

Throughout this book you have read about the great Babe Ruth, and I decided this chapter was a good place to write about his seventeen-year-old, one hundred thirty-pound nemesis, named Mitchell. One of the greatest promoters in baseball, Joe Engel, was the president of the Chattanooga Lookouts, and he decided in 1931, that it was time for Mitchell to help him pull off his greatest publicity stunt, by having Mitchell pitch in an exhibition game against the Powerful New York Yankees. The game took place on April 2, 1931 and Clyde Barfoot started the game for the Lookouts. The first two batters got hits off him and the manager of the lookouts, Bert Niehoff, called time and brought Mitchell in to face the feared Babe Ruth. Babe tipped his hat to Mitchell and reminded Mitchell that there was a runner on first base. Babe swung at the first pitch with his usual enthusiasm and the ball landed in the catcher's glove. The next two pitches were balls and the next pitch sailed by Babe's swinging bat again. The umpire, Brick Owens, called strike three on the next pitch, and as the crowd roared Babe gave an angry look to Brick and sulked to the dugout after kicking the dirt and tossing his bat in anger. The next batter, "The Iron Horse," Lou Gehrig, stepped up to the plate and faced the same fate.

The Yankees went on to win the game 14-4, but the news from that day was historical as seventeen-year-old Mitchell was shown in movie houses all over the country striking out Ruth and Gehrig. Oh, one small detail I forgot to mention. Mitchell was none other than Jackie Mitchell, the first woman to sign a professional baseball contract, but unfortunately the commissioner of baseball, Judge Kenesaw Mountain Landis, voided her contract banning all women from competing in baseball.

Cosmonaut, Valentina V. Tereshkova, of the former Soviet Union was the first woman in space from June 16-19, 1963, and so another barrier was broken by women. When American, Sally Ride, at age 32 entered space in June 18-24, 1983, she made history by becoming America's first woman astronaut-repeating the feat in 1984.

Throughout history, whenever there was a war, the pictures we saw on the newspapers and magazines were the faces of men, like Roosevelt, Eisenhower, Patton, Truman, MacArthur, Omar Bradley, Marshall, Nimitz, Halsey, Churchill, Westmoreland, George Bush, George W. Bush, Schwartzcoff, Franks, and many other Generals and leaders. My personal feeling is that alongside those great men's pictures should be pictures of their wives, because behind every great man it has been proven time and time again stands a great woman.

In time of war there are never enough men to get the job done, and some of the jobs are better suited to women, who were simply better at the job in the first place. But women have always been held back in the Armed Forces, because the prevailing feeling in the services was women were only qualified to do certain jobs, and they did not deserve to be promoted too often. And so women were left out at time of promotion. Then two Positive Thinking dynamos, Mary Hallaren, and Jeanne Holm, came along. Mary was a junior high school teacher at the time of the Pearl Harbor attack. She had no doubt (after all her brothers had enlisted) that her duty was to her country too. This five foot tall dynamo was a hitchhiker, traveling through Canada, Mexico, Europe and China. Mary's confidence and determination was a major factor in her rapid rise through the ranks, until she was finally promoted to full Colonel, taking over the new branch, named appropriately, the Women's Army Corps (WAC's). Women struggled in a male dominated military force, and Mary was a promoter for women's rights for a bigger role in the military. Because of Mary's efforts, women were eventually integrated into all the branches of the Military. Right before her ninetieth birthday this trailblazing, positive thinker was inducted into the National Women's Hall of Fame.

Jeanne Holm was living in Oregon and working as a radio technician for the U.S. Forest Service. Jeanne also felt a need to help her country; started out as a truck driver in her WAC career, and eventually was promoted to Captain. She completed her tour of duty and attended college on the GI Bill, but still was not sure what her career should be. That all changed, as she received a letter from the Defense Department asking her if she would consider duty in the Women's Armed Services after the implementation of the integration act. There was no thinking it over for Jeanne, as she jumped in her car, without much money to her name. She slept in her car as she drove from one end of the country to the other. Jeanne was the first woman to attend the Air Force Command and Staff College. She was a crusader in the Air Force for women with children, who were forced to be discharged, and she convinced the powers to be that the Air force could not make a determination on a woman's ability to raise her children. In 1971, Jeanne was promoted to Brigadier General, and two years later received her second star. Even after retiring in 1975, Jeanne was asked by President Ford to instruct the Justice Department on issues that discriminated against women. And finally, Jeanne was instrumental in changing the attitudes and behaviors on sexual harassment. A former woman truck driver took on a man's world and came out a star with two additional stars on each shoulder.

During World War II, many women took over the jobs of the men in the factories that were drafted. According to records these women served with distinction as welders, pattern makers, riveters, and a myriad of other demanding jobs required to build the necessary weapons and vehicles for the armed services. My personal opinion is the quality of work went up a notch, because women are more detail oriented than men.

Very few people know this next fact, but Jacqueline Cochran, in WW II, formed the Woman's Air Force Service Pilots, U.S. Group. These daring ladies flew not in combat, but delivered much-needed aircraft to the front and were taking a chance of being shot down. Thirty-eight of these brave women died in the line of duty delivering the much-needed aircraft to the front lines.

And flying was not the only arena where women died during WWII, because women served in combat areas as nurses. These brave women wore combat fatigues and helmets, and slept in tents just like the men, and at Anzio, Italy, six nurses died from artillery shells. In a different combat arena in Europe, Mary Louise Roberts, Elaine Roe, and Virginia Rourke, received the Silver Star, the second highest award in wartime for heroism in that theater. You might consider reading the moving book, We Band of Angels, by Elizabeth M. Norman, which tells of the unbelievable suffering nurses faced in World War II after their capture by the Japanese in the Philippines. These brave nurses faced starvation, malnutrition, malaria, and crippling diseases, yet they held their heads high and performed their duty to take care of the sick and injured American soldiers and civilians of different nationalities.

If you can imagine the discrimination white women faced in the armed services, just try to imagine what life was like for an African American. One such woman was Martha Putney. Martha lived in Norristown, Pennsylvania, at a time when most African Americans could only find a job as a domestic. Martha helped get out the black vote for the Republican candidate for Congress and he agreed to help her get an academic scholarship to Howard University. After earning a Master's degree in history and being turned down for a teaching job, due to political cronyism, she went to work as a clerk for the War Manpower Commission. After facing more than her share of racism, she joined the Women's Army Corps during WWII.

Having her Master's in history, Martha understood the importance of the war and knew the world would change dramatically. When the WAC official interviewed her, she stuck to her guns demanding a commission, and after a six-week course she became a fresh new Second Lieutenant, but the discrimination she and other black officers faced was shameful. In one instance, a group of German POW officers were invited into the officers' club at her base in Iowa while the black officers were refused admittance. Not only that, but black musicians were barred from the Army band, so they formed their own band. But bigoted army officials from Washington sent orders to, "get rid of the black band." Martha and others raised objections. Word reached Eleanor Roosevelt, and shortly thereafter, the band was playing again. Nothing like a Positive Thinking woman with determination!

After more ugly incidents, which were quickly resolved, Martha resigned at the end of the war and returned to her old job with the Manpower Commission. In 1947, she was married, but her husband died in 1965 leaving her with one child, so Martha decided to take advantage of the GI Bill and earned her Ph.D. in European history. She taught at Bowie State College for twenty-five years, and earned a reputation the students came to respect as one who you would learn from. Her motto was, "Work hard and if you fail look in the mirror and don't blame others. You have to accept responsibility for your own life." Martha has written, When the Nation was in Need: *Blacks in the Women's Army Corps During World War II.* One of her projects is a book on the history of blacks in combat from the Revolutionary War through Operation Desert Storm. Dr. Putney is a class act and proof that women regardless of color can be successful. Dr. Putney is another Positive Thinker. Gosh, I love writing these great stories about Positive Thinkers!

One of the most dangerous challenges a man can attempt is to fly around the world in a small plane. There is weather and machinery to consider, as well as skill and timing, along with many other factors, as you read in an earlier chapter when Wiley Post and Harold Gatty flew around the world in 1931. Try attempting to fly around the world at age seventy-two as Margaret Ringenberg did in 1994. Margaret did not win the race she entered, but she was not interested in the trophy as much as competing. After all, she had already logged over forty thousand hours flying in small planes, and had her share of trophies. She is a testament to women (and men) everywhere that you can do anything you make up your mind to do. Margaret is a Positive Thinker, knows the **three-word motto** and I would feel completely safe as a passenger in any plane she piloted, because Margaret is a Positive Thinker.

Dian Fossy was born in 1935 and spent 18 years in the Virungas Mountains in East Africa, living among the gorillas, and working to preserve them from being exterminated by poachers. She put her life on the line daily, and founded Karisoke Research Center of Rowanda. She wrote Gorillas in the Mist, and shortly thereafter did pay with her life for protecting this endangered species. In 1988 a motion picture about Dian starring Sigorney Weaver played to large audiences and started a landslide of opposition to poachers in the region. Now the gorillas live in peace and harmony once more, thanks to the willingness of a Positive Thinker to give her life for a just cause.

Women broke another barrier when Sandra Day O'Connor was sworn in as an Associate Justice of the U.S. Supreme Court during President Reagan's term. Positive Thinker, Justice O'Connor, also broke down another barrier when she became the majority leader of the Senate, in the state of Arizona, earlier in her sterling career. There are two women on the Supreme Court now, as Ruth Ginsberg joined her a few years later.

Betty Cuthbert is known as "The Golden Girl". At eighteen years old she won four Olympic gold medals for Australia, the highest number won by any Australian track and field athlete. In beating the world's best, this golden-haired runner raced her way into the hearts of millions of Australians.

When Betty was born, in 1938, her mother was shocked to find she wasn't having just one baby - but two! Betty and her twin sister, Marie, grew up in Sydney during the 1930s depression. To survive the tough times their father ran a plant nursery, and young Betty used to love running barefoot between the rows of plants. *"I always felt free when I ran. I suppose that's what was good about it ."*A trophy for the best girl athlete while at primary school hinted at the victories to come. "I realized from a very early age that God gave me a gift, and that gift was to run, and I wanted to use it to the best of my ability."

In high school, Betty's running skill attracted the attention of athletics coach, June Ferguson. So began one of Australia's most successful sporting partnerships. Betty's tendency to run with her mouth wide open became a trademark characteristic *"Everything I did that required effort, I opened my mouth. Even to catch a ball, I opened my mouth."* At the age of seventeen, Betty set her sights on the 1956 Melbourne Olympics - the first Olympic Games to be held in Australia. "No way did I ever think I was going to win the 100m.""My favorite event was the 200m, so as I won the 100m, I thought it was possible I'd win the 200m." Then came the relay. "A photo finish was called for, and Betty won. The country went mad!

Are you old enough to remember the television program, *'The 64 Thousand-Dollar Question?'* This program was the first installment of, *'Who Wants to Be a Millionaire.'* I remember the contestants being escorted into the sound proof booth and asked the questions. One contestant, Dr. Joyce Brothers, was a boxing expert, and Dr. Brothers stunned the world by answering what the show's executives thought was an "impossible" question to answer. The names and date escape my memory, but the question was who the referee was in a certain boxing match? Up to that point in the questioning, all the questions were about boxers. The show's executives in their arrogance felt no woman would know about referees. When the question was put to Dr. Brothers, a smile crossed her lovely face. Dr. Brothers is a very intelligent lady, and as I think about it, that smile (in my opinion) was because she knew they felt she did not know the answer. So she enjoyed having a surprise waiting for them as she took her time for effect in answering the question. I remember the shocked look of surprise on the hosts' face. Dr. Brothers went on to fame as a psychologist; appeared as a spokesperson for commercials, and she was one of the first people I inducted into the World Positive Thinkers Club. Dr. Brothers made a profound statement about salespeople, when she said, "That person, who does the most effective job of selling in the 1990's, will be that person who does most to reassure the prospect."

During my research, I wanted to know the comparison of success rate among start up women and men entrepreneurs. Was there a difference? Up to that point, I had no idea. It just hadn't occurred to me that one or the other would be more successful as a start up entrepreneur. The study was done purely on an average, because there are more men start-ups than women. To my surprise I discovered that the failure rate for men is 76%, but for women, the failure rate was only 25%. I discovered that women are more detail oriented. Women do the small things better. They are more persistent, and are better at follow up. They are more inclined to pick up the phone or write a letter or e-mail and thank a customer for his or her business. The phone is a natural tool for them, because they have been using it since their early teens. They are better at putting out flyers and posters, and they know how important it is to give a good first impression. They are better at personal grooming. I have found that, through my going out and pretending to be a buyer, women make better salespeople. The average salesman is not as goal oriented as a woman, and in lots of cases, couldn't care less about selling his product or how he dresses. I have found in my industrial selling days that it was very hard to compete against some women.

Joanna L. Krotz is a marketing expert, and in her newsletter that I read occasionally, she talks about the difference between men and women entrepreneurs. In one newsletter a profitability expert, Karen Lund, claims that men are focused more toward vision and analysis, whereby, "women are more focused on how well people are doing." So women are more people oriented, and that comes down to the workers they hire and their customers needs. In my opinion that is the most important ingredient, because you can always hire the numbers crunchers, but if you are not people oriented, you don't have a clue as to who really provides the income.

Joanna Krotz recently reported on the findings of researchers involved in the biology aspect of men compared to women. The research concluded that male brains are ten percent (10%) larger than women, but women have larger nerve fibers, which connect the right brain with the left. The report also reported on female leadership strengths.

- Women are better than men at empowering teams and staff.
- Women encourage openness and are more accessible.

- Women respond more quickly to calls for assistance
- Women are more tolerant of differences, so they are more skilled at managing diversity.
- Women identify problems more quickly and more accurately.
- Women are better at defining job expectations and providing valuable feedback.
- Women are better communicators.

I remember a clerk in a store giving me a hard time once, and I looked at him and said, "Am I the customer, or are you?" He said, "You are." To which I replied, "Then why do you have the role confused? I am income and you are overhead." In my personal experiences and opinion, men sales people are less interested in a customers needs than a woman. Ahemmmmm, unless it is a pretty woman the salesman is waiting on!

One of the biggest fields for women today is the real estate market. If you look in any brochure, you will find it has pictures of the salespeople, and at least seventy percent of the sales people are women. Now granted, some of the women are in the field part time, but that does not take away from the fact that they make money in the profession. Women are natural home lovers, so they can usually give more enthusiasm in showing a home. They can paint a picture of what the home will look like with certain additions or changes. Women are better home decorators than most men, and a classic example of that is the very successful company based out of Texas, Home Interior's, started 44 years ago by Mary Crawley. Mary built a company from scratch to one that reaches across America and into Canada, Mexico and Puerto Rico, with over 70,000 representatives (made up mostly of women) with over $500 million in annual sales. Mary was born in Slater, Missouri in 1915, where many of the people still drive around in ten to forty year old cars. (I can personally attest to that fact, because I lived in Slater for eighteen months). Little did her parents realize that she would be awarded the Horatio Alger Award, which is given to the winner of the best 'rags to riches' accomplishment each year. Mary was also the first woman inducted into the Hall of Fame for Direct Selling Associates. Zig Ziglar, who also is a member of the World Positive Thinkers Club, inspired Mary. She read his books, followed his advice, and started her company with a few dollars and a dream. (Hope you highlighted the preceding sentence). Mary passed away, but her son and his daughter run the company, and sales grow tremendously every year. I have a friend in Canada, who typifies the drive and enthusiasm of the majority of women working for this great company.

One of the great entrepreneurs, Mary Kay Ash, died recently. Mary Kay also built up a multi-million dollar, multi-level marketing cosmetic empire from scratch, and she was very people oriented by awarding excellent bonuses to her top performers, including a new car.

Let's make it three Mary's in a row. This Mary came from a poor family that could not afford to send her to college. One night she had a dream, and in the dream she saw herself on a college campus. The dream showed the buildings in detail. A few weeks later she was called to the pastors office of the local church and was informed that she had won a scholarship to, of all places, St. Mary's, in Ohio. Mary took that scholarship and arrived on a campus that was exactly as in her dream. The buildings looked exactly as the ones in her dream, and while attending college she had another dream to be an insurance agent.

After graduation she went to the local insurance agency to fulfill that dream, because she had decided she wanted to sell insurance to protect people from losing their homes and life savings. The problem was, that in those days women were not considered competent enough to sell insurance. So the agency head turned her down, but Mary was determined, and so she came back day after day to land a job selling insurance. Finally, Mary decided to go over the agency manager's head and went to the local banker, who was the father of her roommate in college. He gave her a recommendation, and when Mary presented the letter to the manager, he was astonished, and hired Mary. Mary Crow became the greatest insurance agent the Equitable Insurance Company ever hired, because she was a Positive Thinker and all three Mary's knew the **three-word motto**.

Do you husbands want to know how to have a better marriage? According to some articles money and sex are the principal marriage problems. But according to a reputable survey, women admitted that "low self-esteem" is rated as the biggest hurdle to marriage harmony. Let me address the problem with sad conviction, because I made the same mistake of thinking that money and sex were my marriage's biggest barriers. If only I had been my wife's best friend! Be as good a friend to your wife as you are to your associates and neighbors. Give her support, and kindness.

"Charity suffers long and is kind." —St. Paul- Corinthians 13:4

For you wives, a bit of advice from Ruth Stafford Peale, is worth heeding after one wife complained to her that her husband worked all the time. In essence Mrs. Peale said, perhaps he was a workaholic, perhaps not, but the point is that maybe he was doing it so that the family could have financial freedom. Don't knock him for that. Support him, like the wife of the CEO of General Motors, Alfred P. Sloan, did. Mrs. Sloan took a deep interest in his business, and learned to understand his problems. Alfred P. Sloan had many experts helping him run one of the world's giant companies, but he said that his wife was the best business advisor he had.

In the late 1970's a survey was taken of top management in some of the nations leading corporations, and in just about every case one very interesting factor stood out. The men interviewed praised their wives, and admitted that they would have failed miserably without the cherished support and advice of their wives.

Dr. James Dobson wrote a wonderful book titled, *What Wives Wish Their Husbands Knew About Women,* and in this poignant book Dr. Dobson reveals that he also came to the conclusion through research, that low self-esteem is the biggest concern and problem with married women. When asked what husbands could do to help their wives overcome those feelings he stated that the key was, "Keeping romantic love alive." In I Peter 3:7 it gives sagacious advice in stating, "You husbands must be careful of your wives, being thoughtful of their needs and honoring them." My personal feeling is that it works both ways, in that wives should return the favor to their husbands. The old saying still holds true, "It takes two to tango."

Some years ago I watched the movie "Fiddler on the Roof." In that award winning movie Tevye asks his wife, Golde, the question of the ages for all sweethearts, "Do you love me?" Golde at first tells him that it is obvious, because she has taken care of the children, milked the cow, washed his clothes and made his meals for 25 years. Tevye asks her again and again she skirts the question. A third time Tevye asks her, and finally she says she loves him. Tevye smiles from ear to ear and says, "After twenty-five years, it's nice to know." We learn from that poignant movie that we should not withhold our love and affection from our mate. Don't let the fact that perhaps our own parents did not show much affection, or that fear of rejection makes us skittish to say, "I love you." We should not be critical, but rather show the caring, affection and friendship we agreed to from the very beginning of the relationship. If you have been thinking lately that you do not tell your mate you love her or him enough times stop reading right now and march into the kitchen or bedroom, or pick up your cell phone and surprise him or her with that wonderful statement. Go ahead do it right now I will wait for you, and I know you will have put a smile on three faces after telling your mate those so very important three words. And after making that wonderful statement write four words right here. Write the words "I did say it." Go ahead I dare you.

"If we discovered that we had only five minutes left to say all we wanted to say, every telephone booth would be occupied by people calling other people to stammer that they loved them. Why wait until the last five minutes?"
— Christopher Morley

If you want to know how to give your spouse a warmer feeling and improve their self-esteem, try following the advice of Philip Zimbardo, a social psychologist at Stanford University. He writes about shyness in his book *Shyness: What is it and what to do about it*. In the book he reveals that shyness is a learned trait and not inherited. He found that children in Israel are less shy than in most other countries, because the children are always praised for their performances regardless of the scope of the performance. The Israeli culture minimizes failure and reinforces good performance. Why don't we take that one step further with our spouses, and as a matter of fact our friends and relatives, and praise and thank them more often for preparing a great dinner or for fixing a leak in the toilet or for taking out the trash? Is that so hard to do or above your station in life? The point is we have to learn to stop asking all the time and start giving, because the result is always the same: something good returns to us. In a husband-wife/parent-child relationship that something is usually love.

Finally, I feel it will be fitting to close this chapter by quoting Susan Taylor. Susan is an African American, who at the time she made the following statement was editor-in–chief of *Essence magazine,* founder of a cosmetic company, creator of a nationally syndicated TV show and a charity worker.

"No matter how frantically busy they are women must take time to ask themselves: 'Are our children being educated? Are our elderly being cared for? What is my purpose? Where am I going?" Women often make the mistake of nurturing everyone but themselves and cluttering their lives with so many activities that they're emotionally and spiritually depleted."

"You're in charge of you. You have everything within you to live fully and victoriously. That's not to say you're not going to weep; that life will not knock you down. But if you're strong inside, you'll get back up."

"Pain can be transforming. Without the pain I have experienced in life I wouldn't be where I am or who I am today. Waking up one morning in my early 20's with a new baby and a broken marriage shook me out of complacency, and sent me on a lifelong journey of self-improvement and positive thinking. I raised my daughter myself for 19 years, until remarrying. Pain has a purpose—to draw us closer to God. Life is peaks and valleys. Ask God: What lesson am I to learn this moment?"

A very profound article was written on March 4, 2005 in the Philadelphia Inquirer, and I quote. Headline—"Positive thinking keeps Hatters at their peak." "Hatboro-Horsham's girls have a winning attitude, which has kept the swimming program among the elite." "Whether they are visualizing future events or viewing past ones, members of the Hatboro-Horsham girls' swim team wear rose-colored goggles." That is a refreshing article in a day where some vilify those teens who strive to win.

The great hymn writer Fanny Crosby lived to the ripe old age of 95 totally blind, yet because of a daily positive attitude Fanny could see better than most people, writing many hymns that inspired millions. Fanny wrote the following poem when she was a young girl.

"Oh, what a happy soul am I,
Although I cannot see.
I am resolved that in this world
Contented will I be.
How many blessings I enjoy
That other people don't;
To weep and sigh because I'm blind
I cannot and I won't."

Here is an additional listing of women who made a difference and forged history.

- Sacagawea—Indian maiden who helped Lewis and Clark.
- Harriet Beecher Stowe—Author of Uncle Toms Cabin
- Susan B. Anthony—Responsible for women gaining the right to vote.
- Gertrude Stein—Great writer and patron of the arts.
- Katherine Hepburn—Academy Award winner
- Julia Child—Pioneer of television cooking.
- Rosa Parks—Civil Rights pioneer
- Agnodice—4th century physician
- Deborah Sampson—Fought as a man in the revolutionary war.
- Ida B. Wells Barnett—Precursor to Rosa Parks
- Nellie Bly—Journalist and best selling author.

MAKE YOUR OWN ADDITIONAL LIST.

"A great man without a great woman backing him is like a library without books."
— Ken Bossone 2003

MAIN THOUGHTS AND CHALLENGES

1. Go back to the beginning of this chapter and review your highlighted sentences.

2. Place the highlighted page numbers on this page.

3. Write the most important highlight and why it is so important to you.

4. Name a woman you admire and why.

5. Write what you will do to make life easier for your mate. You will want to write down what you will do on a daily and weekly basis. Think of your mates' welfare.

Positive Thinking, Nutrition, and Faith Improve Your Health

"Health is not a condition of matter, but of mind."
—Mary Baker Eddy

This chapter can be another controversial one depending on your outlook. However, after my research I am firmly convinced that you can think your way to good health or you can think your way to bad health. Even the great philosopher, and human rights advocate, Voltaire said, "The fate of a nation has often depended on the good or bad digestion of a prime minister." And Bulwer-Lytton, the English novelist, playwright, and politician remarked, "Refuse to be ill. Never tell people you are ill; never own it to yourself. Illness is one of those things which a man should resist on principal at the onset."

Dr. Sarah Jordan of the Lahey Clinic in Boston encountered a patient filled with negative thinking and prescribed a "mind shampooing." So when we have a problem or many problems facing us perhaps we should retire to a quiet place and have a mind shampooing, by clearing our mind and concentrating on positive things to replace the negative. I hope you highlighted this paragraph.

Earlier in this book I wrote about people who overcame illness, like the beauty queen. There are many more documented stories of people who contracted all manner of illnesses and with medicine or nutrition and a positive attitude, recovered, whereas there are patients with the same disease who have not been able to overcome their illnesses. A classic example of overcoming is Lance Armstrong. Lance contracted cancer in five parts of his body and was given a three-percent (3%) chance of recovering. With positive thinking and care Lance overcame the illness and went on a year later to prove the skeptics wrong by winning not once, but seven times in a row the most grueling athletic event in the world: the Tour de France bicycle race, which I wrote about in an earlier chapter. I will give another example of someone who, through positive thinking, became well. The story was told to me by a very reputable source some years ago about a doctor. It takes place when the roads were filled with hitchhikers, and it seemed that every road was filled with men and women with their thumbs stuck out. I always picked up women because I was concerned for their safety and would on many occasions take them directly to their homes with a lecture on how dangerous it was for them to hitchhike. Unfortunately some did not appreciate my lecture, but I continued lecturing them anyway, because I would have felt like a hypocrite if I didn't. After all, I did teach self-defense tactics. This particular doctor had cancer ravaging his body and had less than 6 months to live. While driving to his office one day, he picked up two male college hitchhikers. They thanked him, but commented that he was taking a chance picking up two men while he was alone in the car. The doctor told them that it was no concern of his since he was dying anyway. They queried him on his condition and he casually explained the nature of his illness. To his surprise the hitchhikers became excited and told him they were doing research on his particular strain of cancer, and had found that certain macrobiotics, coupled with positive thinking, could cure his illness. The doctor laughed at such nonsense and wished them well, but they became insistent and urged him to give it a try since he had nothing to lose anyway. The doctor was silent a moment and thought of the burden his wife and children would have to face after he was gone, and with enthusiasm told the hitchhikers he would do it. That skeptical doctor took up positive thinking, and did in fact follow the macrobiotics plan. He was cured to the amazement of his colleagues, and in fact, wrote a book about his cure. "A merry heart doeth good like a medicine." Proverbs 17:22. "God heals and the doctor takes the fee." Benjamin Franklin "A sound mind in a sound body is a thing to be prayed for." Juvenal

The skeptics reading that story will chuckle, because I presented no dates or names, but there is more, so continue to keep an open mind. During the civil war, General Grant, the leader of the Northern armies, had General Lee surrounded near Richmond, Virginia. He was attacking from both sides and the rear; General Sheridan was blocking their front and the siege was going on for nine months. Lee's soldiers were ragged, hungry, and deserting by the regiments. General Grant was suffering from a violent headache, whereby he became so sick that he had to stop at a farmhouse well behind his troops. In his memoirs he stated, "I spent the night bathing my feet in hot water and mustard, and putting mustard plasters on my wrists and the back part of my neck, hoping to be cured by morning." (The next morning he was cured. Not by mustard plasters, but by a horseman racing down the dirt path with a surrender letter from General Lee). Grant continued, "When the officer [bearing the message] reached me, I was still suffering from the sick headache, but the instant I saw the contents of the note, I was cured. Was it his tension, his worries that made him ill? Why was he cured instantly after reading the letter?

There is a compelling story in the 1998 winter issue of *Vital Health News* about Kaye Wyatt. Kaye was sickly from the time she was born. She found it hard to breathe, and due to ignorance the doctors did not know that the thymus gland is the master control gland of the immune system. Her immune system was slowly deteriorating and she constantly fought life-threatening infections. There were many times when she was too weak to pick up a dish to wash it. Even chewing food was painful and she spent over $30,000 for dental work. Kaye had a bad fall and her knee swelled up to the size of a grapefruit. Her husband had purchased colostrum through a naturopathic doctor from Belgium a few days earlier and pleaded with her to take this "miracle health product." Her answer was that she wanted him to help her die, not live with the constant pain anymore. Her husband totally believed in colostrum and forced her to take it. The bruise on the knee had healed by the next morning and Kaye was fighting off the infection. Two years later she has no infections and her vision and speech have improved so dramatically that she gives speeches now and is a marketing executive. Kaye stated, "I think that the 'someone upstairs' knew that if colostrum passed all my stringent tests, I would shout about it loud enough to be heard around the world." Kaye can thank her positive thinking husband and colostrum for her cure. He obviously knows the three word motto and so does Kaye now.

In the third edition of a major health magazine, there is a story about Mindy, from Nova Scotia. For six months Mindy had symptoms of Wegener's Granulomatosis, an autoimmune disease where the immune system attacks itself. This terrible affliction is life threatening and can take over any part of the body. Many patients have kidney failure and need dialysis. In May of 1999 Mindy lay in a hospital bed. Her hearing and speech were gone and nodules had formed on her lungs. Chemotherapy was prescribed along with prednisone, which causes hair loss as well as vomiting and a myriad of side effects.

Mindy's mother refused to submit her daughter to these debilitating conditions and sought help in the nutritional and herb communities. She read an article of the benefits of Moducare, a nutritional product, in *Alive magazine* and did some research on it. Moducare is a plant nutrient with sterols and sterolin and there are over 4,000 scientific and medical studies on this amazing plant nutrient.

Mindy has been on Moducare, and her symptoms have been in remission now since July of 1999 and even her energy levels have been restored. Mindy has her life back thanks to Moducare and a Positive Thinking mother. In another article, Lee Heiman, of New York writes about using Moducare to cure his prostate cancer after the doctors practically wrote him off.

Dr. Karl Menninger, one of the Mayo Brothers of psychiatry, tells about how we destroy our bodies and minds with anxiety, anger, frustration, resentment, rebellion and fear. I am sure you can find a copy of his book in your library. Dr. Edward Podolsky had the following to say, "WHAT WORRY DOES TO THE HEART—HIGH BLOOD PRESSURE IS FED BY WORRY—RHEUMATISM CAN BE CAUSED BY WORRY—WORRY LESS FOR YOUR STOMACHE'S SAKE—HOW WORRY CAN CAUSE A COLD—WORRY AND THE THYROID—THE WORRYING DIABETIC. Dr. W.C. Alvarez, of the Mayo clinic years ago said: "Ulcers frequently flare up or subside according to the hills and valleys of emotional stress." He and his colleagues came to that conclusion after 15,000 patients were treated for stomach disorders at the Mayo Clinic. Four out of five patients had no physical reasons for their stomach illnesses. Dr. Harold C. Habien, of the Mayo Clinic, did a study of 176 business executives and found a third of them suffered heart disease, ulcers, and high blood pressure caused from high tension relations. *Life* magazine once printed that ulcers stood tenth in the list of fatal diseases. Dr. William I.L. McGonigle addressed the American Dental Association and stated, "Worry can cause tooth decay." Worry, fear, and nagging can upset the body's calcium balance and cause tooth decay." Professor William James once said, "The Lord may forgive us our sins, but the nervous system never does." Dr. Alexis Carrel once said, "Those who keep the peace of their inner selves in the midst of the tumult of the modern city are immune from nervous diseases." Dr. Carrel also said, "Businessmen who do not know how to fight worry die young." Dr. James Rouse, Naturopathic physician, stated, "You also know that you need to relax; hundreds of studies confirm that stress leads to increased risk of colds and flu, migraine, PMS, back pain, fatigue, depression, heart disease and the list goes on."

The erudite Plato said, "The greatest mistake physicians make is that they attempt to cure the body without attempting to cure the mind; yet the mind and body are one and should not be treated separately."

Do you believe in miracles? I do, because many have happened to people I know and me. God comes to our aid just when we need it, as happened to me while I was riding my bike in the scorching heat of July. Circumstances had put me in a deep hole financially and I had just enough money for the rent. During my bike rides to meet my "so-called partner" [I could write a complete book about that] for the day's work I always rode up a slight upgrade to get to our meeting place. One day I decided not to go ride up the hill but walk instead. I had no breakfast that day for lack of food and was having hunger pangs. As I got off the bike I looked to my right and noticed a small green piece of paper. As I walked over to it, it became apparent that it was money, and to my complete delight I picked up the twenty dollar bill and tore up the hill on my bike to the nearby restaurant. Now some of you may think this is a coincidence but hold on to your hats. Remember now that I had no money for food. With the balance of that twenty-dollar bill I paid for some phone time on a prepaid phone I had to borrow. Several days later I decided to go for a bike ride as I was getting cabin fever. The heat index was one hundred four degrees, but I did not care as I was getting used to riding in the heat. I came to the same hill; again I decided not to ride my bike up the hill, and got off to walk. I looked to my right and saw a green piece of paper. Nonchalantly, I walked over to the spot and stopped dead in my tracks, because lying there was a fifty-dollar bill in the same exact spot where I found the twenty-dollar bill a few days before. Now I don't know about you, but this to me was no coincidence. The following week I rode my bike the usual four and a half miles to the library, which is my temporary second home. That day the weatherman was talking about thundershowers, but they were not to start until the evening. Wouldn't you know that with my luck it started drizzling around 3pm. It was decision time, so I jumped on my bike and pumped as fast as my now in shape legs would allow up the long half-mile hill until I reached a gas station. Just as I reached the station it started raining harder and suddenly the thunder and lightening exploded. As I stood next to my bike I just knew everything would work out, and sure enough a black pick-up truck with a high cover on the bed pulled up for gas. After he paid for his gas he looked at me and smiled and said, "I bet you need a ride in all this rain." I asked him what direction he was headed and it was in the opposite direction, but he said, "Don't worry about it I will take you home." He handed me his business card and on the bottom was the symbol of the Christian fish. God knew my needs and rescued me, and to my dying day I will thank him and never forget his miracles.

Earlier in the book in chapter eight you read about the unfortunate men who went through the horrors of Bataan and were interned in a prisoner of war camp named Camp Cabanatuan. One of the survivors of that death march was Edward Tommie Thomas, who was suffering from diphtheria. This disease is usually associated with children, but because of the horrendous malnourished state the prisoners were in, diphtheria was rampant, causing in almost all cases death. Diphtheria is usually treated with an antitoxin, but there was not enough to go around. Tommie had lost close to one hundred pounds and noticed that he was having trouble swallowing, while already suffering from malaria. Some of these malnourished men including Tommie, had no difficulty placing both hands around their waist touching their four fingertips to each other. He had to face the fact that he would be facing a slow, agonizing death confined in what was named the Zero-Zero ward. These poor unfortunate heroes had to lay in filth all day coughing up mucus into a little can. In the Zero-Zero ward with Tommie was Armando Trujillo, another diphtheria patient from New Mexico. Finally, because the disease had spread unchecked, Dr. Williard Watrous convinced the Japanese Camp commander, Colonel Mori, that if the antitoxin was not received in time the disease would spread to the Japanese troops. The serum was received a few days later and dispensed immediately, but when Dr. Watrous came to Tommie and Armando there was only enough left for one of them. Without flinching Tommie asked the doctor which of them was worse off. Doctor Watrous sadly exclaimed that Armando was, and again without flinching this brave soldier told the doctor to give the last dose to Armando.

That night Tommie's condition worsened to the point where he could hardly swallow; allowing him hardly any rest from having to spit in his can all night. But next morning Tommie was felling much better, and after the doctors examined him they stood in near shock. The coughing was gone, along with the membrane that covers the patient's throat. Tommie who admitted to not being religious, claims it was a miracle for his unselfish act of allowing a fellow human being to take the only life saving drug available, thereby giving his chance for survival to another. Tommie vowed that since he was spared death he was going to survive the hell he faced every day and walk out of that filthy prison a free man someday. He automatically became a believer in Positive Thinking, and through his faith and positive attitude he did exactly that. For the sake of not allowing this unbelievable episode to become hackneyed I will end by stating that there are many more documented cases of miracles in the lives of the men who had to face death for three years on a daily basis in that horrendous camp. As a matter of fact, a television special aired recently narrated by Scott Glen, about the "Ghost Soldiers" of the 6th Ranger Battalion, headed by Lt. Colonel Muse and Captain Prince, that rescued Tommie and his 512 fellow prisoners at the end of January 1945, and you will find the book *Ghost Soldiers* in most libraries.

Perhaps you have religion, perhaps you do not. Perhaps you are an atheist, or an agnostic or a devout Christian, or Muslim. That does not matter to me, as I am simply reporting the next story as I read it from an authoritative source. The source is none other than the best selling author, Dale Carnegie, who wrote *How to Win Friends and Influence People,* and *How to Stop Worrying and Start Living.* Dale also set up the famous Carnegie Institute for adult night schools, which are all over the world.

Mary was walking downtown in Lynn, Massachusetts, when she slipped and fell on an icy pavement. As a result, she was knocked unconscious, irrevocably injuring her spine, according to the doctor. He gave her no hope of living, and if she did live it would only be by a miracle, however, there was no hope she would ever walk again. She opened her bible, and as she put it,

"I was divinely led to read these words from Saint Matthew:" "And behold, they brought him to a sick man of the palsy; son, be of good cheer; thy sins are forgiven thee. ... Arise, take up thy bed, and go into thine house. And he arose, and departed to his house." "These words of Jesus," she declared, "produced within me such a strength, such a faith, such a surge of healing power that I immediately got out of bed and walked."

Mrs. Mary Baker Eddy declared, "That experience, was the falling apple that led me to the discovery of how to be well myself, and how to make others so. I gained the scientific certainty that all causation was mind, and every effect a mental phenomenon."

And so, Mary Baker Eddy became the founder and high priestess of a new religion: Christian Science—the first established by a woman, which encircles the globe.

Again, let me be emphatic. I am not here to promote any religion. I am simply reporting the facts, which can be substantiated by a little research on your part. My firm conviction, and of many others with more sagacity than I, is that positive thinking, be it associated with religion or medicine or otherwise, can cure illness. And in fact can keep illness away.

I have personally experienced thinking myself back to health and a close friend can confirm it. In January of 2002, I contracted pneumonia. I am certain it was pneumonia, because while I was sick I looked up the symptoms on a medical reference program. I decided to be living proof that I would cure myself with positive thinking and nutrition. Now it was not easy, because I was delirious at one point, babbling to myself. As I was babbling my friend insisted on taking me to the hospital. But under no uncertain terms would I allow myself to be taken to the hospital, so I started thinking positive. I told myself that, "this too shall pass." I got up from the bed and started drinking fluids and taking vitamin C with rose hips. I refused to take medication. My decision was to rest for several days with plenty of fluids and vitamin C, and continue to think my way out of my sickness with positive thinking. After all I would be a hypocrite if I did not believe what I write in this book. It was not easy, but I stayed completely focused and put out of my mind the fact that people die from pneumonia. I would have nothing to do with the negative and every waking hour was filled with positive input.

Slowly I recovered, am fit as a fiddle once more, and if you wish to contact my friend for confirmation you may e-mail me and I will put you in touch with her.

The following is an article from the Internet: *Alternative Medicine for Dummies*, by James Dillard. M.D., Terra Ziporyn, Ph.D.

Change Your Attitude/Why and how to keep the sunny side up...

"All the advice to "keep the sunny side up" if you want to be healthy sounds all warm and fuzzy, but almost too good to be true. Actually, though, a load of evidence shows that your attitude about life can improve your health and even speed your recovery from a serious ailment or surgery. The attitudes that seem to help the most are optimism, hope, and above all, a feeling that you have some impact on the quality of your own life."

Why you should be optimistic?

"No one really understands how or why a positive attitude helps people recover faster from surgery or cope better with serious diseases—diseases as serious as cancer, heart disease, and AIDS. But mounting evidence suggests that these effects may have something to do with the mind's power over the immune system. One recent study, for example, polled healthy first-year law students at the beginning of the school year to find out how optimistic they felt about the upcoming year. By the middle of the first semester, the students who had been confident that they would do well had more and better functioning immune cells than the worried students. (see Suzanne C. Segerstrom, Ph.D., et al., "Optimism is Associated With Mood, Coping, and Immune Change in Response to Stress, Journal of Personality and Social Psychology, Volume 74, Number 6, June 1998.)

"Some researchers think that pessimism may stress you out, too, boosting levels of destructive stress hormones in your bloodstream. Of course, it's also possible that having a positive attitude toward life makes you more likely to take better care of yourself. And more likely to attract people into your life (and keep them there)—Which in and of itself may boost your health."

"We're not saying that you should deny life's darker side or interpret every calamity as a blessing. But when calamity does strike, try not to give in to despair or fatalism. Concluding that you personally have been singled out for suffering, refusing to see any silver lining, abandoning all hope may not only be a recipe for illness: Such attitudes are also not such great ways to go through life. Try to recognize that your grief and pain, however real and deep, are only part of the larger picture—and that this picture includes many elements of pleasure, success, and meaning."

"Another approach is to try to "use your pain" for good. Many people who have suffered from life threatening and incapacitating illnesses – including cancer, heart attack, and the like – say that they consider their illness to be "a gift. The illness taught them to value each day, appreciate the moment, and get their priorities straight. Sometimes they discover that they have the power to do things they never knew they could."

"Losing a breast to cancer, for example, has led some women to stop pouring all their energies to cultivating perfect bodies. As a result, they discover other interests and talents, such as French literature, tutoring, or race walking. Being forced to give up a high-powered job because of a disabling illness has given other people the time they always wished they had to pursue sculpting, chamber music, gardening, or other passions. We're not saying that you should wish cancer, heart disease, or AIDS upon yourself, of course; but of you keep an upbeat perspective, even life's blows can bring rewards beyond your wildest imaginings."

"Remember that even if you can't change the circumstances of your life [here is where I disagree with the writer of this article; you can change your circumstances as this book has set out to do and proves] you can change your attitude! If you need help, talk to a professional about whether psychotherapy, support groups, or other structured approaches might help you."

"Attitude definitely seems to influence the course of illness. But some people take this link too far and make you feel that your bad attitude caused your disease or is keeping you from healing. Walk the other way if anyone makes you feel guilty for being sick or treats your physical ailments as if they were emotional or mental problems (included are physicians who banish you to a psychiatrist when you have no obvious signs of physical illness)."

[Again, I slightly disagree with the writers, as numerous examples prove many illnesses come from our mental attitude. I quoted the great, Plato, earlier, who lived almost 2500 years ago. His Academy in Athens has had a tremendous influence on today's colleges and universities all over the world. His school taught philosophy, law, scientific research, and mathematics. Plato's influence has spread to Judaism, Christianity and even into Islam. Again, I quote one of the greatest minds the world has ever had the good fortune to have grace this wonderful planet. Plato said, "The greatest mistake physicians make is that they attempt to cure the body without attempting to cure the mind; yet the mind and body are one and should not be treated separately." For my money I will stick with Plato and his thinking].

[What is usually prudent is to get a second opinion, and even a third. If it proves that there is no physical aliment, then research on your part should follow as to which psychologist or psychiatrist has had the most success in curing patients, [that is if you still don't feel qualified to do it on your own after reading this book], then consider setting up an appointment with him or her. The One, in my opinion, who has had the most success, is our Creator. Abraham Lincoln said, "I have found myself on my knees more often than not, as there was no place else to go." Speaking of getting down on your knees, I have to tell you about the late great Senator Everett Dirkson, of Illinois. In 1948, while he was a Representative in the House of Representatives in Washington, D.C., he noticed one eye was blurred. After many consultations with specialists he became convinced that the eye had to be removed. After taking a train to Baltimore to be operated on at Johns Hopkins Hospital, he shocked the doctors by telling them that he was not going through with the operation. When they asked him why, he responded by telling them he had been to another doctor. When they asked him whom, he calmly stated, "Coming over on the train I got down on my knees and had a little talk with the Lord, and I am not going through with this operation." Dirkson had a talk with the Big Doctor, and after resting over a period of time his sight improved. He then decided to run for the Senate, and Senator Everett Dirkson became one of the most respected public servants ever to grace the halls of Congress.]

Continuing the article—

"By now, almost everyone has heard of the Type A personality: the driven workaholic who supposedly is at high risk for heart attack. Well, credible evidence is starting to show that being a Type A personality is not the only risk factor. Shouldering any kind of negative emotion—especially powerlessness, hostility, anger, suspicion, and restlessness—may not only increase your odds of heart disease, but jeopardize your health in general."

"No one can avoid those feelings all the time, of course. But the happiest people somehow know how to buffer them by keeping life's inevitable tragedies from spoiling the good stuff. And these folks may be the healthiest people as well. This section fills you in on the growing evidence that you may be able to improve your physical health just by changing the way you think and feel about your life."

"Feeling that you have some say in your own life seems to be good for you—both emotionally and physically. People who don't believe that they have any control over their lives develop a sense of passivity and helplessness—and this sense has been linked to poor health in the same way that feeling loved and hopeful have been linked to better health."

"If you have any doubt about just where your attitude stands, see whether you have the characteristics for what some people call "the survivor personality." According to Bernie Siegel, M.D., at the March 1998, Casa Colina Whole Health Forum, survivors:

- Find meaning in their work, daily activities, and personal relationships.
- Express anger appropriately.
- Ask for help. Survivors know that they can't control everything.
- They can express their needs to friends, family, and health professionals and complain when their needs are not met.
- Say no to non-priorities.
- Make time for play.
- Learn from their pain and depression—and then get on with living.
- Choose healthy behaviors that meet their own needs—not someone else's ideas about what's good for them.

"Don't let outside duties keep them from meeting their basic needs. Survivors remember that they are precious people first, and mothers, employees or otherwise upstanding citizens second."

"Evidence shows that social support can come in the form of four-legged friends as well. In fact, having a furry friend in your life can be just as good for your health—maybe even better—than a human confidant, at least if you're an animal lover." (And you're not allergic of course!)

"Pet ownership has been linked to many benefits, including reduced blood pressure, increased mental alertness, lowered rates of depression, better survival rates from heart disease, and –for people with physical disabilities—well being in general. Some hospitals, hospices, and nursing homes even have formal "pet therapy" programs (specially trained animals visiting patients). Dogs seem to be the most healthful to patients, but any pet will do."

"Some people attribute these benefits to a pets unconditional love—something you can't expect even from the most loving spouse. Plus, people with pets may get more exercise, and caring for a pet engenders positive emotions such as responsibility, empowerment, and love."

"One (of many) reasons that your attitude can affect your health is that a bad attitude can drive other people away. And interaction with other people is vital for your health. Human beings are social animals. So it's no surprise that people thrive when they have good relationships with friends, family, and people in general. More surprising perhaps, is that these relationships can also affect physical well-being—and not just because being nasty to your doctor or shouting obscenities at her receptionist will keep you from getting optimal treatment."

"The power of intense social support to help you better cope with physical illness goes above and beyond the powers of medications and other therapies. According to psychotherapist Joan Borysenko: "The[scientific] literature says clearly that although good habits are important—eating right, exercise, not smoking, etc.—none are as important as high self-esteem and the ability to give and receive love and develop intimacy with other humans."

[Approximately five years ago a very good businesswoman friend, who lives in West Chester, Pennsylvania, with sterling business credentials and I were talking about the power of acupuncture. She told me that one of the artists she gives some work to gets migraine headaches and flies to Canada to have acupuncture treatments performed by a Chinese doctor. After having this treatment she comes home and does not experience migraine headaches for over six months. When she again experiences another headache, she confidently flies to Canada for her treatment, having no doubt about the doctor's ability to heal her again. With that in mind, I quote again from *Alternative Medicine for Dummies*].

"How can sticking a needle in your neck make you healthy? Supposedly that needle unblocks a path of "vital energy" (qi in Chinese) that the acupuncturists believe flows through your whole body. When this flow gets blocked or unbalanced, you get sick."

"To figure out where to put the needles, acupuncturists rely on a dot-to-dot map of invisible channels—or meridians—through which the qi flows. By stimulating any of the 365-or-so dots, called acupuncture points, along this map, acupuncturists can supposedly fix the flow of qi."

"The reason that a needle in your wrist may affect your lungs is that the meridians connect to various internal organs. The details don't matter—but the idea that everything's interconnected does."

"All acupuncture is based on stimulating acupuncture points and getting the qi back in balance. But acupuncturists use other ways to accomplish this balance besides sticking in needles and twisting them around, including:"

• Acupressure. During this needle-free form of acupuncture (called shiatsu in Japan), the acupuncture points are stimulated with finger pressure.
• Cupping. The acupuncturist puts a small heated cup over the acupuncture point or painful muscle, creating a vacuum to suck out or blow around the qi.
• Electroacupuncture. During this labor saving technique, the needle manipulations are done by an electric current applied to the acupuncture point.
• Moxibustion. The acupuncturist burns a powered herb called mugwort to warm up the needles – or stimulates the acupuncture points directly by burning the herb on or near them."

"Perhaps you don't buy the whole idea of invisible vital energy, explaining just how acupuncture works can be challenging. But whatever the explanation, increasing scientific evidence suggests that it does work."

"Frankly, the facts that acupuncture works are pretty mind boggling. To do acupuncture "right," just jabbing the needle in the right spot isn't enough. That kind of approach would be more typical of our western biomedicine – find what's wrong and fix it. The patient doesn't have to do anything. In traditional Chinese medicine, the needle can't go in until the patient has his or her spirit in order. You also have to adjust the treatment to the season, sun, moon, planets, stars, and atmosphere. The facts that acupuncture works at all are a testament to its power." It is also a testament to positive thinking, because the patient has to believe in the healer and be in a positive frame of mind to make the procedure successful."

According to Howard Ringold, former Executive Editor of the magazine *Hotwired,* and author of *Higher Creativity, The cognitive Connections,* and They *Have a Word for It,* the Koreans call the healing trance a *kut.* I was in Korea for almost a year, so I can attest to the following. "The healer (shaman) goes into a trance, and temporarily adopts the personalities of various gods and spirits in a phenomenon known to anthropologists as "spirit possession."

One of the techniques that works for me is using magnets on a sore spot.

I have been using magnets for over a year for tennis elbow and for knee strain with great success. The magnets make the pain go away and if I am re-injured I simply use the magnets and the pain subsides.

Peter Kulish has a degree in Advanced Biomagnetics from the Broeringmeyer Institute, Murray, Kentucky. In his book, 'Conquering Pain,' he first addresses what pain is and then shows scientific ways to overcome the pain with magnets. Peter states, "Pain is the response to the disorganization of cellular functions and nerve connections which occur as a result of stress." He goes on to state, "Biomagnetism amplifies the body's normal electrical currents to immediately reorganize the distressed metabolic nerve functions. This results in the reduction and elimination of pain."

This writer refuses to attempt to pass himself off as a licensed healer of either the mind or body. I must admit however, the stories and facts I have dug up in my research stagger the imagination, and so I am happily reporting them to you, for you to make up your own mind.

Dr. Norman Vincent Peale, the world's second greatest Positive Thinker, wrote many books. The prevailing theme in his millions of copies sold was that positive thinking and faith in God will overcome any obstacle, be it mental or physical. In his ministry, Dr. Peale treated patients in his clinic with a qualified Christian psychologist, accompanied with a faith in God approach by himself or another minister.

Dr. Peale was not the only person who believed prayer overcame illness and other problems. The great heavyweight boxing champion, Jack Dempsey, always said bedtime prayers, and he prayed before every fight for courage and confidence. The famous "long count" when he fought Gene Tunney is another story, which I would love to tell anyone willing to listen. I read a book about Dempsey, which shows pictures proving Dempsey received, in my opinion, a raw deal. The "Grand Old Man" of baseball, Connie Mack, said he would not go to bed without saying his prayers. The famous pilot Eddie Rickenbacker, who for 21 days was adrift in the ocean, was confident his and the lives of his comrades were saved by prayer. The late Edward. R. Stettinius, former executive with General Motors, United States Steel, and former Secretary of State, prayed for wisdom every morning and night. J. Peirpont Morgan, the greatest financier of his period, prayed on Saturdays at Trinity Church on Wall Street. General Eisenhower took only the Bible with him when he flew to England to take charge of all the Allied

Forces during WW II. General George S. "Old Blood and Guts" Patton, the most feared General by the Germans in World War II, prayed before every battle. During one particular battle, the Allies needed air cover, but it was too foggy for our planes to fly. General Patton ordered the Chaplain to write a prayer to ask God to lift the fog, so the Chaplain reluctantly wrote the prayer. General Patton approved it and no sooner had they prayed the prayer than the fog lifted, assuring the allies victory. No wonder the Germans feared General Patton more than any other World War II Allied commander.

During World War I, the Germans pinned down a company of American soldiers in a forest in France. The Americans prayed for victory, and suddenly millions of Angels appeared to both the Germans and Americans. The Germans became frantic; threw down their weapons and ran away, thereby saving the Americans.

Olympian, Reverend Bob Richards, tells of the time he helped Milt Campbell around the track after Milt had just scored a big upset in the Olympics, and all Milt could say was, "God did it, God did it, God did it." Billy Mills, a product of a poor American Indian family, scored the biggest upset in Olympic history. When Reverend Richards asked him what was going through his mind, Billy said, "Bob, I just kept praying and trying."

Bill Russell was the player/coach of the Boston Celtics and at half time during the basketball world championships he got everyone in a circle. He then asked Bailey Howell to lead the team in prayer. We are talking about big strong athletes here, who know the **three-word motto**.

Do you believe in faith healing? That is a subject for the ages! In the Bible, stories abound about Christ healing the sick and infirmed and bringing people back to life. What most people do not know is that Elijah of the Old Testament brought back to life the son of a widow in the town of Zarephath, sometime between in the years 874-853 B.C. This was during the time of the reign of King Ahab and the evil Jezebel. Elisha became the prophet after Elijah, and during his travels stayed in the home of a wealthy Shunammite woman in the town of Shunem. The woman was childless and Elisha assured her that a year later she was to give birth to a son. The son grew up, but one day complained of headaches to his father. A short time later the boy died, so the mother traveled to Mount Carmel to have Elisha bring the boy back to life. Elisha lay on the boy and prayed, and the boy was brought back to life.

On television there was a series called, "Mysteries of the Bible." Many scholars gave irrefutable proof of the Bible stories, while some scholars disputed the stories. So while I give the facts as I believe them, I do not necessarily expect you to believe all or any of the stories. I am simply giving the facts, as I believe them. In my opinion and in the opinion of many scholars (most of them more educated than me) these stories are based on fact. It is a simple matter of faith.

Perhaps you might look into the stories that abounded regarding Sleeping Lucy. Lucy Ainsworth was born in 1819, in Calais, Vermont, to a poor family. Eventually Lucy would come to the attention of not only her neighbors but to much of the whole world after her "gift" surfaced in 1833. A neighbor, Nathan Barnes had lost his gold watch and after Lucy and her family helped look for the watch, with no results, Lucy went home. After feeling strange and tired she took a nap, and when she woke up she blurted out that she knew where the watch was. When they looked in the tall grass under the hammock where Nathan was asleep there it was. After many more like experiences suddenly Lucy fell ill, and took to her bed for two years, eventually slipping into a coma. Her brother prayed for her and suddenly she spoke in a strange voice, "I will get well if you get what I tell you and give it to me." She described some strange roots and herbs and after administering it as they were told she recovered. Lucy and her family decided that she had experienced a miracle and that she should share her healing powers. The only condition was that she could only be asleep to be able to diagnose the illness and cure for others, thus earning her the title of "Sleeping Lucy." She eventually ran a world medicine-by-mail-business recommending remedies consisting of herbs, barks and roots which always seemed to work, thereby angering more traditional healers who treated illnesses by bloodletting, blistering and dangerous drugs like mercury and laudanum. During her 53 years of healing she became known as "the greatest medical clairvoyant of the nineteenth century."

Speaking of faith, I once asked an atheist if I could prove with scientific fact, credible witnesses, legal scholars, and evidence based on excavation that Christ existed would she (the atheist) then believe that Christ existed. Without blinking an eye, the atheist said that, yes, she would believe based on those facts. I looked her right in the eye and said, "That is the difference between atheists and Christians." I told her she could give the same evidence that Christ did not exist, and I would still believe in His existence. I will never forget that incident, because we were on an airplane and she was sitting next to me with a few hours left on the flight. The second I finished my statement; she slumped in her seat, stared straight ahead, and did not say a word for the rest of the flight. I remember a frightened look on her face, and you can bet the mortgage that she had a lot to think about.

"I believe in the sun even when it is not shining. I believe in love even when I feel it not. I believe in God even when he is silent."
— Anonymous

Father Bill Kiel realized his calling at the age of 55, and went into the Seminary to study to become a priest. Father Kiel was stationed at St. Mary's in Uniontown, Pennsylvania, near Pittsburgh. On June 13, 1996, Father Kiel laid hands on Tom Oshnock, who was diagnosed with cancer being given very little time left to live. His sister Jo Ann told me that it was raining buckets that day. A warm feeling shot through Tom's body as Father Kiel put his hands on him, and suddenly the rain stopped. A few seconds later, two water drops fell on Tom's arm. Tom went to the doctors who declared him completely healed.

Dr. John Taylor told about a faith healer he investigated in the south of England. This faith healer's patient was a middle-aged woman who had suffered badly from arthritis for 18 years. "The pain in her knees and ankles," Dr. Taylor reports, "was so intense that she could no longer climb the stairs of her house or hold a saucepan. She took 15 aspirins a day to reduce the pain. She visited a faith healer with an open mind. The healer ran her fingers down the woman's spine causing "hot spots of pain." At the end of the first session," Dr. Taylor continues, "All pain had been removed from the patient's back. In three weeks, the patient was much better during the treatment, and she stopped taking the aspirin and other drugs. Within a year she was cured and could even go dancing. Granted, the woman took drugs that were supposed to alleviate the pain, but she did not improve until the faith healer worked with her." I personally am convinced that the patient had to think positive for the faith healing to work, because as Plato said, "The mind and body are as one."

Dr. Taylor also told about astrologer Sybil Leek. Sybil was suffering from an infected insect bite that caused unbearable pain, which forced her to depend on crutches or a wheelchair. While attending a conference in Hawaii, she met a medicine woman named Moana. They held hands and Sybil felt an electrical force flowing through her leg. The pain left. Sybil threw away her crutches and walked barefoot on the beach. At the end of the second week her ulcers healed without hospitalization or drugs of any kind. A doctor confirmed her previous condition, and was at a loss to explain the healing.

Finally, Dr. Taylor reported about Frenchman Serge Perrin, who suffered terribly from thrombosis (blood clot). The doctors told him to make his funeral arrangements. Perrin's wife begged him to make a pilgrimage to Lourdes, which he did on May 1,1970, whereby he was completely cured to the utter amazement of the doctor who was treating him. "His case was hopeless," the doctor reported. Perrin became a true believer in faith healing and positive thinking!

If you believe that you can have an affliction cured you have won half the battle, which was proved by Dr. Akers time and time again. He had an interesting (to say the least) medicine to cure warts. When patients applied his red liquid for a month the warts disappeared. For years this formula worked on his patients, and Dr. Akers finally revealed that when he gave the "medicine" to patients they firmly believed that the three ounces of water and two drops of red food coloring was real medicine.

I am going to give you one of my recipes for relaxing and curing many mental and physical maladies. Some years ago, I can't quite remember when, while driving in congested traffic I picked up a pair of Chinese exercise chime balls I had purchased in Korea and started twirling them in my right hand. I noticed that after five minutes of twirling them, the melodic chime and twirling completely relaxed me. After several months I noticed a strange thing happening to my right hand. Where before my middle finger was afflicted with arthritis, it was no longer a problem. The pain was gone. In fact the finger became flexible and no longer stiff, and as a matter of fact I prided myself on showing people how far backwards I could bend the finger. Some of my more squeamish friends and relatives just about passed out from seeing my finger bend backwards.

If you will purchase a pair in one of the many Chinese gift shops for around five dollars you will notice one thing as you twirl them in your hand. If you watch the underside of your wrist you will notice the blood vessels moving thereby improving circulation to the heart. The muscles and tendons are also affected, which also makes your movements more flexible. Make sure that if you have small hands that you purchase the small pair, so that it will be easier to twirl them at first and consequently you will learn to twirl them faster and faster as time goes by. Carry them in your purse or pocket so that you can use them in times of stress in your office or car. I recommend twirling them for five minutes at a time to start. Your hands will ache a little, but after your body gets used to them it will go away. The Chinese and most Asian people swear by them and they are a cousin to the "worry stone." The worry stone is a jade stone, egg shaped on the top, and flat on the bottom so that you can hold it easier and run your thumb on the flat surface. The purpose is supposedly to take your mind off the problem. Personally, I don't like the term "worry" so my recommendation is the Chinese chime balls, and to this day, many years later I still use them.

For you ladies suffering through the anguish of menopause I have a remedy that if you will just do a little research you will be pleasantly surprised at how well it works. It is the herb Maca, discovered by a female doctor in Peru. I personally have witnessed a friend going through hot flashes among many other menopausal symptoms. She finally agreed to go to a reputable health food store after reading the information about Maca, which I showed her on the Internet. [It is relatively inexpensive considering the other medical options, including hysterectomy, which another friend went through]. My friend purchased the herb and after following the directions for thirty days noticed the hot flashes diminishing. In ninety days the hot flashes were completely gone as well as some of the other symptoms, with no side effects. Just make sure you purchase the Peruvian herb, if you decide to try it after doing a little research. I refuse to guarantee any product-rather I consider myself an exponent of possibilities.

The Magic of Believing, written by Claude Bristol, became a best seller, and in this profound book he reveals how hundreds of people believed their way to success. How does faith really work, you may ask. Succinctly put, it is nothing more than conviction and then commitment.

"The best doctors in the world are Doctor Diet,
Doctor Quiet, and Doctor Merryman."
— Jonathon Swift

"Do not worry, eat three square meals a day, say your prayers, be courteous to your creditors, keep your digestion good, exercise, and go slow and easy."
— A. Lincoln

"A state of faith allows no mention of impossibility."
— Tertullian-Chief founder of Christian Latin Theology…

"A strong, positive attitude will create more miracles than any wonder drug."
— Patricia Neal
1963 Academy Award winning actress, and former cancer patient

MAIN THOUGHTS AND CHALLENGES

1. Go back and review your highlighted sentences.

2. Write the page numbers of the highlighted sentences on this page.

3. Write the most important highlighted sentence and why it is so important to you.

4. Write instances where you personally have experienced a change in your physical well being through nutrition and/or positive thinking.

5. Write instances where a relative or acquaintance has experienced well being through nutrition and/or positive thinking.

6. Do some research on this subject on your own if it has too many question marks for you.

Chapter 14

MIND OVER MATTER

*"If I have the belief that I can do it,
I shall surely acquire the capacity to do it,
even if I may not have it at the beginning."*

—Mahatma Gandhi

If anyone would know about mind over matter, it would surely be the great Gandhi, because this small frail man was mainly responsible for leading his fellow countrymen out of the bondage of Great Britain.

Gandhi was born in Porbandar, near Bombay, India, and was married when he was only 13 years old. When he was 19, he defied custom, and moved overseas to study in London, but he was snubbed because he was a dark skinned Indian. He studied Thoreau's principal of nonviolence. He became the first "colored" lawyer admitted to the Supreme Court in Natal, in South Africa. In 1906, he started his peaceful revolt; was jailed twice, and in 1914 he returned to India where he led the peaceful revolt once more. Thousands of Indians followed him in his quest for "home rule", and in 1947, India finally gained its independence from Great Britain. In 1982, a stirring movie staring Ben Kingsley, which won several Academy awards was based on Gandhi's life. Gandhi proved that man could overcome all sorts of adversity when the mind is determined to overcome. Another clear-cut example of positive thinking! Ghandi knew the **three-word motto**.

In 1971, Felicia Parise, a laboratory assistant at the Maimonides Medical Center in New York, moved a bottle, which was a quarter full of medicine, six inches without touching it. She made no physical contact. The additional amazing thing was that she could stop it at will and reverse it while members of the scientific community watched her perform this unbelievable feat.

"The difference between a successful person and others is not a lack of strength, not a lack of knowledge, but rather a lack of will."
— Vince Lombardi

There are many reference books used for this chapter. There has to be, because it probably is the most controversial of all the chapters. But through all my research, I am firmly convinced that mind over matter proves the word impossible does not exist ninety nine percent of the time. Throughout history people have overcome all manner of difficulty and so called impossible feats, and you have read some of them in this book.

Dr. John Taylor, Professor of mathematics at Kings College in London, is a distinguished physicist and mathematician, (written about earlier) and the author of a key introduction to quantum mechanics. Dr. Taylor encountered Uri Geller, a psychic who could bend spoons using his mind, and afterward he made up his mind to examine the supernatural, knowing that he would be ostracized by some of his peers in the scientific community. The skeptics (and there are many) opposed to the paranormal, tend to be irrational in their opposition to those scientists they oppose.

Dr. Taylor explored the many phenomena of the paranormal. He delved into psychic healing, clairvoyance, telepathy, precognition, psycho kinesis, and unsolved problems. Before I go any further, can you explain the unsolved phenomena of the 'Bermuda triangle?' There are many theories about the triangle and unfortunately many missing aircraft and boats in that area. How about the Philadelphia experiment? In October of 1943, scientists actually made the U.S.S. Eldridge, a US Naval ship disappear from Philadelphia, Pennsylvania, reappearing in Norfolk, Virginia, three hundred miles away. This story is documented in the Naval Archives, was recently documented in a television special, and an authoritative book is written about it involving Einstein. Can you explain that? How about the Dragons Triangle 100km south of Tokyo or UFO's? Keep an open mind and do some research.

Dr. Taylor stated, "There is a whole range of phenomena that some of us may experience at one time or another, and which runs counter to common sense." Dr. Taylor goes on to state, "All of these powers presently involve unknown powers of human beings beyond the more limited five senses to which we are so accustomed." (In 1977, 1,188 professors at major universities took a poll. Sixteen percent agreed that ESP was real. Forty nine percent believed it was possible. The American Menninger Foundation studies ESP, and realizes we have to put more research into ESP to stay ahead of Russian research. Russian defectors have reported that the Russians are looking for military uses for ESP and there is an alarm in U.S. military circles that the Russians will use "thought control" against us. In 1977, Robert Toth, writer for the Los Angeles Times, was arrested by the KGB and charged with stealing "state secrets" about parapsychology.)

Dr. Taylor excitedly reported what happened on November 23, 1973. "It all started for me on the evening of Friday, November 23, 1973. I had been invited by the BBC to act as scientific hatchet man on Uri Geller during his appearance on David Dimbleby's "Talk In." This was transmitted live, and since it was being screened just after the "Miss World" competition, it had many millions of viewers. I myself felt keyed up, both because of the live transmission (where mistakes can't be remedied) and also because of Gellar's supposed powers. I was almost sure he would not be able to do what he claimed—bend spoons or forks, start watches and guess pictures sealed in envelopes. Yet there was a small doubt in my mind. What if he could do these things?"

"On being introduced to Geller, I found him to be an engaging and friendly young man, without a hint of the deviousness supposedly associated with him. Almost immediately after the program started a BBC assistant brought in a tray of assorted pieces of cutlery. Geller selected four big, solid forks and handed one to each of us on the program, (myself, Dimbleby, and Lyall Watson, the biologist and author), keeping one for himself. We sat and held them for a minute or so until suddenly Geller claimed that Watson's fork was bending. Indeed it was, and I watched in utter amazement as Geller gently stroked the neck of the fork to cause it to break into two pieces. I could have sworn that the fork had not been forcefully bent back and forth during the program and I am certain that the many viewers at their television sets would have supported me in this."

"Geller then demonstrated his telepathic powers by attempting to reproduce the picture of a yacht (in silhouette) which had been drawn before the program by a young BBC employee and sealed in an envelope. Again I had not expected much success, but Geller was absolutely accurate. I was once more astonished by this prowess: it just could not happen."

"The final item had to do with starting or stopping watches. A number of broken watches had been gathered and Geller held his clenched fists over them, willing them to start again. As amazingly as before, he proceeded to make one of them start, and even more amazingly caused the second hand of another to become buckled under the watch glass."

"There was an enormous uproar in the studio as the "Talk-In" program ended. The invited audience milled about, talking at the top of their voices about what they had seen demonstrated by Geller; some saying how it was impossible (the complete skeptics) and others that there were even more exciting things that could be achieved by such powers (the believers)."

"What was more interesting for me was the response of the viewing audience. The BBC telephone lines were completely swamped by callers saying that they had experienced in their own homes the various phenomena Geller had demonstrated. Knives, forks, spoons and even pots and pans had apparently become bent, in some cases without any direct contact with them. Watches (and even electric clocks), hitherto unusable, had started on command. Many callers had guessed the sealed picture of the yacht."

"The scientific framework with which I viewed the world up until then was crumbling about my ears." (If you will go to your local library and ask for John Spencer's book, *The Paranormal,* you will see a picture of Uri Geller gazing at a spoon he has just bent. You will even find that the famous Marie Curie was a believer in the Paranormal).

I must tell you, as I finished quoting Dr. Taylor's above statements, I sat in my chair slightly drained. Just reading the words are a drain, because the paranormal is so powerful. And even though I am a confirmed believer in mind over matter and overcoming the impossible, it still seems like a dream world at times. But I have had my own experiences, so I can believe.

What do you think about intuition? If you are a woman your intuition is usually better than a mans, particularly when it comes to judging people on a first impression basis. I have an old dear friend, who is a great judge of character, and she was right on the money when her husband praised a young man they had hired and eventually rose in the ranks of the company. She constantly warned her husband, who was the president, that this particular man was deceitful and that they should not allow him executive status. She could just feel it. Her husband refused to believe her and sang the praises of this man and began to treat him like a son. Her husband suffered a heart attack and this man came into the hospital to visit. Over time when the husband was recovering he convinced the husband to change the stock in the company to him so that the company could continue if the president should pass away. Again she warned her husband not to take such drastic measures, but the husband ignored her warnings and even rebuked her for her mistrust. Well, why should I tell you the rest of the story, for you know the outcome. That's right; the man took over the company. When the husband came back to work his personal items were in cardboard boxes, and he was escorted out of the building, which he had occupied for over thirty years. This man even had the unmitigated gall to try to convince my friend to stay with the company after taking over. The crowning blow was that this man went to church every single day, and made the comment to my friend while trying to convince her to stay, "We don't need that old man, but you can stay." If only we would listen to women when they use their intuitive instincts.

In March of 1990, I was working around the Philadelphia airport industrial section. At that time I was selling industrial abrasives and I remember it as though it was yesterday. I was about to call on the La France Company, which makes the metal plaques that go on the sides and front of trucks like Mack or Peterbuilt, but something told me to stop and go to dad's house and check on him. Dad was in a wheelchair and it broke my heart to see my once strong father like that. I just could not ignore the strong voice inside me, and so I backed out of the parking lot and drove thirty miles to dad's house. When I opened the door with my key I called out to dad but he didn't respond. I checked the bedroom and finally walked into the kitchen, and there was dad lying on the floor bleeding with a gash in his head for who knows how long. I tenderly picked him up and kidded him while cleaning him up and bandaging him up. To this day I know how important it is to listen to your instinct, for if I hadn't that day dad would have bled to death and I would have never forgiven myself if I hadn't listened to that little voice.

Do you believe in angels? Well even though this book is written for you I have the power of the computer keys, so I am going to write something that has been on my mind for a long time. I believe that intuition mostly comes from angels. After all if you read the bible there are many references to angels, as a matter of fact hundreds of references, i.e. Genesis 16:7, Genesis 28:12, Exodus 33:2, Psalm 34:7, Psalm 34:7, Job 33:23-24, Daniel 6:22, to Revelation 5:2. Still don't believe in angels? Perhaps you need to read a few books written by retired minister and best selling author, Charlie Shield, who is an expert on the subject.

On April 2, 1993, I took my ninety-five year old father to the hospital, for what I just knew was the last time I would see him alive. I felt it. He had been rushed to the hospital twice before and was written off by the doctors and nurses, but he recovered, amazing everyone. But this time I knew it and I believe he knew it was his last day alive. Dad was a fighter, and as he lay on that hospital bed he grabbed the sheets and tried to pull them away. I remember the fighting look on his face, as though to say, "This is the end Ken, but I will still fight to stay alive."

The next morning I drove to Cape May Villas, New Jersey, where Dad owned a summer home, as I had to clear the house out and sell everything in a garage sale to help pay his bills. At the end of the day, there were a few items left, and one in particular was an unplugged electric coo-coo clock. I picked it up and noticed the time was 9:30. I really didn't think anything about it until I arrived home and my wife told me my brother called to tell me Dad had passed away. So I picked up the phone and called my brother. Without even thinking, I asked him when Dad had died. His answer floored me: it was 9:30.

Dr. Taylor also talks about psycho kinesis (PK), whereby all sorts of objects are moved by will. The American parapsychologist, Pamela Painter de Maigret, visited Alla Vinogradova, a Russian while a television studio in Moscow filmed the following. "Alla appeared to be under considerable tension despite her great warmth. As the filming began she rubbed her hands together, and then reached toward a round aluminum cigar tube, which lay near one edge of the table. She stopped her hand about six inches from it. Staring at it, she raised and lowered her hand quickly several times, never coming closer than five or six inches from the tube. Then with a look of immense strain and concentration she turned the palm of her hand forward and appeared to 'push' at the cylinder. It rocked back and forth several times, and then slowly began to roll across the plastic tabletop away from her hand. When the cylinder neared the outer edge Alla quickly reached over the tube and put her hand on the far side of it. It stopped suddenly six or eight inches from her hand, rocked a few times and then started to roll in the opposite direction. Alla's hand was always at least half a foot away from both the table and the cylinder."

A good friend of mine, Patty Jolliff, from Slater, Missouri, told me that her father was suffering from cancer. Early one morning in January, of 1996, she woke up and looked at the clock. Patty said she could not get back to sleep, and while she was sitting at the kitchen table drinking coffee, she felt hands resting on her shoulders comforting her. The hospice called to tell her of her father's death, which occurred at the exact time she woke up.

Patty also told me about a close family friend, Jerry Tinkam. A picture of Jerry hung on the picture galley with other friends and family. Months after Jerry passed away; no one in the family could stand to see the picture hanging on the wall, so Patty's father took the picture down and put it in a lock box in the garage. It wasn't a week later when the picture reappeared on the wall. No one admitted to hanging the picture back on the wall. Patty's father would take the picture down and hide it again, and every time the picture reappeared on the wall. He had the key to the lock box so no one else could have put it back on the wall except Patty's father. Finally in desperation he simply gave up and put the picture back on the wall. To this day, the family gets goose bumps thinking about that episode.

One of the amazing phenomenons is a Poltergeist ("noisy ghost"). This is where objects are thrown around or moved. No one else is in the room but the observer, yet the objects are tossed about or moved.

Reasonable people would think that a lawyer usually is credible. A lawyer named Adam, in the town of Rosenheim in Bavaria, in 1967, told a very strange story. He reported short circuits in the telephone wiring, and the lighting in the ceiling turned out of their fittings 90 degrees, partially falling out. Adam called in the experts, but they could not offer a credible explanation. The electric company replaced the lighting, but the lighting broke and even burst. Suddenly the lamps started swinging, and even the pictures on the wall turned themselves. The pictures even fell off the wall as though the wire holding them on the wall was cut. To add to the confusion drawers slid out of the desks, and finally, a three hundred-pound oak cupboard moved eighteen inches from its original spot. After two policemen using all their strength moved it back to its original position, it moved itself again. The final blow was that the phone company put in a single phone line after Adam complained of phone charges that were not his. The time clock with the number 0119 received eighty-five calls on October 17, yet Adam claimed the phone hardly rang that day.

The great Oscar winning actor, James Cagney, told of two startling experiences about death. Jimmy claimed to his two children that disinterest and boredom could kill even a very healthy person. A friend of his, was, "dying out of it." He was having difficulties in his personal life and it was affecting his weight, because of a loss of appetite. Jimmy asked his good friend, Actor, Ralph Bellamy, to go with him to the friend's house to try to cheer him up. They took him for a long drive and told jokes and small talk. Later on they took him for another drive to try to get him to become interested in life again but to no avail. He simply was, "Dying out his whole life scheme." "The doctors couldn't find anything wrong with him; he no longer maintained an interest, and so he just finished living."

Jimmy told of another incident regarding a friend who was suffering from several strokes and was in, "terminal condition." Jimmy went to see this friend in the hospital and started a conversation, talking about things that would be of interest to his friend. This man was suffering from terrible hiccups and perspiration was pouring off his body. But after a half-hour of chatting with Jimmy his right arm which usually was useless and lying across his chest was up behind his head and the perspiring had stopped. His speech was slurred, but at least he was receptive and responding after lying in the hospital bed almost comatose. Not many days later he was up and around and he lived for four more years.

Jimmy was not only a great actor and positive thinker but he was a fantastic hoofer, (dancer). I am convinced that Jimmy knew the **three-word motto**, because he could have given up many times while working as a struggling actor. At the time he told this final story he was sixty-five years old and in great health, but 45 years earlier he had injured his arm and bursitis had set in. He was on his boat one day and the discomfort became unbearable, causing terrible pain all the way up to his head. The pain was so excruciating that he was rocking back and forth. Finally he said to himself, "The hell with it," and got up and started swinging his arm twenty-five times one way and twenty-five times another. The pain was gone and he told his brothers, who were doctors, about it and they were shocked. They told him he was taking a terrible chance by doing it, but the pain was gone and he never suffered from bursitis again. I can validate that story, because I had the same problem after banging my elbow. My wife insisted I visit a specialist and I took all sorts of tests. The conclusion was that my elbow had to be operated on to open the bursa sac. I remember looking at the doctor and telling him that I would simply think it away while using proper nutrients. He gave me a disgusted look and wished me luck. In fifteen days after lightly exercising the arm and taking B-Complex, vitamin A, E, and alfalfa the pain was almost gone. In forty-five days the pain was completely gone, saving me much more pain from the operation as well as a hefty sum of money.

Near Chicago, Illinois, drivers have picked up a hitchhiker named Resurrection Mary. Mary stands at the side of the road wearing a turn of the century white dress with her thumb out. After being picked up she asks the driver to drive her to Resurrection Cemetery. When they get there Mary jumps out and starts running into the cemetery, slowly disappearing after she gets several yards. At the Willow brook Ballroom dance club (where Mary used to dance) near Justice, Illinois, outside of Chicago, she has appeared to the dancers on occasion. The people who have witnessed this phenomenon are credible and reliable, and as a matter of fact a television special reported about Mary.

Frank Spaeth compiled and edited stories from Fate Magazine and wrote a storybook titled *Phantom Army of the Civil War and Other Southern Ghost Stories.* It is a collection of first-hand encounters with ghosts and haunted mansions of the South, with many credible stories, which pertain to soldiers who fought in that terrible war. Another poltergeist historian is Mark Nesbit, who has been researching ghosts for twenty years, and has several interesting accounts from none other than the historic Civil War battle fought at Gettysburg, Pennsylvania. The battle took place on July 1-3 in 1863 with 51,116 casualties, and park rangers today tell tales of visitors to the park who swear they have seen Civil War Soldiers. In Gettysburg College not too long ago, two college administrators were finished work and took the elevator to the first floor to leave the building. They pushed the button for the first floor, but the elevator took them to the basement. When the door opened they viewed a scene too unbelievable to contemplate. Right before their stunned eyes were Civil War soldiers lying on gurneys, screaming while being operated on by doctors. One doctor beckoned to them to come in to the room to assist in removing the limbs of the soldiers lying on the tables. These two women were frightened out of their wits and pounded on the elevator buttons to be able to get away. Finally the door closed and they were able to get to the first floor and breathlessly report what they had witnessed. When the campus guards went to the basement on the same elevator everything was normal, including the janitor vacuuming the floor.

Stevens Hall on Gettysburg College campus was built between 1865 and 1868, and has its own story. It was originally a preparatory school and the headmistress was a martinet. Several of the girl students hid a little boy in their room who the headmistress was mentally abusing. One night she knocked on their door to see if the little boy was in the room. The girls hid the boy on the outside window ledge and then let the headmistress in the room. After searching she made the girls come downstairs while she grilled them for another hour in front of the fireplace while the poor little boy stood freezing on the ledge. When the frantic girls opened their window the boy had disappeared, so they ran downstairs and looked outside all around the window, finding no tracks or marks of any kind. Every once in a while students who occupy the room in recent times hear strange noises at the window and actually see a blue face of a little boy, or writing on the window that spells out, "help me."

Now I know skeptics will laugh at these stories and all ghost stories, including the Bermuda Triangle and the rest of this type of experience. So, until it happens to them they will be unbelievers like the people were before they experienced the unbelievable themselves. But the true Positive Thinker keeps an open mind, because even some Presidents of the United States became convinced that Lincoln haunts the Lincoln Room in the White House. As a matter of fact, several of the Presidents have reported their dogs barking furiously then running away from the room, yet no one was to be seen.

Many people have been hired by the police or relatives to find missing persons, and several years ago I became friendly with a paralegal from New Jersey, who prefers to remain anonymous. She is a very intelligent lady who is not prone to getting excited. She told me about her missing niece and how she was found. Being very close to her niece, she had heard of a lady on the West Coast who finds missing persons through what is called distant viewing. She decided to call the lady, and when the lady answered the phone, she immediately said, "You are looking for your niece." After the initial shock, my friend admitted that she was. The lady told her that she should have the police look on a certain level of a mountain where the niece and her boyfriend had been climbing. But, my friend never mentioned the mountain climbing. It turned out the niece was found buried on that level, on that mountain, and the clues led to the arrest of the boyfriend.

An expert, named Gerard Croiset, has helped discover many missing people. He discovered the body of Lesley Ann Downey, who was missing in what was known as the famous "Moors murder case." After being given all the clues by the police, he announced the child was dead and buried in a certain area near water. The police charged two people with Lesley's death, as well as two boys they had also murdered. During Gerard's ride with the police, he took them to several places the abductors had taken the girl, which was later proved in the trial. Was it lucky guessing? Why did he solve the case in an hour when the police had been investigating for a year? Dr. Taylor claims that the descriptions of distant scenes by the 'Expert,' "could be more fantasy than the result of real paranormal powers." Yet, the fact remains there are hundreds of people with distant viewing powers who have helped the police solve non-solvable crimes.

And finally Dr. Taylor stated, "There is presently a great deal of interest in the way the control of the mind over bodily health can be increased. Groups of terminal cancer patients are being taught meditation practices in an attempt to increase resistance to the spread of their disease. There are biofeedback methods to help the patient learn to reduce his or her levels of tension, as we mentioned earlier. These techniques seem of value, especially in the reduction of pain, though have not yet been fully assessed."

Remember now, the aforementioned information was stated in 1980, over 20 years ago. Medicine has taken quantum steps in not only cures with medicine but in the field of mind over matter in conjunction with medicine. Doctors are now becoming believers, where they were once skeptical.

Here is another controversial subject that baffles many in the scientific community: ESP. Dr. Louisa E. Rhine, wife of Dr. Joseph B. Rhine (Dr. Rhine was endorsed by the president of the American Institute for Mathematical Statistics in 1937 and as a pioneer in parapsychology organized Parapsychology Laboratory) has studied many spontaneous experiences at the Institute for Parapsychology in Durham, North Carolina. She has one of the most extensive collections of these cases—over 12,000 of them—sent in by interested laymen. Dr. Joseph Rhine stated, "Several years ago, I lived in Virginia. One evening after dark, my wife fell down a long flight of stairs, breaking her left arm above the wrist. The next morning my daughter, living in Colorado, complained to her husband that her left arm pained her awfully and that she could see nothing but mother. I wrote them about the accident. My daughter came immediately to Virginia to care for her mother. She stayed just a month. I took her to the train, which left at 10:45 A.M. She was now on her way back to Colorado. That evening while doing chores around sundown, a wasp stung me in the right eyelid."

"The next morning my eye was swollen entirely shut and was very painful. As soon as my daughter arrived home, she reported as follows: "Dear Mamma, I had a nice trip home and found the folks all well. But what is the matter with Daddy's eye? My right eye is paining me so I can hardly stand it, and I see nothing but Daddy. I don't think he is blinded, but his eye is swollen shut. Write me at once."

As an exponent of the Martial Arts, and certified Black Belt, I can attest to the amazing and superhuman feats performed by the top practitioners. If you were to ask a top martial artist what his or her most important weapon is, the answer will be on the lines of a state of mind rather than a physical secret fighting move. The mental component of the martial arts is known as the *zanshin* (zon-SHEEN). It is a state of calmness and assuredness and is displayed in the face of danger or combat. The martial artist faces his opponent, is in a relaxed state, and concentrates on his energy center, the *hara* in the center of his body. The first opponent to lose his concentration winds up losing. This *zanshin* is valuable in everyday life. When you are confronted by a roadblock or tense situation, simply relax your muscles and breath deeply, close your eyes for a second while you do this then open your eyes, stare straight ahead and say to yourself, "I can, I will."

I own a rare copy of *What is Karate,* written in 1963, by the Master, Masutatsu Oyama. On the twelfth page of this profound book is a picture of Oyama standing under a waterfall, (that is close to forty feet high), cascading onto his naked shoulders, while deep in concentration. He does not feel the sharp needle stings from the falling water. Oyama stated, "The essence of Karate, therefore, is nothing else than a training of mind over body."

On pages 128 and 129 it shows a color photo of Oyama, knocking off the horn of a charging bull with his bare hand, using a chopping motion with the side of the palm known as the 'Shuto.' I personally have witnessed the top experts performing unbelievable feats, including snatching an arrow out of the air shot at their heart from twenty five-yards away.

Oyama said, "Is there a limit to man's power? Why can a man's fist break a stone, which can not be broken with an iron hammer? Strength itself is not the answer."

"One day I visited Shohkakuji Temple in Nagasaki. The old priest of this temple is the one who had learned the art of Chinese *Hsing-i* (Karate) and *Ch'an* (Zen). This old priest showed me a part of his training practices during my visit. What I saw was a scene almost too dreadful to behold. He put some oil around his hand and thrust it with a yell, into boiling water in a big pot hung over the hearth."

"As I was watching it in surprise, he slowly counted from one to ten and pulled his hand out of the boiling water quickly. "Look at my hand." He showed me his hand with a smile; not only was it not scalded but had gone through no change whatsoever. I could never forget the words he mentioned," "You can do anything if you will. Act only with self-confidence."

Some people say you have to be born with the right disposition, or you have to have rich parents or relatives, yet psychoanalysts and evangelists contend you can achieve such a state through faith and time, with work mixed in towards achieving that state of mind.

In the book of Daniel, chapter three, he writes about Shadrach, Meshach, and Abednego. They were Israelites who had refused to worship the ninety-foot tall golden image King Nebuchadnezzar had built on the Plain of Dura. They knew the penalty was to be thrown into a blazing furnace. The king was furious and ordered the furnace heated seven times hotter than usual, whereby the heat killed the soldiers that threw the three men into the furnace. We all know the rest of the story. The three men walked out of the furnace without so much as one hair of their heads scorched, nor was there the smell of smoke on their clothes and Nebuchadnezzar swore he saw four men walking in the furnace. Their complete self-confidence and faith in God saved them, and we all know the story of Daniel in the lion's den.

Now this and the other stories have been authenticated, but it is up to you to believe in mind over matter and the paranormal. Do a little research. It will be fun, and you will be pleasantly surprised at what you might find. Oh by the way, have you been highlighting?

"Canst thou not minister to a mind diseased.... Raze out the written troubles of the brain? Therein the patient must minister to himself"
— Shakespeare

Blind Milton said, "The mind is in its own place, and in itself can make a heaven of hell or a hell of heaven."

"Every day give yourself a good mental shampoo."
—Sarah Jordan, M.D.

"Some things have to be believed to be seen."
— Ralph Hodgson-

"When you are at peace with yourself any place is home."
— Author Unknown

MAIN THOUGHTS AND CHALLENGES

1. Go back to the beginning of this chapter and review your highlighted sentences.

2. Place the highlighted page numbers on this page.

3. Put down the most important highlighted sentence and why it is important to you.

4. Do you believe in mind over matter? Yes or no

5. If you do not believe then you need to do some research on your own. After researching write the results for this chapter.

Chapter 15

THE POSITIVE THINKER PUTS IT ALL TOGETHER

"You cannot depend on your eyes when your imagination is out of focus."

—Mark Twain

What do you want from this book? And, as a matter of fact, what do you want from any self-help book? First off you want to be inspired. You need to learn new things, which are valuable to you and can be used in your daily life. You want the book to keep your interest. The book should give you motivation to want to do better, giving you direction and suggestions for accomplishing your goals and aspirations. It should give reliable information, and most of all it should make you want to change for the better. Of all the palpable suggestions and direction in this book, you have to decide which ones are the most important in using your God given talents, working hand in hand with goals and the profound **three-word motto** of all Positive Thinkers. Changing your self-image is an intelligent start if you think negatively too often. Maybe it is a quote, or story, or an example that will change your thinking, as is the case with many Positive Thinkers who were once negative thinkers. Hopefully you have highlighted messages that are meaningful to you. If not then you only have yourself to blame for not following advice, not from just me but the winners and great thinkers of the world. I humbly believe that I am simply their messenger. This book will work for those who will keep an open mind and memorize the **three-word motto**.

If you look around, you will see many similar stories in everyday life situations as well. There are many stories of people and business leaders who have faced defeat, bankruptcy, scandal, malicious gossip, drug and alcohol addiction, sickness and many other maladies. They have fought back and won. They have faith in themselves, and in many cases a higher power. They refuse to stay down for the count, because they know the **three-word motto** to achieving their goals, winning in life and true happiness. When you set your mind to accomplish something don't ever quit until you have accomplished it. If you face an obstacle, figure a way around, under, over, or through, and keep focused on the **three-word motto** until you have won.

Know that you can accomplish anything you set your mind to, as long as you know your physical limitations. Once you do, then you can learn to use your real talents. For example: David Young, a nuclear physicist, stated, "When I was a small boy I lived on a farm here in California. I loved the outdoors, and spent every minute that I could exploring the wonders of nature in the hills that surrounded our valley."

"One afternoon I was walking along the top of a high ridge and I spotted a hawk in a tall tree that leaned away out to overlook our fertile acres. I saw a nest in that tree, and I felt sure that there must be some eggs in that nest. I wanted those eggs so badly, but I knew it was impossible to reach that nest without breaking the tree limb and falling down the mountainside.

"So I closed my eyes and prayed. I prayed for God to let me fly up to that nest just like the hawk so I could get those eggs. And as I prayed I thought that I ought to show God I had some faith too, so I flapped my arms up and down as fast as I could just like wings. I was so sure that God would hear my prayer and answer it, but of course, nothing ever happened.

"And then the hawk flew into the air so gracefully from the nest. I was so envious. But as it flew away, a feeling of understanding came over me, young as I was, that God could not interrupt or change the orderliness of His creation so that little boys could fly."

"From then on I think I knew deep down inside me that to be happy, one had to follow his inner guidance, so that he might do that which God had given him the talent to do. And that he should also accept the limitations that had been placed on him as exactly that—limitations—and nothing more. Only then could a person realize his true potential, do great things, and fulfill his own individual destiny!"

St. Francis of Assisi is credited with the following popular verse. **I'll**

"God grant me the serenity to accept
The things I cannot change,
Courage to change the things I can,
And wisdom to know the difference."

Never The distinguished dean of American psychologists, Professor William James of Harvard, has been written about in many of the previous pages of this book. He wrote six sentences that have had a profound, exciting effect on many lives. Professor James wrote, "In almost any subject, your passion for the subject will save you. If you care enough for a result, you will most certainly attain it. **Quit** If you wish to be good, you will be good. If you wish to be rich, you will be rich. If you wish to be learned, you will be learned. Only then you must really wish these things and wish them with exclusiveness and not wish one hundred incompatible things just as strongly."

By getting this book into your hands and giving you hope I will be happy. And if that is the only good thing that happens to me then that is all right too. I have my self-respect and faith in my abilities and faith that God will take care of me. I will continue to face obstacles and I will overcome them. I refuse to shy away from them, because I accept obstacles. Do I encourage them? Not on your life! That would be foolhardy. But I know they are a part of life, and I know that everyone faces problems. The **three-word motto** has been burned into my being. I know that things could get worse. I even find that hard to believe, but I am prepared for worse than I have faced in my life up to this point. And finally, I have burned into my soul, my whole being the fact that: <u>It's when things seem worst that we must not quit.</u> There is no room in my vocabulary for "no mas," (no more). Those are the two words Roberto Duran uttered from his corner in the eighth round in his championship fight with Sugar Ray Leonard in 1980, in Montreal, Canada, that I wrote about in an earlier chapter. He gave up; he quit. The interesting thing was that he was not beaten physically, but he was frustrated and humiliated. Keep "no mas" out of your vocabulary, and you will realize the joyful experience of winning in life. You will be known as a WINNER. And you will be happy! Finally, here are the three words that will change you into a constant winner. I know you are ready for them now. "Read the three bold words on page 235, and then write them boldly down here and highlight them.

Now you know the profound life changing **three-word motto** of all winners combined with goals, and frankly, after reading this profound book I am positive you will want to change for the better. E-mail me at mail@worldpositivethinkersclub.com and I will help you stay on target. And if you wish to join the **World Positive Thinkers Club** go to www.worldpositivethinkersclub.com.

Once you burn the **three-word motto** into your very soul you will be known as a winner, a Positive Thinker and a leader, and will never have been happier in your life. The following prose will give you a succinct definition of what you will be as a leader, if you have decided to change your self-image and become a **Positive Thinker**.

"A **leader** is a person just like you, who sometimes in his life had the vision to see the vast abundance in life, and developed the determination to collect his God-given fortune in the richest nation in the world. When this time came in his life he must have had a personality around him whom he admired. This personality, this person, he called a leader, so he followed him and learned the ways of success. He found that a leader believes in and follows the Golden Rule: "Do unto others as you would have them do to you. He saw the leader give his all, all of his time, all of his knowledge, all of his strength, all of his honest sincere devotion to his task. He saw that the leader was an unselfish person. He saw him laugh with tears and cry with tears when victory and defeat came his way. He knew his leader had humility. He learned that this person, this leader, was a disciple of the principles he believed in, and used them as guidelines in his everyday work. This positive attitude, this dedication to following a track, the ideas and execution of ideas, this combination of fundamentals, this personality, this man who knows where he is going, knows how to get there, and knows how to take men with him, *this person is a leader.*" —Author unknown

And the leader knows the **three-word motto**! "I'll NEVER QUIT." Finally, on the following page of this book I leave you with a poem I have memorized and repeat to myself almost daily. You have come this far, which means you plan to be a daily Positive Thinker. I strongly suggest you consider memorizing the poem or at least keeping it handy.

When things go wrong, as they sometimes will,
When the road you're trudging seems all-uphill,
When the funds are low and the debts are high,
And you want to smile, but you have to sigh,
When care is pressing you down a bit—
Rest if you must, but don't you quit.

Life is queer with its twists and turns,
As every one of us sometimes learns,
And many a fellow turns about
When he might have won had he stuck it out.
Don't give up though the pace seems slow—
You may succeed with another blow.

Often the goal is nearer than
It seems to a faint and faltering man;
Often the struggler has given up
When he might have captured the victor's cup;
And he learned too late when night came down,
How close he was to the golden crown.

Success is failure turned inside out—
The silver tint of the clouds of doubt,
And you never know how close you are,
It may be near when it seems afar,
So stick to the fight when you're hardest hit,
It's when things seem worst that you mustn't quit.

MAIN THOUGHTS AND CHALLENGES

On the following pages write all your goals. Break them down by week, month and main goal. If you desire to put down yearly goals as well as a five-year goal that is even better. The most important goal is your main goal in life and you must carefully think out a time frame for it. That goal along with the three- word motto must be on your 3 X 5 cards that you will concentrate on at least three times a day. Remember to procure a separate calendar on which to mark your goals.

This possibly is a new way of life for you and so you must allow three weeks for all this to sink in and take hold of you. If you miss reading your goal every day or weekly goals you must start over until you get in the habit of attaining the small things. No, it will not be automatic at first for most people as change can be harder for some than others. But you must know that all skills and any program be it learning yoga or the martial arts or a trade take learning and practice. Just remember that if you follow the chapter reviews and perform them religiously, that coupled with your imbedding the **three-word motto** into your very soul you will meet your goals and aspirations. You will in fact enjoy all or most of the benefits written on the back cover of this book.

You will have to make some sacrifices, like giving up some of your television time. If you aren't willing to do that then you need to reevaluate your priorities.

Do I wish you to face the trials and tribulations I have faced in my life, some of which are described in the epilog? Not on your life, because I would not wish that on my worst enemy. Just know that I had no idea that I would be facing these horrible experiences, but it was God's will that I face my trials and tribulations as my life unfolded. That has made me stronger and convinced me that I am certainly qualified to write this book and give you valuable life changing advice.

If I were to leave this earth tomorrow, I would still make sure that this important book became your valuable property. My goal has been to get this book in your hands in the year 2005, and that is going to happen ten years from the time I started writing it. You can be assured that I will reach that very, very important goal.

Epilogue

When I started writing this book in 1995, I had no idea that I would go through the heartbreaking experiences I have encountered. I have faced financial catastrophe; loss of family; living in a homeless center after being thrown out on the street with no notice; being betrayed by friends; threatened with death; loss of drivers license and automobile, and walking or riding up steep hills on a bike on major highways while inhaling fumes and dirt, and blinding rain stinging my eyes. And I had to face the further humiliation of being yelled at by passing vehicles and purposely run off the road. I've even had people throw things at me, like a cup of cold lemonade, trash or pennies. I have walked miles to the store or library in the bitter cold or searing heat, while being attacked by dogs and kids shooting stones at me with a slingshot. And recently, I trusted a man to join in partnership with him in his building business, only to find out later he is on disability, and is an alcoholic and pathological liar. And so by trusting him and moving to another state I have worked only six days out of ninety, thereby leaving me just enough money for mostly peanut butter and jelly sandwiches (without the peanut butter and jelly) and rent. He says he will be there to pick me up for a job, but never shows up or he arrives three hours later in a pick up truck or station wagon, both littered with trash on the floor. The first time I got in the passenger seat I gagged, not just from the garbage, but from his body odor as well. The excuses he gives are mind boggling, and I was reduced to picking up coins on the shoulders of the roads to get something to eat.

Through it all I have felt mental and physical pain, but my attitude has been positive and my resolve has been strong, because I knew that I could not write a book of this genre and quit when the going became tough. That would make me a hypocrite, and I could not bear to give up and quit in the game of life, especially for the sake of my oldest son. And most of all, I have believed with all my heart that this book belongs in your hands, so I have refused to quit. Just as the best selling book, *Think and Grow Rich* changed millions of lives and was the force in putting more millionaires on the IRS record books, this book has been a labor of desire to help you to become a true winner; help you to finally learn how to meet goals and know how to be truly happy.

Every once in a while someone comes along like the former running back for the New York Giants and broadcaster, Frank Gifford, who admits he never has goals. Frank says, "I just chugged along and did the very best I could with every opportunity I had. And when I came to a crossroads, I took what I thought was the best I could and never looked back, and bemoaned not having done this or having done that." Well, that is OK for tremendously gifted people like Frank Gifford, but ninety-nine percent of the gifted athletes and winners will tell you that no matter how gifted they were they still set goals. And I will add that Frank never quit once he set his mind to something. No winner ever quits. So in reality Frank had goals. He made up his mind to accomplish the task at hand. He just didn't think he had goals. When the rubber meets the road he will admit that he knows the **three-word motto**.

I truly believe with all my heart that it has been my destiny to suffer what I have gone through, so that I could speak with authority on how to face adversity and practice the **three-word motto**. My pains have been nothing compared to the pain and suffering winners like Lance Armstrong, and Joni Eareckson Tada, and Shirley Cheng have overcome.

It is up to you now to make a decision to move on to greatness and become a dedicated Positive Thinker, and be happy constantly. Dr. Norman Vincent Peale said, "Become a possibilitarian. No matter how dark things seem to be or actually are, raise your sights and see possibilities – always see them, for they are always there."

Make a decision to become a Positive Thinker today and vow to get the negativity and negative thinkers away from you. Forget the past. Read the lines you have highlighted in this book weekly, and remember one thing. There will be skeptics who will say this will never work, but they say that about other books and programs too. There is no one book or program that satisfies or works for everyone. If that was not true then there would be no atheists, because they would take the bible seriously. Make up your mind to change your self-image, and never, never, never quit once you make up your mind as to what you want. That is the difference between the people who set goals and those who achieve them. If you don't achieve the goal in a set period of time you must reset it. You don't simply say, "Well all these programs don't work, because I have tried them." You did not try them, you simply set a goal and if you did not achieve it on the first or second or third or fourth try you gave up. No, that will never work. Imbed the **three-word motto** into your very soul and you will succeed.

It is convenient to take the easy road and simply say, "Well that will work for some people, but not me." Thomas Edison, the greatest inventor the world has ever known, was a man who was not afraid of hard work and long hours. Edison was considered one of the greatest people to put on a thinking cap. He once said, **"There is no expedient to which a man will go to avoid the labor of thinking."** Don't let that happen to you. Think of the roses, not the thorns, and put the three special words on three 3 X 5 cards along with your goal. **"I'll never quit."**

Yogi Berra said it with humor when he said, "If you don't know where you are going you might not get there." So know where you are going and make Yogi happy. Combined with goals and the **three-word motto** you will not fail. **"I'll never quit."** You will succeed! You will succeed! You will succeed! One of the cards goes on your bathroom mirror; one goes on your refrigerator, and one at a place at work or car dash, where you will see it plainly. You must imbed those three words in your mind, heart and soul. "I'LL NEVER QUIT." You must give yourself three weeks to allow the principles of Positive Thinking and the **three-word motto** to sink in and take hold of you, like it took hold of the blind man, who walked across America in 1984. [I recommend that you highlight the previous sentence.]

On June 2, 1995, Captain Scott O'Grady was shot down over Bosnia. While the enemy forces were searching for him for six days, he never gave up his belief in God and that he would be rescued. He never quit while eating insects and grass. Captain O'Grady is a Positive Thinker, and he knows the **three-word motto**.

I suppose you are wondering what has happened to me. That could take up another entire book as a sequel, but I feel you are owed a happy ending to my quest for happiness. My so called partner picked up our commission for a job we completed, (which he underbid) and met me at the bus station with my half. That half paid for a bus ticket to Daytona Beach, Florida and enough for an inexpensive motel for a few days. As he left a feeling of great relief came over me, and I vowed to never look back as I boarded the bus that in my mind was delivering me to freedom.

During my time in Missouri I had linked up with a woman who assured me she could get me an investor so that I could go on tour to bring this book to you. But my intuition told me her many aggrandized statements were equivocal to say the least, because she turned out to be a complete phony. In her e-mails to me I noticed they were incongruous and she bunched words together, and yet she claimed to be a PR expert. But she did connect me to a man who was CEO of a company in Pennsylvania, whom I eventually e-mailed my book and he showed interest. After looking up his web site I was impressed, and on the phone he was enthusiastic about the book.

He is considered by some to be a marketing master and I truly believe his mother and father whispered in his ear at birth telling him to never quit. He is one of the most enthusiastic people I have ever met and could be considered ranked with the best of the best in the sales field. However, after working with him for eight months I have my own personal opinion.

And so I decided it was time to get back to my native Pennsylvania and my children and meet this man to see what he could do for me. But first I wanted to get to Florida and get away from it all, and so off I went with a determination to complete my quest for completing this book and rise from the ashes. I did not really feel I was in the ash pile, because the positive thinker in the game of life just feels that he is giving the rest of the world a head start.

I really had no idea where I was going to stay during my week in Florida, but as a positive thinker I was not the least bit concerned. On the bus I met a nice fellow from Chicago, who told me about an inexpensive motel on the beach, and so when I exited the bus in front of the motel I thanked my lucky stars and my guardian angel once more. What a surprise when I opened the door to the room, as it was a dingy old room with an odor. But I didn't care, because I was free of the terrible bonds, which held me for so many months and was positive I was headed to my karma.

That week was a mixture of relaxing and going over my thoughts. I walked the beautiful beach, and flushed out the flotsdam of my life while soaking in the refreshing rays of the sun, knowing I was definitely on my way to greatness. Of this I had no doubt, even though my funds were limited. As a positive thinker I had no doubts whatsoever as to my reaching my goal of getting this book into your hands, and so I walked the beach with a happiness in my soul. And my long treks to the library in the searing sun furthered my determination and strengthened my will. It was so hot that some days I had to carry an open umbrella to keep the scorching heat off me during my mile and half walk each way.

During my time in the library I checked the maps and sent e-mails to the CEO and others as well as checking the latest news. I also read history books, which had become my passion years ago: to increase my knowledge. But all the while I focused on my goal of getting back to my indigenous Pennsylvania, and linking up with a man I was sure could help me with my goal of getting this important book into your hands. There was just one problem. I had no money for bus fare and only enough for food, and so on my last day in Florida I realized that I was going to have to hitchhike in an era where hitchhikers are viewed with suspicion and almost contempt.

Some of you reading this book will probably think I must be crazy to hitchhike in an era where many hitchhikers can be mugged or can be the mugger; however I knew that I could take care of myself since I hold the Black Belt. But after walking 3 miles lugging my worldly possessions I realized I had to get a ride soon headed north. As luck would have it, and my angels constant guidance, a man in a pick-up I met in a grocery store took me the final 3 miles to route 95, where I was ready to stick out my thumb for the first time in over forty years. Did I think this was the lowest point in my life? Not at all! I looked at this as an exciting adventure and a golden opportunity to get this compelling book into your waiting hands. For you see, I have constantly visualized millions of eager readers perusing the many exciting pages of this one of a kind book. And so I stuck out my thumb with a renewed determination.

No, I did not get a ride immediately. As a matter of fact I stood out in that scorching sun for 5 hours before a retired Army sergeant picked me up in a recent model mini-van. We talked about his tenure in the Army and his family and when he reached his exit he took me an additional mile so I could get to a truck stop.

Now the fun began, because I had to figure out a way to get a ride north, and so I sat on an outside bench and started chatting with the drivers telling them of my quest. In no time one fellow gave me advice on how to link up with the truckers and what to say. However the truckers were at the stop for the night and it was time for me to find a place to stay. The fellow I met advised me to go to the television room with him and we could sleep there in the chairs. As I look back on that first night of many nights of sleeping in chairs looking over my shoulder, wondering if I was going to be tossed out to the pavement I have to chuckle. Here I was a man with no place to call home. That dear reader is known as a homeless person. But I felt no loss of dignity, because I knew it was my station in life in order to experience travails and want, to be able to write and talk with authority on the subject of rising from the ashes and meeting goals. I do know the **three-word motto**.

That whole next day was spent searching for a ride to head north and unfortunately no trucker could help me. And so I spent another night in the television room trying to get comfortable enough to sleep. But some of the truckers put the word out and sure enough the next day I linked up with a trucker who took me to another truck stop in North Carolina. From there I got another ride in a beat up van driven by a hippie type with a life in shambles. I have to laugh now as I write this, because here I was a struggling author riding in a beat up van littered with trash not knowing where I would sleep that night, but I was not the least bit concerned as I silently chuckled.

That night I slept in another truck stop television room where the chairs were falling apart. But my stay was short lived as I received a ride from a trucker headed to Virginia Beach, Virginia who needed a helper to help him unload. He then headed north and dropped me off at a major entrance to route 95 and after 3 hours of sticking my thumb out a pick up truck with two Viet Nam Vets picked me up. What a riot as I had to sit in the bed of the truck to the next truck stop. They left me off at another truck stop, gave me some money for food and wished me God speed. The next morning I hitchhiked again and a corporal in the Marines saw my sign I had written. It simply stated, "Vet headed North." He and his wife could not have been nicer and dropped me off at another truck stop a hundred miles further north. Again I slept in the truck stop and the next morning a trucker took me to a rest stop in Delaware just south of the Pennsylvania border. One more trucker heading to Philadelphia had pity on me and took me to Delaware Avenue just below Veterans Stadium where I walked into the Holiday Inn and tried to sleep. But it did not last long as security asked me to leave. Luckily it was only two hours before the busses were to start their rounds and so I stood at the bus stop until a bus picked me up and took me to the train station. Using part of my last five dollars I purchased a ticket to the last stop on the rail line and caught a bus to Jenkintown where my destiny awaited me.

I feel it is important and my obligation to thank those many truck drivers who were taking a chance by giving me rides, because in most cases it is against company policy. These brave men leave their families for days and sometimes weeks on end to make a decent living and were taking a chance for me. I will be forever indebted to them.

Ahhhhhh, now the fun begins! I exited the bus in Jenkintown and realized I got off too far away from where I was to meet my destiny, and so once more I lugged my sole possessions another half mile to an office building which I thought was the offices of IMC. But disappointment met me, because no one at the reception desk heard of IMC. One of the receptionists handed me a phone book and sure enough the company was listed in a building just one block away on the other side of the road. I am dying to tell you the rest of the story, but I need a break. So let's take a powder room break and I will be right back to tell you what excitement awaited me. Oh, and you too!

"I'll never quit."

Well here I am back again sitting in my bedroom excitedly typing away. Ahhhhhhh, a bedroom where I have a computer a desk and a bed. Those of you who were never deprived of those luxuries will never understand how much you miss that kind of luxury until you are homeless.

I met the CEO, and he is a dynamo of a man, who just celebrated his 75th birthday this past week. When I arrived at his office I was impressed with the enormity of it all, with plush carpeting and impressive desks and offices. It turned out I arrived one day early for my appointment, and no one had any idea that I had hitchhiked all the way from the East coast of Florida to meet my appointed time in destiny to complete an exciting journey. We chatted for a bit and then I met with some of his clients to listen to them talk about their projects. The next day I met the CEO officially and we chatted for an hour on what I could do to build the World Positive Thinkers Club and get my book published. No, I should say your book, for this book is also dedicated to you. After meeting with him I decided I wanted to stay and do what I could in the funding arena with him, as I have that knowledge and most of his clients come in for funding as well as marketing. He asked me if I wanted to stay and I told him that was a great idea, as I spied the couch in one of the three meeting rooms. That couch was my resting place over night for three weeks. I have to laugh when I think of the mornings I went into the men's room to shave and half bathe.

Now I have my own bedroom, and have a car of my own after five years of walking and taking public transportation. A very nice office is now mine to use with computer and the necessities needed to run a business, including a color printer and many brains to pick to put this book into the proper format to be printed.

I am funding director now at IMC and now have an exciting website for the World Positive Thinkers Club, with many prominent business and educational leaders gracing the board of advisors. The website will sell my book and offer many free services and discounted gifts. One of my favorite people and motivators, Glenn W. Turner, has asked me to write his business plan and come on board his management team. Glenn was a share cropper's son with a harelip; plowing fields barefoot behind a mule and dropped out of school in the eighth grade. This fantastic man borrowed $5,000.00 and turned it into $200,000,000.00 in five years; was railroaded to jail by greedy politicians and now is making a comeback at the exciting age of 69. And the heartbreaking part still rambles on, as many people Glenn helped to become millionaires turn their backs on him now, but Glenn knows the **three-word motto**.

After working with Glenn for a time I decided it was time to get back to this book so that I could meet my ten year goal of getting it into your hands, and so after shaking hands with Glenn I went on my way to meet the most important goal in my life.

I gave up ten years of my life and a handsome income to write this book with a compelling desire to help you, and I remember a 1958 movie titled 'The Matchmaker' with Shirley MacLaine, Shirley Booth, Anthony Perkins, Paul Ford and Robert Morse. At one point Shirley Booth says, as she stares intently into the camera lens, "Money, is like manure. Pardon the expression, but it is not worth a thing unless it is spread around to encourage young things to grow." I wrote this book to encourage you to grow.

It has been an exciting journey for me up to this point, and I am looking forward to meeting you in person at book signings. Think Positive now, smile often and burn into your very soul the three profound words that will change your life forever:

We can do anything we want to do if we stick to it long enough."
— Helen Keller

"Grant me the courage not to give up even though I think it is hopeless."
— Chester W. Nimitz, Admiral

"Never, never, never, quit."
— Winston Churchill

"They never told me I couldn't"
— Tom Dempsey

"Inside of a ring or out, ain't nothing wrong with going down.
It's staying down that's wrong."
— Mohammed Ali

"This I do believe above all, especially in times of greater discouragement, that I must believe—that I must believe in my fellow men, that I must believe in myself, that I must believe in God—if life is to have any meaning."
— Margaret Chase Smith

"A positive attitude may not solve all your problems,
but it will annoy enough people to make it worth your while."
— Author unknown

"He that endureth to the end shall be saved"
— Matthew 10:22

World Positive Thinkers Club
PO Box 951687 Lake Mary, Fl. 32795
E-mail mail@worldpositivethinkersclub.com

March 20, 2005
Mr. Bill Belichick-Head Coach
New England Patriots
Foxboro, Ma. 02035

Dear Bill,

Welcome to the World Positive Thinkers Club. This is a non-profit non-dues paying club consisting of Positive Thinkers like you. The club is made up of people from all walks of life, including the late President Ronald Reagan, the late Dr. Norman Vincent Peale, (Author of the best selling, *The Power of Positive Thinking*) Mrs. Norman Vincent Peale, Eric Fellman, (president of the Center for Positive Thinking), Reverend Bob Richards (two time Olympic pole vault champion), Bobby Shantz (1952 MVP & 8 time gold glove winner), Hank Aaron, the late Jackie Robinson, Joe Girard (Listed in the Guinness Book as the world's greatest salesman), Jim Palmer (Hall of Fame baseball pitcher), the late Margaret Gorman (the first Miss America), Anthony Rossi (retired as the worlds greatest vacuum cleaner salesman), Charlton Heston, Stan (The Man) Musial, the late Johnny Unitas, Tom Hopkins, John Madden, Zig Zigler, Cal Ripkin, Chuck Norris, Mike Ditka, Sally Starr, Thelma Gray (Advertising Woman of the Year & PR Hall of Fame member) the late Hank Stram, Dr. Joyce Brothers, Joni Earickson Tada (paraplegic artist) Dorothy Dent (Famous Artist) Lance Armstrong, Oprah Winfrey, Tom Brady, Payton and Eli Manning, Andy Reid, Paul Mckinney, Esq, and many other Positive Thinkers too numerous to list.

The purpose of the club is to recognize & honor Positive Thinkers who overcome difficulties, are an inspiration to others, are willing to help others become positive thinkers, and thus join the winner's circle. You will receive newsletters, and there will be get-togethers, as well as a junior division for high school seniors and a children's charity. The World Positive Thinkers Club Winners list will be printed in the front of my book titled, Why Do Positive Thinkers Win. The website is to be **www.worldpositivethinkersclub.com**

As president of the club I have the prerogative of installing new members, and so, I welcome you into the Club Winners Circle with hearty congratulations.

Positive regards,
Ken Bossone
President
Encls: Membership card
Certificate   Newsletter

Index

While reading this book insert page numbers and comments next to names that interest you.

— God Jesus Christ

Aaron, Hank 173
Abbott, Jim 69
Abednego 231
Adams, Edie 43
Adams, Samuel 43
Aeschylus 176
Ahab, King 212
Ainsworth, Lucy 213
Akers, Dr. 215
Alcott, Louisa May 153
Ali, Mohammed 70-71-172
Amelio, Gil 120-121
America, Miss 81
American Menninger Foundation 221
Andrews, Dana 149
Anthony, Susan B. 196
Arbanis, Fred 70
Arc, Joan of 182
Armstrong, Lance 85-98-99-198
Armstrong, Neil 60
Arnold, Hap, General 115
Ash, Mary Kay 192
Ashe, Arthur 34
Assisi, St Francis 235
Astair, Fred 152
Astroth, Joe 156
Aurelius, Marcus 46
Aughey 75
Autry, Gene 131
Bach, Richard 153
Bakken, Jill 112
Baldwin Locomotive 147
Ball, Lucille 153
Barber, Red 156
Barkley, Charles 105
Barrymore, Lionel 41
Bataan 62-202
Bates, William Dr. 94
Beethoven 69-153
Bell, Alexander G. 42
Bellamy, Ralph 226
Benoit, Joan 22
Bermuda Triangle 220-228
Berra, Yogi 58-102-115
Berry, Ray 70
Bismark 48
Black Sox 29
Boaz (Old Testament) 183
Bok, Edward 165
Bolitho, William 42
Bonds, Barry 173
Bordes, Lla 32
Boston Red Sox 125
Bowman, Dana S.F.C 140-141
Boyd, Belle 181
Bradley, Omar General 185
Brand, Dorothea 49
Briskin, Sam 41
Bristol, Claude 216
Brooks Herb 124

Brosius, Scott 122
Brothers, Joyce Dr. 189
Brown, Ed 83
Buchanan, James President 66
Burk, Lee 103
Burnes, Robert 71
Bush, Bob 44
Cabanatuan 202
Caesar, Julius 146
Cagney, James 63-226
Campbell, Milt 212
Carell, Alexis Dr. 201
Carlyle, Thomas 156
Carnagie, Dale 33-43-50
Carnegie, Andrew 23-37-46
Carson, Johnny 146
Caruso, Enrico 136
Cauthen, Steve 134
Chambers, R.E. General 42
Chan, Jackie 135
Chandler, Happy 91
Chaplin, Charlie 104
Chappell, Matthew Dr. 50-96
Charles, Ray 69
Cheng, Chi 175
Chrysler, Walter 23
Churchill, Winston 154-247
Cicero 129
Cleveland, Grover, President 180
Cliff, Montgomery 84
Cobb, Ty 77
Colette 104
Confucius 46-170
Cook, Robin 89
Court, Margaret 174
Cousins, Norman 103
Crawley, Mary 191
Croiset, Gerard 229
Crook, Wm. H., Colonel 89
Crosby, Fanny 69-195
Crow, Mary 192
Culleston, Bill, Lt 144.
Curtis, Tony 40
Custer, Elizabeth 183
Custer, George Armstrong, General 183
Cyrus 48
Daily, Dan 40
Dangerfield, Rodney 17
Daniel (Old Testament) 231
Darrow, Clarence 95
David, King 108
Davis, Betty 149
Davis, Jefferson 88
Dean, Bonnie St. John 72-73
Demetris, Roberta 129
Demosthenes 53
Dempsey, Jack 57-70-211
Dempsey, Tom 111-112-247
Devers, Gail 72
Dewey, James Dr. 65-94
Dickens, Charles 162
Dillard, James Dr. 205
Dimbley, David 221
Dirkson, Everett 207
Disney, Walt 127
Dixie 39-181
Dobson, James, Dr. 193
Donlan, Mike 31
Doubleday, Abner General 29
Douglass, Kirk 68
Downey, Lesley Ann 229
Dragons Triangle 220

Duell, Charles 171-176
Duran, Roberto 235
Durante, Jimmy 71-136
Earhart, Amelia 183-184
Eddy, Mary Baker 197-204
Edison, Thomas 42-69-79-153
Edmonds, Emma E. 181
Einstein 49-59-153-169
Eisenhower, Dwight D. President 70-211
Elam, Jason 112
Eldridge, U.S.S. 220
Elija 212
Eliot, T.S. 42
Elisha 212
Eller, Carl 109
Elway, John 118
Emerson, Ralph Waldo 56-126
Epictetus 96
Escalante, Jamie 170
Esther (Old Testament) 182
Evaluations, federal Employee 148
Evans, Dale 85
Everett, Chris 174
Facinda, John 51
Feller, Bob 174
Feshbeck, Seymore Ph.D 109
Fillmore, Millard President 66
Fisher, Mel 48
Fitzgerald, F. Scott 17-152
Flemming, Peggy 175
Flowers, Vonetta 112-113
Flutie, Doug 119
Forbes, B.C. 24-154
Ford Henry 21-70-138
Ford, Whitey 156
Forston, Ben 59
Fosdick, Harry Emerson 102
Fossey, Dian 188
Foster, Jay 92
Franklin, Benjamin 43-51-198
Frost, Robert 26
Ft. Union Military Academy 39
Gabor, Zaa Zaa 80
Garcia (Message to) 148
Garfield, James President 66
Gates, Bill 44-99
Gates, Elmer Ph.D. 102
Gatty, Harold 35-188
Gehrig, Lou 184
Geller, Uri 221
George III, King 43
Gettysburg College 227
Ghandi, Mahatma 219
Ghost Soldiers 203
Gibson, Bob 173
Gifford, Frank 239-240
Gilkey 50
Ginsberg, Ruth 188
Girard, Joe 123-124
Gisolo, Margaret 33
Gladstone, William 159
Glass, Bill 109
Golde 193
Goliath 108
Gomez, Lefty 91
Gonne, Maude 113
Gonzalex, Louis 122
Gorman, Margaret 81
Graham, Billy 105
Grant, Ulysses S., President 183-199
Greenhow, Rose O'Neal 181
Griffey, Ken Jr. 92

Griffith, Clark 31
Gund, Gordon 71
Habien, Harold Dr. 200
Hall, Brian 68
Halleran, Mary 185
Halsey, Bull Admiral 127-185
Haman (Old Tastament) 182
Hamlet 138
Hammerstein, Oscar 31
Hammerstein, Stella 31
Hanks, Tom 33-45
Hannah, Mark 139
Harding, Warren G. President 66
Harrison, Rex 55
Hartel, Lisa 117
Hause, Connie 156
Hawthorn, Nathanial 61
Henie, Sonja 175
Henry, Patrick 43
Hepburn, Audrey 55
Herman, Fred 96
Hill, Napoleon 23-24-37-46
Hill, Paul 156
Hillary, Sir Edmond 153
Hindenberg 81
Hite, Mabel 31
Hodgson, Ralph 232
Hofheing, Roy Judge 32
Hollingsworth, H. L. 97
Holm, Jeanne 185
Homa, Masahara General 62
Hope, Bob 80-95
Hopkins, Tom 171
Iaccoca, Lee 41-121
Inge, W.R. 92
Irving, Washington 56
Ivestor, Doug 132
JFK 67
Jackson, Andrew, President 66
Jackson, Horatio N. Dr. 45
Jackson, Reggie 32
James, Harry 84
James, T.F. 138
James, Wiliam Ph.D. 50-64-94
Jefferson, Thomas President 43
Jenner, Bruce 59
Jesebel 212
Johnson, Lyndon B. President 89-127
Johnson, Magic 71
Johnson, Rafer 118
Johnson, Walter 175
Jolliff, Patty 90-119
Jones, Dub 109
Jones, Tommy Lee 145
Jordan, Michael 60 -71-117
Jordan, Sarah Dr. 232
Joyce, James 45
Kahanomoku, Duke 167
Karate 167
Kekcheyev, K. 94
Keller, Helen 247
Kelvin, Lord 25
Kerr, Deborah 84
Kettering, Charles 157
Kevlar 42
Kiel, Father Bill 214
King, Bernard 117
King, Billy Jean 70-174
King, Edward General 62
Klima, Mita 174
Klug, Chris 123
Knieval, Evel 167

Koen, Fanny Blankers 21
Koenig, Mark 174
Koppel, Ted 71
Koufax, Sandy 174
Krotz, Joanna l. 190
Krumboltz, John Ph.D. 124
Kulish, Peter 211
Kwan, Michelle 175
Lamar, Hedi 43
Lancaster, Burt 84-173
Landis, Kenesaw Mountain Judge 42-184
Langer, Ellen 124
Larson, Don 111
Lee, General 199
Leek, Sybil 214
Lemiux, Mario 116
Lemon, Jack 40
Leonard, Sugar Ray 172-235
Lilienthal, Otto 26
Lincoln, Abraham, President 66-78-87
Lindbergh, Charles 151-152
Lipinski, Tara 175
Lombardi, Vince 150 -151-169-220
Longworth, Alice Roosevelt 145
Louganis, Greg 117
Louis, Joe 172
Love, Bob "Beanball" 71
Lozanov, George Dr. 65
Loy, Myrna 149
Lynn, Loretta145
MacArthur, Douglas General 162
Maca 216
Mack, Connie 116-175-211
MacLaren, Jim 68-69
Maglie, Sal 111
Maltz, Maxwell Dr. 46-64-103-130
Man O War 174
Manley, Charles M. 26
Mantle, Mickey 32-111-121
Marble, Alice 70
March, Frederick 149
Marciano, Rocky 172
Maris, Roger 173-175
Marshall, George C. General 185
Marshall, Jim 109
Mary, (Resurrection) 227
Mash 28
Matthew, Saint 204-247
Matthias, Bob 70-173
Maugham, W. Sommerset 177
Mays, Willie 173
McBride, Mary 131
McGonigle, Wm. I.L. Dr. 200
McGwire, Mark 173
McKinley, William President 139-148
McPHail, Larry 31
Meninger, Karl Dr 200.
Meshack (Old Testament) 231
Michelangelo 175
Mier, Golda 71
Miller, Michael, Dr. 103
Mills, Billy 212
Mindy 200
Mineau, Kris Colonel 139-140
Mitchell, Dale 111
Mitchell, Jackie 32-184
Mohammed 179
Moliere 93
Monroe, Marilyn 40
Mordecai (Old Testament) 182
More, Hannah 27-78
Morgan, J. Pierpont 23-211

Mori, Colonel 202
Morley, Christopher 194
Mortman, Doris 96
Moses, Grandma 89
Motta, Dick 115
Muse, Henry Lt. Colonel 203
Mumford, Mr. 29
Murphy, Audie 107-108
Muto, Tony 81
Myers, F.M.H. 49
Naomi (Old Testament) 182
Navritalova, Martina 174
Neal, Particia 217
Nebuchadnezzar, King 231
Nevers, Ernie 108
Newcomb, Simon 25
Newman, Cardinal 59-135
Newmann, John von Dr. 132
Nicholson, Jack 71
Niettzche 62
Nightengale, Earl 27-157-177
Nightengale, Florence 182
Nimitz, Chester Admiral 247
Noonan, Fred J. 184
Oakley, Annie 175
O'Connor, Sandra Day 188
O'Donnell, Rosie 33
O'Grady, Scott 241
O'Hara, Maureen 40
Oprah 57
O'Reilly, Josh 163
Osler, William Dr. 50
Owens, Jesse 107
Oyama, Matsutatsu 230
Paige, Satchel 32
Parise, Felicia 219
Parks, Rosa 196
Parry, Neil 68
Patton, George S. General 35 -162-212
Paul, Saint 40-80
Pavlov 50 -111
Peale, Norman Vincent Dr. 45-48-50-80
Peale, Ruth Stafford Mrs. 80-193
Pennock, Charlie 106
Penny, J.C. 124
Pennypacker, Paul Chief 146
Perrin, Serge 215
Picasso, Pablo 144-175
Piniella, Lou 92
Plato 46-206
Pocker, Vic 128
Podolsky, Edward Dr. 200
Post, Wiley 35-188
Presley, Elvis 136
Prince, Robert, Captain 203
Putney, Martha, Dr. 187
Pyle, Gomer 132
Quezon, Manuel 47
Reagan, Ronald President 89-142-143
Rae, Sergeant 162
Reese, Pee Wee 91
Reeve, Christopher 141
Retton, Mary Lou 60-173
Rhine, Joseph B. Dr. 229
Rhine, Louisa Dr. 229
Richards, Bob Reverend 60-212
Rickenbacker, Eddie 211
Ride, Sally 185
Ringenberg, Margaret 188
Ringold, Howard 210
Rizzo, Frank Mayor 51
Robbins, Anthony 22

Roberts, Cavett 78
Robertson, Cliff 48
Robinson, Jackie 159
Robinson, Sugar Ray 122
Rogers, Maxwell Mrs. 17
Rogers, Roy 85
Rogers, Will 36-104
Rohn, Jim 22
Roosevelt, Eleanor 54-187
Roosevelt, Franklin D. President 18
Roosevelt, Theodore President 38-45
Rouse, James Dr. 201
Rowling, J.K. 136
Rudy 84
Russell, Bill 212
Russell, Harold 150
Ruth, Babe 29-30-184
Ruth (Bible) 182
Ruyan, Jim 70
Ryan, Nolan 175
Sanders, Colonel 159
Saul, King 108
Schindler, John A. Dr. 94
Schlater, Preacher 164
Schmidt, Mike 32
Schwab, Charlie 23
Scott, George C. 81
Secagawea 196
Secretariat 174
Seneca, Marcus 97-177
Servco, Robert 160
Shakespeare, William 101-129-138
Shantz, Bobby 91-102
Shaw, George Bernard 75
Shedd, William 39
Shields, Charlie 224
Simmons, Jean 68
Sinatra, Frank 84
Smith, Al 58
Smith, Kate 115
Smith, Margaret Chase 247
Socrates 46
Spacek, Sissy 145
Spaeth, Frank 227
Spahn, Warren 175
Spalding, Albert 29
Stables, Ron 57
Stargell, Willie 32
Starr, Sally 51
Stauback, Roger 118
Stettinius, Edward R 211.
Stevens Hall 228
Stevens, George 41
Stevenson, Robert Louis 97
Stewart, Jimmy 41
Stone, W. Clemment 46
Stones, Dwight 135
Sullivan, John L. 139-172
Sullivan, Tom 71
Summers, Andrew Lt. 148
Swift, Jonathon 216
Switt, Loretta 28-48-123
Tada, Joni Earickson 24-98-240
Taft, President 183
Takacs, Koroly 118
Tandy, Jessica 138
Taylor, John Dr. 214-220
Taylor, Mary 81
Taylor, Susan 194
Tereshkova, Valentina 184
Tertullian 217
Tevye 193

Thatcher, Margaret 71
Thomas, Edward (Tommie) 202
Thoreau 150
Thorp, Jim 155-173
Tinkam, Jerry 225
Tolstoy, Leo 104
Torre, Joe 174
Trevino, Lee 66
Triple Crown 174
Trujillo, Armando 202
Truman, Harry President 61
Trump, Donald 120
Tunney, Gene 57-70
Turner, Glenn W. 246
Twain, Mark 27-88-157
Uecker, Bob 46
Unitas, Johnny 118
Vinogradova, Alla 224
Waitley, Dennis 60
Wagner, Honus 173
Waldo, Albigence 29
Wal-Mart 147
Walton, Sam 147
Waltrous, Willard Dr. 202-203
Warner, Pop 173
Washington, George President 29-43-44
Watson, Lyle 221
Wead, Frank Spig 40
Weaver, Sigorney 188
Webster, Daniel 28-37-157
Weiner, Norbert Dr. 132
Whitney, Willis 36
Whittle, Frank 27
Wiggam, Albert E. Dr. 135-136
Wilder, Billy 40
Williams, Ted 32-173
Wilson, Harold 107
Wilson, WodrowPresident 89-110
Winfrey Oprah 57-97-159
Witt, Katarina 175
Wonder, Stevie 69
Woods, Tiger 175
Wright Brothers 25-26-27
Wyatt Kaye 199
Wyler, William 41-149
Xerxes 182
Yamaguchi, Kristi 175
Young, Cy 173
Young, David 234
Zaharis Babe Diedrickson 155-172
Ziglar Zig 50-67-97-98
Ziporyn, Terra, Dr. 205